THE OFFICIAL theory test for car drivers and motorcyclists

VALID FOR TESTS TAKEN FROM 4 SEPTEMBER 2000

London: The Stationery Office

Written and compiled by the Publications Unit of the Driving Standards Agency (DSA)

Questions and answers are compiled by the Question Development Team of the DSA with support from the National Foundation for Educational Research

Published by The Stationery Office with the permission of the Controller of Her Majesty's Stationery Office on behalf of the Driving Standards Agency.

Third impression 2001

First published 1996

ISBN 0 11 5521186

A CIP catalogue record for this book is available from the British Library

Other titles in the Driving Skills series

The Official Theory Test for Drivers of Large Vehicles

The Official Motorcycling Manual

The Official Driving Manual

The Official Guide to Compulsory Basic Training for Motorcyclists

The Official DSA Guide for Driving Instructors

The Official Bus and Coach Driving Manual

The Official Goods Vehicle Driving Manual

The Official Guide to Tractor and Specialist Vehicle Driving Tests

The Official Driving Test

The Official Theory Test CD-ROM - 'Your Licence to Drive'

The Official Guide to Accompanying Learner Drivers

Acknowledgements

The Driving Standards Agency would like to thank their staff and the following organisations for their contribution to the production of this publication.

National Foundation for Educational Research

Transport Research Laboratory

Department of Environment, Transport and the Regions

Driver & Vehicle Testing Agency, Northern Ireland

Every effort has been made to ensure that the information contained in this publication is accurate at the time of going to press. The Stationery Office cannot be held responsible for any inaccuracies.
Information in this book is for guidance only.

All metric and imperial conversions in this book are approximate.

Information

Theory Test

DSA Bookings and Enquiries: 0870 01 01 372
DVTA (Northern Ireland) Booking and Enquiries: 0845 6006700

Faxes: 0870 01 04 372
Minicom: 0870 01 06 372
Welsh speakers: 0870 01 00 372

Postal applications to:
Driving Standards Agency or Driver and Vehicle Testing Agency
PO Box 148
Salford M5 3SY

Driving Standards Agency:
(Headquarters)
Stanley House
Talbot Street
Nottingham NG1 5GU

Tel: 0115 901 2500
Fax: 0115 901 2510

Driver & Vehicle Testing Agency
(Headquarters)
Balmoral Road
Belfast BT12 6QL

Tel: 02890 681831
Fax: 02890 665520

Driver Vehicle Licensing Authority
(GB Licence Enquiries)

Tel: 01792 772151
Fax: 01792 783071
Minicom: 01792 782787

Driver and Vehicle Licensing Northern Ireland
Customer Services
Tel: 02870 341469
02890 250 500 (24 hours)
Minicom: 02870 341 380

Website addresses:
DSA: www.driving-tests.co.uk
DVTA: www.doeni.gov.uk/dvta

The Driving Standards Agency (DSA) is an executive agency of the Department of the Environment, Transport and the Regions (DETR).

You'll see its logo at test centres.

DSA aims to promote road safety through the advancement of driving standards, by

- establishing and developing high standards and best practice in driving and riding on the road; before people start to drive, as they learn, and after they pass their test
- ensuring high standards of instruction for different types of driver and rider
- conducting the statutory theory and practical tests efficiently, fairly and consistently across the country
- providing a centre of excellence for driver training and driving standards
- developing a range of publications and other publicity material designed to promote safe driving for life.

DVTA

The Driver & Vehicle Testing Agency (DVTA) is an executive agency within the Department of the Environment for Northern Ireland. Its primary aim is to promote and improve road safety through the advancement of driving standards and implementation of the Government's policies for improving the mechanical standards of vehicles.

DSA Website

www.driving-tests.co.uk

DVTA Website

www.doeni.gov.uk/dvta

CONTENTS

With the ever-increasing volume of traffic on the roads today, it's important to make sure that new drivers have a broad spread of driving knowledge. Since July 1996 new car drivers and motorcycle riders have been required to pass a separate theory test before obtaining a full driving licence. This is a major step towards improving road safety in the UK.

The performance of all aspects of the theory test is continually monitored, and the question bank is regularly updated to take account of changes to legislation and best driving practices. This book contains the entire theory test question bank, set out in an easy-to-read style, with plenty of illustrations. To assist preparation for the test, it explains why the answers are correct and identifies good driving practice.

However, to properly prepare for the test, you should study the source material; this consists of

The Highway Code
Know Your Traffic Signs
The Official Driving Manual
The Official Motorcycling Manual

All are published by The Stationery Office and available from good bookshops.

The Driving Standards Agency has produced a video *An Inside View*, which gives an insight into how to prepare for the next step, the practical test. Available from TSO by telephoning 0870 600 5522..

To help you practise for the test the Driving Standards Agency have produced a CD-ROM that contains the question bank. The Official Theory Test CD-ROM - 'Your Licence to Drive' is available from all good booksellers.

Using these training aids will give you an extensive knowledge of driving theory, and will help you towards a better understanding of practical driving skills.

Robin Cummins
The Chief Driving Examiner
Driving Standards Agency

ABOUT THIS BOOK

This book tells you about the touch screen theory test.

This book will help you to

- study for your theory test
- prepare and be successful.

Part One gives you information on how to get started.

Part Two tells you about the test itself.

Part Three shows you the questions that may be used in your test. Don't worry, you won't have to answer all of them. Your test will have 35 questions.

Books for study

To prepare properly for the theory test DSA strongly recommends that you study the books from which the questions are taken. These books, known as the source material, these consist of: *The Highway Code, Know Your Traffic Signs, The Official Driving Manual* and *The Official Motorcycling Manual*.

These books will help you to answer the questions correctly and will also guide you when studying for your practical test. Keep them so that you can refer to them throughout your driving life. You can find them in most booksellers, together with relevant books from other publishers. Information about these, and other DSA products appears at the back of this book.

The Driving Standards Agency has also produced a CD ROM containing all the questions, which allows you to practise mock theory tests.

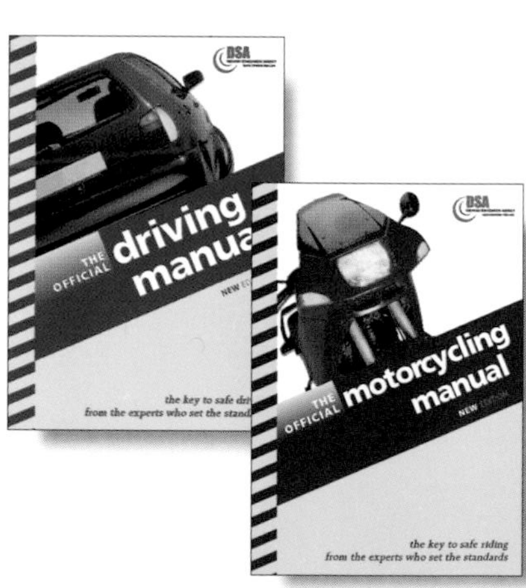

It's important that you study – not just to pass the test but to become a safe driver.

To ensure that all candidates are tested fairly, questions used in the theory test are under continuous review. *Some of the questions used will be changed periodically to reflect changes in legislation, or as a result of customer feedback. There may be questions in your test that do not appear in this book.* The information needed to answer all questions is readily available in the books recommended for study on the previous page.

Driving is a life skill.

Your driving tests are just the beginning.

When you pass your theory test you will be given a certificate. **This has a life of two years from the date of your test.** You will have to take and pass your practical test within this two-year period. If you don't, you will have to take and pass the theory test again before a booking for a practical test can be accepted.

Some of the questions in this book will not be used in Northern Ireland theory tests.

These questions are marked with this symbol.

If you're a motorcycle rider there will be some specific questions on motorcycling.

In this book these questions are marked with this motorcycle symbol.

PART ONE GETTING STARTED

If you want to drive a car

DSA in Great Britain, and DVTA in Northern Ireland, approve instructors to teach learner drivers for payment. These instructors have their standards checked regularly.

Approved Driving Instructors (ADIs) must

- pass a series of difficult examinations
- reach a high standard of instruction
- be registered with DSA or DVTA
- display an Approved Driving Instructor's certificate (except in Northern Ireland).

These professional instructors will give you guidance on

- what books to read
- your practical skills
- how to study and practise
- when you're ready for your tests
- further training after passing your practical test under the 'PASS PLUS' scheme.

DSA and the main bodies representing ADIs place great emphasis on professional standards and business ethics. A code of practice has been created, setting a framework within which all instructors should operate. Details of this can be obtained from DSA headquarters; Tel: **0115 901 2500.**

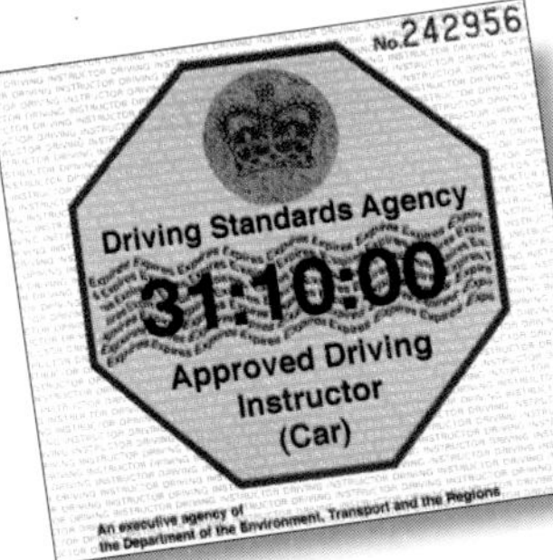

If you want to ride a motorcycle

Before you take your practical motorcycle test you must attend and successfully complete a Compulsory Basic Training (CBT) course (except in Northern Ireland). CBT courses can only be given by training bodies approved by DSA. Frequent checks are made to ensure a high standard of instruction.

The course will include

- classroom training
- practical skills training.

You can find out about CBT courses from

- DSA Tel: **0115 901 2500.**
- your motorcycle dealer
- your local Road Safety Officer (by contacting your local council)

DSA also produces *The Official Guide to Compulsory Basic Training for Motorcyclists,* which will give you details about the course.

You'll have to answer specific questions on motorcycling in the theory test. DSA's *The Official Motorcycling Manual* tells you about motorcycling skills in more detail. Books from other publishers are also available. In addition, you should buy and study a copy of *The Highway Code, The Official Driving Manual, and Know Your Traffic Signs.*

Keep them and refer to them after you've passed your tests. Make sure that you have the latest copy of *The Highway Code* as it's updated periodically.

Information about these and other DSA products appears at the back of this book.

Applying for your licence

You'll need to apply for a provisional driving licence, as you must produce it at the theory test centre. An application form D1 (DL1 in Northern Ireland) can be obtained from any post office.

When you receive your photocard provisional licence, check that all the details are correct. Don't drive until you've done so.

Residency requirements

You can't take a test or obtain a full licence unless you are normally resident in this country. Normal residence means the place where you reside because of personal or occupational ties. However, if you moved to the United Kingdom (UK) having recently been permanently resident in another state of the EC/EEA (European Economic Area), you must have been normally resident in the UK for 185 days in the 12 months prior to your application for a driving test or full driving licence.

About the theory test

During your test questions will appear on a computer screen. You will select your answers by simply touching the screen.

This 'touch screen' system has been carefully designed to make it easy to use.

You can work through a practice session to get used to the system before starting your test. Staff at the test centre will be on hand to help you if you have any difficulties.

The screens are easy to read. Only one question will appear on the screen at a time. You will be able to move backwards and forwards through the questions. You will also be able to 'flag' questions that you want to look at again. It is easy to change your answer.

Some questions ask you to select more than one answer option. The system will alert you if you have not completely answered a question.

Does everyone have to take the theory test?

Foreign licence holders:

If you hold a foreign driving licence issued outside the EEA, first check with the Driver Vehicle Licencing Authority (Tel: **01792 772151**) whether you can exchange your driving licence. If you cannot exchange your licence, you will need to take a theory and practical driving test.

Any particular enquiries about whether a theory test is required should be addressed to the Theory Test Unit, Driving Standards Agency, Stanley House, 56 Talbot Street, Nottingham, NG1 5GU
Tel: **0115 901 2500.**

Can I take my practical test first?

No. You have to take and pass your theory test before a booking for the practical test is accepted.

How many questions are there?

There are 35 questions in the test. You should try to answer all of them. To pass you must answer at least 30 question correctly.

How long do I have to complete the test?

Each test session lasts for 40 minutes. You can take all this time if you need to. The time remaining for your test is displayed on screen.

Where do I have to go to take the test?

There are over 150 test centres throughout England, Scotland, Wales and Northern Ireland. Most people have a test centre within 20 miles of their home, but this will vary depending on the density of the population in your area. You can find a list of test centres at the back of this book.

When are the test centres open?

Sessions are provided on weekdays, evenings and on Saturdays. However, where demand is less than 100 tests per year test sessions may be less frequent.

Will I know the result straight away?

Not straight away but you should receive your result at the test centre within 30 minutes of completing the test.

If I don't pass, when can I take the theory test again?

You will have to wait a minimum of three clear working days before you take the theory test again. If you fail your test you've shown that you aren't fully prepared. Good preparation will save you time and money.

Is the test only available in English?

No. The test is available in the following languages

Albanian	Gujarati	Spanish
Arabic	Hindi	Tamil
Bengali	Kurdish	Turkish
Cantonese	Portuguese	Urdu
Farsi	Punjabi	Welsh

You will be able to listen through a headset to the test being read out in any of these languages.

Northern Ireland tests are available in Cantonese, Bengali and Urdu only.

Can I bring a translator with me?

Yes. If you don't speak any of the languages available you're allowed to bring a DSA or DVTA approved translator with you when you take your test. The Special Needs team at the booking office will tell you who is approved. When you have made arrangements with the translator you should tell the booking office who you intend to bring with you.

If you bring an approved translator with you the responsibility for the contractual arrangements, including the fee charged, is between you and the translator.

Are there any provisions for special needs?

Every effort has been made to ensure that the theory test can be taken by all candidates. It's important that you state your needs when booking so that the necessary arrangements can be made.

There is an English language voiceover, on a headset, to support candidates with dyslexia and other reading difficulties. You can also ask for up to double the normal time to take the test. As evidence of this requirement you will be asked to provide a letter from a teacher or educationalist, a psychologist or doctor (if appropriate). If it isn't possible to get this confirmation from a relevant professional, DSA, or DVTA, will consider a letter from an independent person who knows about your reading ability. This could be your employer, but if you are unsure about who to ask please telephone the Special Needs section on 0870 01 01 372 (Fax 0820 01 04 372) or on 0845 600 6700 in Northern Ireland.

DSA and DVTA are unable to take responsibility for the safe return of any original documentation sent, so it is advisable to send copies only.

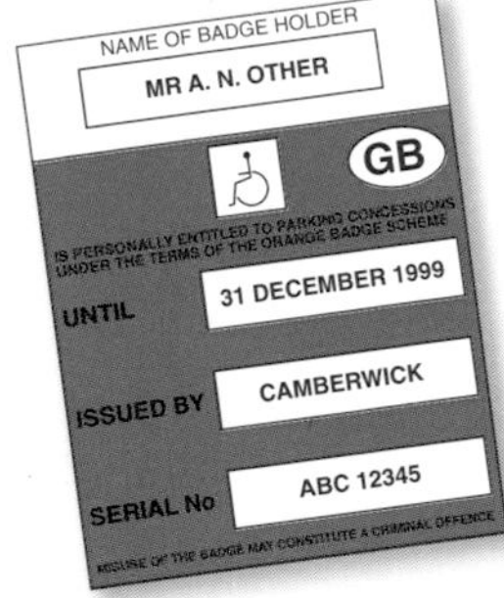

A test with video in British Sign Language is available on screen for candidates who are deaf or who have other hearing difficulties. A BSL interpreter or lip speaker can be provided if requested at the time of booking.

If you require wheelchair access and your nearest test centre doesn't provide this, DSA or DVTA will arrange for you to take the test at a location suitable for you, such as a library or job centre, or take you to another test centre where the facilities are provided.

How do I book a test?

The easiest way to book a test is by telephone, using your credit or debit card. The person who books the test must be the card-holder.

If you book by this method you'll be given the date and time of your test immediately. You can do this by calling **0870 01 01 372** or **0845 600 6700** for Northern Ireland at any time between 8 am and 6 pm Monday to Friday. When you phone you should have ready your

- DVLA/DVLNI driving licence number
- credit or debit card details.

If you're deaf and need a minicom machine telephone **0870 01 06 372**.

Welsh speakers can telephone **0870 01 00 372**.

You'll be given a booking number, and sent an appointment letter that you should expect to receive within four days of your call. If not please contact the booking office to check that the appointment was made.

Alternatively you can book a test by post. Application forms are available from

- theory test centres
- driving test centres
- your Approved Driving Instructor.

You should receive an appointment letter within 10 days of you posting your application form. If not, please telephone the booking office to check that your application was received and that a test appointment has been made.

DSA and DVTA cannot take responsibility for postal delays. If you miss your test appointment you will lose your fee.

How do I cancel or postpone a test?

To cancel or postpone a theory test appointment you should contact the booking office at least **three clear working days** before the test date otherwise you will lose your fee. Only in exceptional circumstances like documented ill-health or family bereavement can this rule be waived.

At the test centre

Make sure that you have all the necessary documents with you.
You'll need

- your signed driving licence and photo identity, or
- both parts of your signed photocard licence.

The form of photographic identification acceptable at both theory and practical tests is as follows

- **your photocard driving licence**
- **your passport**, which doesn't have to be a British passport
- ***cheque guarantee card or credit card** bearing your photograph and signature
- **an employer's identity or workplace pass** bearing your photograph and name or signature or both
- **Trade Union Card** bearing your photograph and signature
- **Student Union Card** with reference to either the NUS or an education establishment/course reference number. The card must bear your photograph and name or signature or both
- **School Bus Pass** bearing the name of the issuing authority and your photograph and signature
- ***card issued in connection with sale and purchase of reduced-price railway tickets** bearing the name of the issuing authority and your photograph and signature. This is a card issued by a Railway Authority or other authorised body to purchase a reduced-price railway ticket (e.g. a Young Persons Railcard)
- ***Gun Licence**, including a Firearm or Shotgun Certificate, which bears your photograph and signature
- ***Proof of Age Card** issued by the Portman Group bearing your photograph and signature

Remember...

No photo
No licence
No test

If you don't have any of these you can bring a signed photograph, together with a statement like the one shown below, that it's a true likeness of you. Both the statement, and the back of the photograph must be signed by the same person. This can be any of the following

- *Approved Driving Instructor, but not a trainee (pink licence) holder
- *DSA-certified motorcycle instructor
- Member of Parliament
- medical practitioner
- *local authority councillor
- teacher (qualified)
- Justice of the Peace
- civil servant (established)
- police officer
- bank official
- minister of religion
- barrister or solicitor
- *Commissioned Officer in Her Majesty's Forces
- *LGV Trainers on the DSA Voluntary Register of LGV Instructors.

*Not valid in Northern Ireland.

If you don't bring these documents on the day, you won't be able to take your test and you'll lose your fee. If you have any queries about what photographic evidence we will accept, contact the enquiry line on **0870 01 01 372** or **0845 600 6700** in Northern Ireland.

Arrive in plenty of time so that you aren't rushed. The test centre staff will check your documents and ensure that you receive the right category test. If you arrive after the session has started you may not be allowed to sit the test.

I (name of certifier), certify that this is a true likeness of , who has been known to me for (number) months / years in my capacity as

Signed
Dated
Daytime phone no.
ADI/CBT Instructor no.

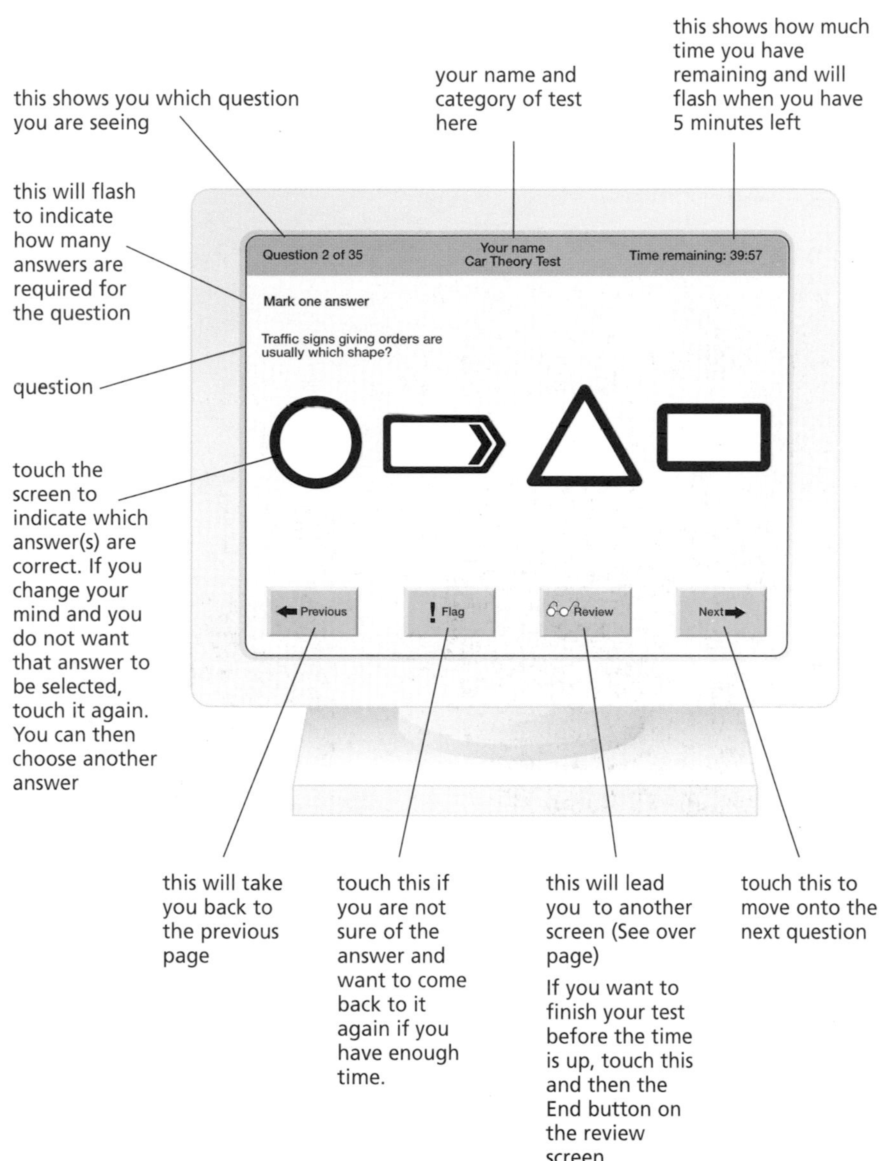
this shows you which question you are seeing
your name and category of test here
this shows how much time you have remaining and will flash when you have 5 minutes left
this will flash to indicate how many answers are required for the question
question
touch the screen to indicate which answer(s) are correct. If you change your mind and you do not want that answer to be selected, touch it again. You can then choose another answer
Question 2 of 35
Your name
Car Theory Test
Time remaining: 39:57
Mark one answer
Traffic signs giving orders are usually which shape?
Previous
Flag
Review
Next
this will take you back to the previous page
touch this if you are not sure of the answer and want to come back to it again if you have enough time.
this will lead you to another screen (See over page)
If you want to finish your test before the time is up, touch this and then the End button on the review screen
touch this to move onto the next question

Reviewing questions

When you press the review button you will see this screen.

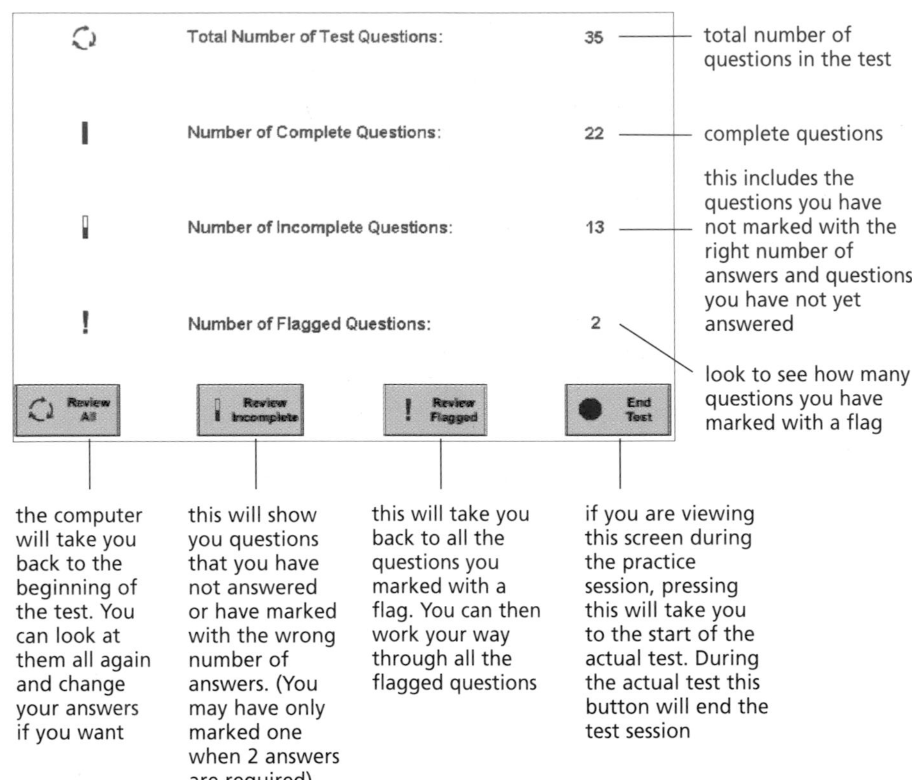

When you have finished your test you may be shown some trial questions. These help us to see if we will use them in future theory tests. They **do not** count towards your final score.

We want to ensure that customers are completely satisfied with the level of service we provide. You will be shown some questions designed to give us some information about you and how satisfied you are with the service you have received from us. Your answers will be treated in strictest confidence. They are **not** part of the test and will not be used in determining your final score. You will be given a choice of whether you wish to complete the survey.

Test Content

At the start of the test you'll have the opportunity to complete some practise questions.

Most questions will ask you to mark ONE correct answer from four. Other questions will ask for TWO OR MORE correct answers from a selection. Some of the questions will show you a picture. This is to test your knowledge of traffic signs or your ability to spot a hazard. Look at the question carefully.

The questions will cover a variety of topics relating to road safety. Touch the box alongside the answers you think are correct.

Some questions will take longer to answer than others. There are no trick questions. If you're well prepared you won't find them difficult.

Take your time and read the questions carefully. You're given plenty of time, so relax and don't rush. Try to answer all 35 questions.

When you think you've finished, use the 'review' feature to check your answers before you end your test.

At the conclusion of the test you may be asked to complete trial questions for next years question bank. You will also be asked to complete a customer satisfaction survey. Both these help DSA and DVTA develop the test and the service provided.

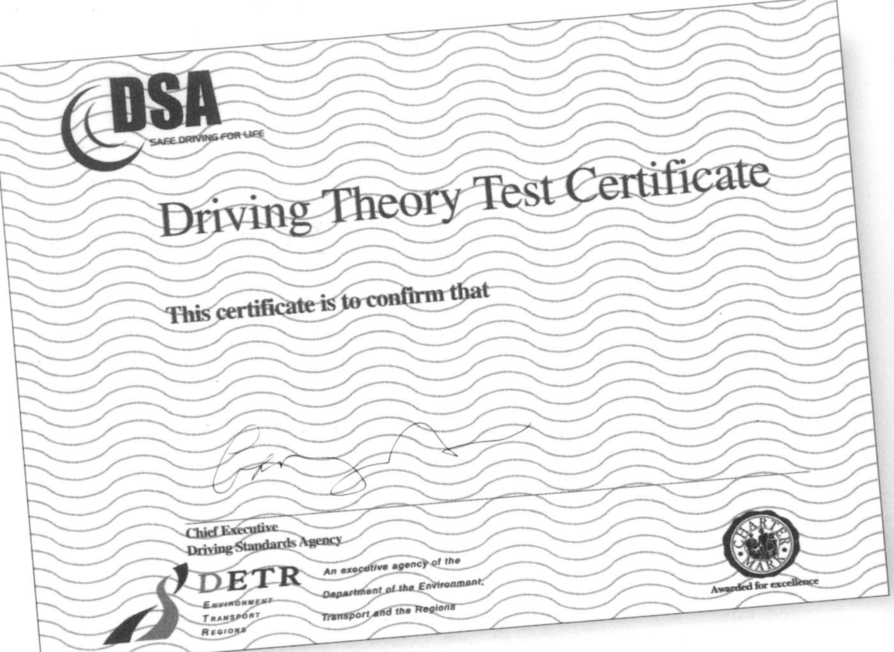
DSA
SAFE DRIVING FOR LIFE
Driving Theory Test Certificate
This certificate is to confirm that
Chief Executive
Driving Standards Agency
DETR
Environment
Transport
Regions
An executive agency of the
Department of the Environment,
Transport and the Regions
CHARTER MARK
Awarded for excellence

About Part Three

In this part of the book you'll find questions that might be used in your theory test. The answers have been provided to help you to study.

For easy reference and to help you to study, the questions have been divided into topics and put into sections. Although this isn't how you'll find them in your test it's helpful if you want to refer to particular subjects.

The questions are in the left-hand column with a choice of answers beneath. On the right-hand side of the page you'll find the correct answers and a brief explanation of why they are correct. There will also be some advice on correct driving procedures.

DON'T JUST LEARN THE ANSWERS. It's important that you know **why** the answers are correct. This will help you with your practical skills and prepare you to become a safe and confident driver.

Taking exams or tests is rarely a pleasant experience, but you can make your test less stressful by being confident that you have the knowledge to answer the questions correctly.

Make studying more fun by involving friends and relations. Take part in a question-and-answer game. Test those 'experienced' drivers who've had their licence a while: they might learn something too!

If you're taking a motorcycle theory test

In this part of the book the specific

questions for motorcyclists are marked with a motorcycle symbol.

Most of the other questions refer to all road users, so you should study these too. Some will appear in your test with slight changes, for example 'rider' instead of 'driver' or 'headlight' instead of 'headlights'.

SECTION 1 ALERTNESS

This section looks at alertness and attention when you're driving.

The questions will ask you about

- **Observation**

  look all around for other road users and pedestrians.

- **Anticipation**

  look ahead and giving yourself enough time to react to hazards.

- **Concentration**

  be alert at all times when driving or riding.

- **Awareness**

  understand the actions of other road users.

- **Distraction**

  don't become distracted whilst driving or riding. Your attention must be on the road.

- **Boredom**

  could make you feel sleepy. Keep your mind on your driving.

Question 1.1

Mark one answer

Before you make a U-turn in the road, you should

- [ ] give an arm signal as well as using your indicators
- [ ] signal so that other drivers can slow down for you
- [x] look over your shoulder for a final check
- [ ] select a higher gear than normal

Answer

look over your shoulder for a final check

If you want to make a U-turn, slow down and ensure that the road is clear in both directions. Make sure that the road is wide enough to carry out the manoeuvre safely.

Question 1.2

Mark one answer

To move off safely from a parked position you should

- [ ] signal if other drivers will need to slow down
- [ ] leave your motorcycle on its stand until the road is clear
- [ ] give an arm signal as well as using your indicators
- [ ] look over your shoulder for a final check

Answer

look over your shoulder for a final check

If you're intending to move off from the side of the road on a motorcycle you must take a final look around over your shoulder. There may be another road user not visible in your mirrors.

Question 1.3

Mark one answer

As a driver what does the term 'Blind Spot' mean?

- [ ] An area covered by your right hand mirror
- [ ] An area not covered by your headlights
- [ ] An area covered by your left hand mirror
- [ ] An area not seen in your mirrors

Answer

An area not seen in your mirrors

Modern vehicles today provide the driver with well-positioned mirrors which are essential to driving safely. However, they cannot show every angle of the scene behind. It is essential you are aware of this and check over your shoulder to see any dangers not reflected in your mirrors.

Question 1.4

Mark two answers

Objects hanging from your interior mirror may

- restrict your view
- improve your driving
- distract your attention
- help your concentration

Answers

- **restrict your view**
- **distract your attention**

Ensure that you can see clearly through the windscreen of your vehicle. Stickers or hanging objects could affect your field of vision or draw your eyes away from the road

Question 1.5

Mark two answers

You are most likely to lose concentration when driving if you

- use a mobile phone
- listen to very loud music
- switch on the heated rear window
- look at the door mirrors

Answers

- **use a mobile phone**
- **listen to very loud music**

Distractions which cause you to take your hands from the steering wheel are dangerous. You should be in full control of your vehicle at all times.

Question 1.6

Mark four answers

Which FOUR are most likely to cause you to lose concentration while you are driving?

- Using a mobile phone
- Talking into a microphone
- Tuning your car radio
- Looking at a map
- Checking the mirrors
- Using the demisters

Answers

- **Using a mobile phone**
- **Talking into a microphone**
- **Tuning your car radio**
- **Looking at a map**

Planning your journey is important. A few sensible precautions will allow you to

- tune your radio into frequencies in your area of travel
- take planned breaks (which can be used for phone calls)
- plan your route (make notes of road numbers and junction numbers if necessary). This will avoid the need to look at maps while driving.

Question 1.7

Mark one answer

When riding, your shoulders obstruct the view in your mirrors. To overcome this you should

- indicate earlier than normal
- fit smaller mirrors
- extend the mirror arms
- brake earlier than normal

Answer

- **extend the mirror arms**

It's essential that you have a clear view all around. Check the position of the mirrors before you move off.

Question 1.8

Mark two answers

You want to change lanes in busy, moving traffic. Why could looking over your shoulder help?

- Mirrors may not cover blind spots
- To avoid having to give a signal
- So traffic ahead will make room for you
- So your balance will not be affected
- Following motorists would be warned

Answers

- **Mirrors may not cover blind spots**
- **Following motorists would be warned**

Before you change lanes you need to know that there's a safe gap to move into. Looking over your shoulder

- allows you to see into the area not covered by the mirrors and which could hide another vehicle
- warns following motorists that you want to change lanes.

Question 1.9

Mark one answer

You are about to turn right. What should you do just before you turn?

- Give the correct signal
- Take a 'lifesaver' glance over your shoulder
- Select the correct gear
- Get in position ready for the turn

Answer

- **Take a 'lifesaver' glance over your shoulder**

When you're turning right plan your approach to the junction. Signal and select the correct gear in good time. Just before you turn give a 'lifesaver' glance to the rear for a final check behind and alongside.

Question 1.10

Mark one answer

What is the 'lifesaver' when riding a motorcycle?

- A certificate every motorcyclist must have
- A final, rearward glance before changing direction
- A part of the motorcycle tool kit
- A mirror fitted to check blind spots

Answer

- **A final, rearward glance before changing direction**

This action makes you aware of what's happening behind and alongside. This glance should be timed so that you still have time to react if it isn't safe to perform the manoeuvre.

Question 1.11

Mark one answer

You are driving on a wet road. You have to stop your vehicle in an emergency. You should

- apply the handbrake and footbrake together
- keep both hands on the wheel
- select reverse gear
- give an arm signal

Answer

- **keep both hands on the wheel**

As you drive look well ahead and all around so that you're ready for any hazards that might occur. There may be occasions when you have to stop in an emergency. React as soon as you can whilst keeping control of the vehicle.

Question 1.12

Mark one answer

You see road signs showing a sharp bend ahead. What should you do?

- Continue at the same speed
- Slow down as you go around the bend
- Slow down as you come out of the bend
- Slow down before the bend

Answer

- **Slow down before the bend**

Road signs might give you warning of a hazard ahead. Always look and plan well ahead. This will avoid the need for late, harsh braking. Your motorcycle should be upright and moving in a straight line when you brake. This will ensure maximum control when dealing with the hazard.

Question 1.13

Mark three answers

As you approach this bridge you should

- move into the middle of the road to get a better view
- slow down
- get over the bridge as quickly as possible
- consider using your horn
- find another route
- beware of pedestrians

Answers

- **slow down**
- **consider using your horn**
- **beware of pedestrians**

This sign gives you a warning. You can't see over the bridge for oncoming traffic so you must be cautious; slow right down. Consider the possible hidden hazards and be ready to react if necessary.

Question 1.14

Mark one answer

When following a large vehicle you should keep well back because

- it allows you to corner more quickly
- it helps the large vehicle to stop more easily
- it allows the driver to see you in the mirrors
- it helps you to keep out of the wind

Answer

- **it allows the driver to see you in the mirrors**

You also need to keep well back so that you get the best view of the road ahead.

Question 1.15

Mark one answer

In which of these situations should you avoid overtaking?

- Just after a bend
- In a one-way street
- On a 30 mph road
- Approaching a dip in the road

Answer

- **Approaching a dip in the road**

As you begin to think about overtaking ask yourself if it's really necessary. If you can't see well down the road, stay back and wait for a safer place to pull out.

Question 1.16

Mark four answers

Which of the following may cause loss of concentration on a long journey?

- Loud music
- Arguing with a passenger
- Using a mobile phone
- Putting in a cassette tape
- Stopping regularly to rest
- Pulling up to tune the radio

Answers

- **Loud music**
- **Arguing with a passenger**
- **Using a mobile phone**
- **Putting in a cassette tape**

You should not allow other factors to distract you from driving. You need to concentrate fully to ensure you are safe on the road. Loud music could mask other sounds, such as the audible warning of an emergency vehicle.

Any distraction which causes you to take your hands off the steering wheel unnecessarily is dangerous.

Question 1.17

Mark one answer

You should not use a mobile phone whilst driving

- until you are satisfied that no other traffic is near
- unless you are able to drive one handed
- because it might distract your attention from the road ahead
- because reception is poor when the engine is running

Answer

- **because it might distract your attention from the road ahead**

Driving requires all your attention and concentration at all times. Don't be distracted by unnecessary mobile phone calls. Be safe, switch off your phone while driving.

Question 1.18

Mark one answer

Your vehicle is fitted with a hands-free phone system. Using this equipment whilst driving

- is quite safe as long as you slow down
- could distract your attention from the road
- is recommended by The Highway Code
- could be very good for road safety

Answer

- **could distract your attention from the road**

Using a hands-free system doesn't mean that you can safely drive and use a mobile phone. This type of mobile phone doesn't lessen your responsibility to keep yourself and other road users safe at all times.

Question 1.19

Mark one answer

Using a hands-free phone is likely to

- improve your safety
- increase your concentration
- reduce your view
- divert your attention

Answer

- **divert your attention**

Unlike someone in the car with you, the person on the other end of the line is unable to see the traffic situations you are dealing with. They will not stop speaking to you even if you are approaching a hazardous situation. You need to be concentrating on your driving all of the time, but especially so when dealing with a hazard.

Question 1.20

Mark one answer

Using a mobile phone while you are driving

- is acceptable in a vehicle with power steering
- will reduce your field of vision
- could distract your attention from the road
- will affect your vehicle's electronic systems

Answer

- **could distract your attention from the road**

Driving today requires all of your attention, all of the time. Any distraction, however brief, is dangerous

Question 1.21

Mark one answer

This road marking warns

- drivers to use the hard shoulder
- overtaking drivers there is a bend to the left
- overtaking drivers to move back to the left
- drivers that it is safe to overtake

Answer

- **overtaking drivers to move back to the left**

You should plan your overtaking to take account of any hazards ahead. In this picture the marking indicates that you are approaching a junction. You will not have time to overtake and move back into the left safely.

Question 1.22

Mark one answer

You are travelling along this narrow country road. When passing the cyclist you should go

- slowly, sounding the horn as you pass
- quickly, leaving plenty of room
- slowly, leaving plenty of room
- quickly, sounding the horn as you pass

Answer

- **slowly, leaving plenty of room**

Look well ahead and only pull out if it is safe. You will need to use all of the road to pass the cyclist so be extra cautious.

Look out for entrances to fields where there could be tractors or equipment pulling out.

Question 1.23

Mark one answer

Your vehicle is fitted with a hand-held telephone. To use the telephone you should

- reduce your speed
- find a safe place to stop
- steer the vehicle with one hand
- be particularly careful at junctions

Answer

find a safe place to stop

Your attention should be on your driving at all times. Never attempt to dial or reach out for your phone while on the move. This could mean taking your eyes off the road. In only a second your vehicle will travel about 27 metres if you are travelling at 60 mph.

Question 1.24

Mark one answer

Your mobile phone rings while you are on the motorway. Before answering you should

- reduce your speed to 50 mph
- pull up on the hard shoulder
- move into the left-hand lane
- stop in a safe place

Answer

stop in a safe place

Plan your journey and take breaks to keep in touch if necessary. When driving on motorways, you can't just pull up to answer the mobile phone. Be safe, switch it off and use the mail retrieval service to get any messages when you are parked in a safe and proper place.

Question 1.25

Mark one answer

To answer a call on your mobile phone while travelling you should

- reduce your speed wherever you are
- stop in a proper and convenient place
- keep the call time to a minimum
- slow down and allow others to overtake

Answer

stop in a proper and convenient place

No phone call is important enough to endanger someone's life. If you must be contactable when driving, plan your route to include breaks where you can catch up on telephone messages in safety.

Always choose a proper and convenient place to take a break

Question 1.26

Mark one answer

Your mobile phone rings while you are travelling. You should

- stop immediately
- answer it immediately
- pull up in a suitable place
- pull up at the nearest kerb

Answer

pull up in a suitable place

Always use the safe option. It is not worth taking the risk of endangering other road users. Make sure that you pull up in a place that does not obstruct other road users. The use of a message service can enable you to complete your journey without interruptions, and you can catch up with your calls when you take your rest breaks.

Question 1.27

Mark one answer

You should ONLY use a mobile phone when

- receiving a call
- suitably parked
- driving at less than 30 mph
- driving an automatic vehicle

Answer

suitably parked

It it far more convenient for you, as well as being safer, if you are parked in a safe and convenient place when receiving or making a call. You will be free to take notes or refer to papers, which would be not be possible while driving.

Question 1.28

Mark one answer

What is the safest way to use a mobile phone in your vehicle?

- Use hands-free equipment
- Find a suitable place to stop
- Drive slowly on a quiet road
- Direct your call through the operator

Answer

Find a suitable place to stop

If the use of a mobile phone causes you to drive in a careless or dangerous manner, you could be prosecuted for those offences. The penalties include an unlimited fine, disqualification and up to two years imprisonment.

Question 1.29

Mark one answer

You are riding at night. You have your headlight on main beam. Another vehicle is overtaking you. When should you dip your headlight?

- When the other vehicle signals to overtake
- As soon as the other vehicle moves out to overtake
- As soon as the other vehicle passes you
- After the other vehicle pulls in front of you

Answer

As soon as the other vehicle passes you

At night you should dip your headlight to avoid dazzling

- oncoming drivers
- drivers in front.

If you're being overtaken, dip your headlight as the other vehicle comes past. When you dip you'll see less of the road so look ahead for hazards on your side of the road before dipping.

Question 1.30

Mark one answer

On a motorcycle you should only use a mobile telephone when you

- have a pillion passenger to help
- have parked in a safe place
- have a motorcycle with automatic gears
- are travelling on a quiet road

Answer

have parked in a safe place

It's important that you're in full control of your machine at all times. If you need to use a hand-held phone you must stop at a safe place before you do so.

Question 1.31

Mark two answers

On a long motorway journey boredom can cause you to feel sleepy. You should

- leave the motorway and find a safe place to stop
- keep looking around at the surrounding landscape
- drive faster to complete your journey sooner
- ensure a supply of fresh air into your vehicle
- stop on the hard shoulder for a rest

Answers

- **leave the motorway and find a safe place to stop**
- **ensure a supply of fresh air into your vehicle**

Plan your journey to include suitable rest stops. You should take all precautions against feeling sleepy whilst driving. Any lack of concentration could have dire consequences.

Question 1.32

Mark one answer

You are riding at night and are dazzled by the headlights of an oncoming car. You should

- slow down or stop
- close your eyes
- flash your headlight
- turn your head away

Answer

- **slow down or stop**

If you're riding a motorcycle, taking a hand off the handlebars to adjust your visor might lead to loss of control. A dirty or scratched visor could cause dazzle and impair vision further. Whether riding or driving, slow down or stop until your eyes have adjusted.

Question 1.33

Mark two answers

You are driving at dusk. You should switch your lights on

- even when street lights are not lit
- so others can see you
- only when others have done so
- only when street lights are lit

Answers

- **even when street lights are not lit**
- **so others can see you**

Your lights are there to help others on the road see you. It can be necessary to turn on your lights during the day due to bad light or heavy rain. In these conditions the light might fade before the street lights are timed to switch on. Be seen to be safe.

Question 1.34

Mark one answer

Why are these yellow lines painted across the road?

- To help you choose the correct lane
- To help you keep the correct separation distance
- To make you aware of your speed
- To tell you the distance to the roundabout

Answer

To make you aware of your speed

These lines are often found on an approach to a roundabout or a dangerous junction. They give you extra warning to adjust your speed. Look well ahead and do this in good time.

Question 1.35

Mark one answer

You are riding along a motorway. You see an accident on the other side of the road. Your lane is clear. You should

- assist the emergency services
- stop, and cross the road to help
- concentrate on what is happening ahead
- place a warning triangle in the road

Answer

concentrate on what is happening ahead

Always concentrate on the road ahead. If you become distracted you may not see a hazard ahead until it's too late to avoid it.

Question 1.36

Mark one answer

Which of the following should you do before stopping your vehicle?

- Sound the horn
- Use the mirrors
- Select a higher gear
- Flash your headlights

Answer

Use the mirrors

Before pulling up you should check for following traffic. Also assess what is ahead and give the correct signal if it helps another road user.

Question 1.37

Mark one answer

You are approaching traffic lights that have been on green for some time. You should

- accelerate hard
- maintain your speed
- be ready to stop
- brake hard

Answer

be ready to stop

The longer that traffic lights have been on green, then the greater the chance of the sequence changing, so always allow for this when driving and be prepared to stop.

Question 1.38

Mark one answer

In motorcycling, the term 'lifesaver' refers to

- a final rearward glance
- an approved safety helmet
- a reflective jacket
- the two-second rule

Answer

a final rearward glance

Mirrors on motorcycles don't always give a clear view behind. There will be times when you need to look round to see the full picture.

Question 1.39

Mark one answer

Riding a motorcycle when you are cold could cause you to

- be more alert
- be more relaxed
- react more quickly
- lose concentration

Answer

lose concentration

Keeping warm can be a problem. Proper motorcycle clothing isn't cheap, but it will keep you warm and is essential in cold weather. It also offers some safety benefits in the event of an accident.

Question 1.40

Mark one answer

You are riding at night and are dazzled by the lights of an approaching vehicle. What should you do?

- Switch off your headlight
- Switch to main beam
- Slow down and stop
- Flash your headlight

Answer

- **Slow down and stop**

If your view of the road ahead is restricted because you are being dazzled by approaching headlights, slow down and if necessary stop.

Question 1.41

Mark three answers

When you are moving off from behind a parked car you should

- look round before you move off
- use all the mirrors on the vehicle
- look round after moving off
- use the exterior mirrors only
- give a signal if necessary
- give a signal after moving off

Answers

- **look round before you move off**
- **use all the mirrors on the vehicle**
- **give a signal if necessary**

Before moving off you should use all the mirrors to check if the road is clear. Look round to check the blind spots and give a signal if it is of help to other road users.

SECTION 2 ATTITUDE

This section looks at your attitude to other road users.

The questions will ask you about

- **Consideration**

  consider other road users. Be positive but treat them as you would wish to be treated.

- **Close following**

  don't follow too closely. As well as being dangerous, it can feel threatening to the driver in front.

- **Courtesy**

  treat other road users as colleagues or team members. They too are trying to complete their journey safely.

- **Priority**

  be aware that all rules on priority won't always be followed by other road users. Try to be calm and tolerant if other drivers or riders break the rules.

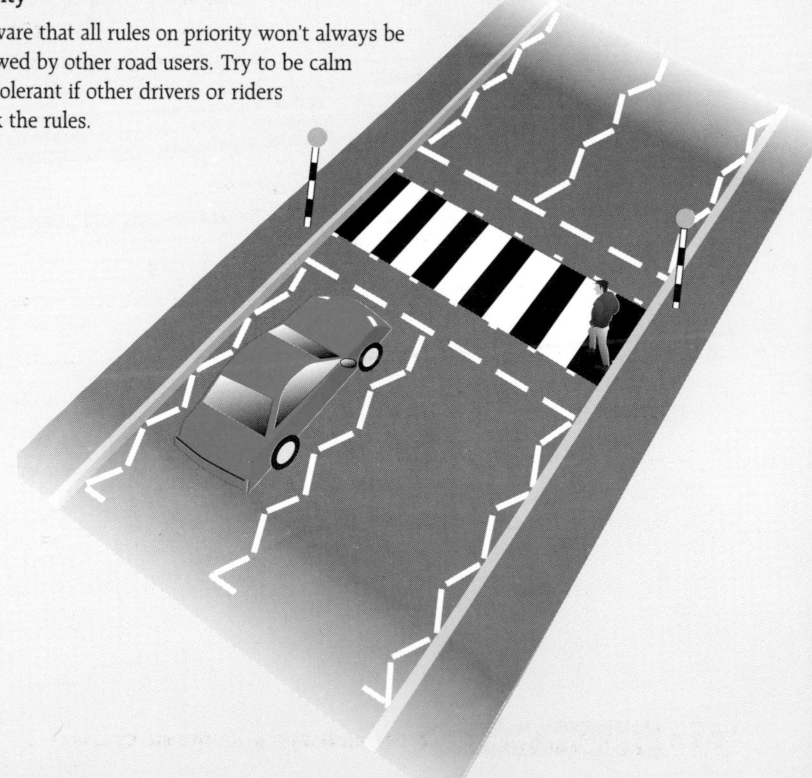

Question 2.1

Mark one answer

A pelican crossing that crosses the road in a straight line and has a central island MUST be treated as

- one crossing in daylight only
- one complete crossing
- two separate crossings
- two crossings during darkness

Answer

- **one complete crossing**

The lights that control the crossing show to both directions of traffic. If a pedestrian from either side is still crossing when the amber light is flashing, you must wait.

Question 2.2

Mark one answer

You are approaching a pelican crossing. The amber light is flashing. You **MUST**

- give way to pedestrians who are crossing
- encourage pedestrians to cross
- not move until the green light appears
- stop even if the crossing is clear

Answer

- **give way to pedestrians who are crossing**

While the pedestrians are crossing don't

- encourage people to cross by waving or flashing your headlights – others may misunderstand your signal
- rev your engine impatiently.

Question 2.3

Mark one answer

You are approaching a zebra crossing. Pedestrians are waiting to cross. You should

- give way to the elderly and infirm only
- slow down and prepare to stop
- use your headlights to indicate they can cross
- wave at them to cross the road

Answer

- **slow down and prepare to stop**

Zebra crossings have

- flashing amber beacons on both sides of the road
- black and white stripes on the crossing
- white zigzag markings on both sides of the crossing.

Where pedestrians are waiting to cross, slow down and prepare to stop.

Question 2.4

Mark one answer

You are riding towards a zebra crossing. Pedestrians are waiting to cross. You should

- give way to the elderly and infirm only
- slow down and prepare to stop
- use your headlight to indicate they can cross
- wave at them to cross the road

Answer

slow down and prepare to stop

It's courteous to stop if you can do so safely, especially if

- anyone is waiting on the pavement with a pram or pushchair
- children or the elderly are hesitating to cross because of heavy traffic.

Question 2.5

Mark one answer

At puffin crossings which light will not show to a driver?

- Flashing amber
- Red
- Steady amber
- Green

Answer

Flashing amber

A flashing amber light is shown at pelican crossings, but puffin crossings are different. They are controlled electronically and automatically detect when pedestrians are on the crossing.

The phase is shortened or lengthened according to the position of the pedestrians.

Question 2.6

Mark one answer

You are approaching a red light at a puffin crossing. Pedestrians are on the crossing. The red light will stay on until

- you start to edge forward on to the crossing
- the pedestrians have reached a safe position
- the pedestrians are clear of the front of your vehicle
- a driver from the opposite direction reaches the crossing

Answer

the pedestrians have reached a safe position

The electronic device will automatically detect that the pedestrians have reached a safe position. Don't proceed until the green light shows it is safe to do so.

Question 2.7

Mark one answer

You could use the 'Two-Second Rule'

- before restarting the engine after it has stalled
- to keep a safe gap from the vehicle in front
- before using the 'Mirror–Signal–Manoeuvre' routine
- when emerging on wet roads

Answer

- **to keep a safe gap from the vehicle in front**

To measure this, choose a reference point such as a bridge, sign or tree. When the vehicle ahead passes the object say to yourself 'Only a fool breaks the Two-Second Rule.' If you reach the object before you finish saying this you're TOO CLOSE.

Question 2.8

Mark one answer

A two-second gap between yourself and the car in front is sufficient when conditions are

- wet
- good
- damp
- foggy

Answer

- **good**

In good, dry conditions an alert driver who's driving a vehicle with tyres and brakes in good condition needs a distance of at least two seconds from the car in front.

Question 2.9

Mark one answer

'Tailgating' means

- using the rear door of a hatchback car
- reversing into a parking space
- following another vehicle too closely
- driving with rear fog lights on

Answer

- **following another vehicle too closely**

'Tailgating' is used to describe this dangerous practice, often seen in fast-moving traffic and on motorways. Following the vehicle in front too closely will

- restrict your view of the road ahead
- leave you no safety margin if the vehicle in front stops suddenly.

Question 2.10

Mark one answer

You are driving on a clear night. There is a steady stream of oncoming traffic. The national speed limit applies. Which lights should you use?

- Full beam headlights
- Sidelights
- Dipped headlights
- Fog lights

Answer

Dipped headlights

You should always be sure that you can be seen by other traffic. Use the main beam of your headlights only when you can be sure that you won't dazzle other traffic.

Question 2.11

Mark one answer

You are following this lorry. You should keep well back from it to

- give you a good view of the road ahead
- stop following traffic from rushing through the junction
- prevent traffic behind you from overtaking
- allow you to hurry through the traffic lights if they change

Answer

give you a good view of the road ahead

By keeping well back you will increase your width of vision around the rear of the lorry. This will allow you to see further down the road and be prepared for any hazards.

Question 2.12

Mark one answer

You are driving behind a large goods vehicle. It signals left but steers to the right. You should

- slow down and let the vehicle turn
- drive on, keeping to the left
- overtake on the right of it
- hold your speed and sound your horn

Answer

- **slow down and let the vehicle turn**

Large long vehicles need extra room when making turns at junctions. They may move out to the right in order to make a left turn. Keep well back and, in this case, don't attempt to pass on the left.

Question 2.13

Mark one answer

You are following a vehicle on a wet road. You should leave a time gap of at least

- one second
- two seconds
- three seconds
- four seconds

Answer

- **four seconds**

Wet roads will increase the time it will take you to stop. The 'Two-Second Rule' will double to AT LEAST FOUR SECONDS.

Question 2.14

Mark one answer

You are driving along this road. The red van cuts in close in front of you. What should you do?

- Accelerate to get closer to the red van
- Give a long blast on the horn
- Drop back to leave the correct separation distance
- Flash your headlights several times

Answer

- **Drop back to leave the correct separation distance**

There are times when other drivers make incorrect or ill-judged decisions.

Be tolerant and try not to react aggressively or retaliate. Always consider the safety of other road users, your passengers and yourself.

Question 2.15

Mark one answer

You are waiting in a traffic queue at night. To avoid dazzling following drivers you should

- apply the handbrake only
- apply the footbrake only
- switch off your headlights
- use both the handbrake and footbrake

Answer

apply the handbrake only

You should consider the driver behind; brake lights can dazzle.

However, if you are driving in fog it's safer to keep your foot on the footbrake. In this case it will give the following vehicle extra warning of your presence.

Question 2.16

Mark one answer

You are driving in traffic at the speed limit for the road. The driver behind is trying to overtake. You should

- move closer to the car ahead, so the driver behind has no room to overtake
- wave the driver behind to overtake when it is safe
- keep a steady course and allow the driver behind to overtake
- accelerate to get away from the driver behind

Answer

keep a steady course and allow the driver behind to overtake

Keep a steady course to give the driver behind an opportunity to overtake safely. If necessary, slow down. Reacting incorrectly to another's impatience will only lead to danger.

Question 2.17

Mark one answer

You are driving at night on an unlit road following a slower moving vehicle. You should

- flash your headlights
- use dipped beam headlights
- switch off your headlights
- use full beam headlights

Answer

use dipped beam headlights

If you follow another vehicle with your headlights on full beam it could dazzle the driver by reflecting on the interior mirror. Leave a safe distance. Your dipped light beam should fall short of the vehicle in front.

Question 2.18

Mark one answer

A long, heavily-laden lorry is taking a long time to overtake you. What should you do?

- Speed up
- Slow down
- Hold your speed
- Change direction

Answer

- **Slow down**

A long lorry with a heavy load will need more time to pass you than a car. It won't be able to accelerate to pass you quickly, especially on an uphill stretch of road. Ease off the accelerator and allow the lorry to pass.

Question 2.19

Mark one answer

You are using a slow-moving vehicle on a narrow winding road. You should

- keep well out to stop vehicles overtaking dangerously
- wave following vehicles past you if you think they can overtake quickly
- pull in safely when you can, to let following vehicles overtake
- give a left signal when it is safe for vehicles to overtake you

Answer

- **pull in safely when you can, to let following vehicles overtake**

Don't

- wave the other traffic on – they may not have seen your signal
- show discourtesy by not pulling in at a safe place.

Try to be courteous and considerate to other road users. Imagine how you would feel if you were the following driver or rider.

Question 2.20

Mark one answer

You are using a slow-moving vehicle on a narrow road. When traffic wishes to overtake you should

- take no action
- put your hazard warning lights on
- stop immediately and wave it on
- pull in safely as soon as you can do so

Answer

- **pull in safely as soon as you can do so**

Try not to hold up a queue of traffic. This might lead to other road users becoming impatient. If you're driving a slow-moving vehicle and the road is narrow, look out for a safe place to pull in.

Question 2.21

Mark one answer

You are driving a slow-moving vehicle on a narrow winding road. In order to let other vehicles overtake you should

- wave to them to pass
- pull in when you can
- show a left turn signal
- keep left and hold your speed

Answer

- **pull in when you can**

Don't frustrate other road users by driving for long distances with a queue of traffic behind you. This could lead them into losing concentration or making ill-judged decisions.

Question 2.22

Mark one answer

You are riding a motorcycle and following a large vehicle at 40 mph. You should position yourself

- close behind to make it easier to overtake the vehicle
- to the left of the road to make it easier to be seen
- close behind the vehicle to keep out of the wind
- well back so that you can see past the vehicle

Answer

- **well back so that you can see past the vehicle**

You need to be able to see well down the road and be ready for any hazards that occur. Staying too close to the vehicle will leave you insufficient separation distance and also reduce your view of the road ahead.

Question 2.23

Mark three answers

Which THREE of these emergency services might have blue flashing beacons?

- Coastguard
- Bomb disposal
- Gritting lorries
- Animal ambulances
- Mountain rescue
- Doctors' cars

Answers

- **Coastguard**
- **Bomb disposal**
- **Mountain rescue**

These vehicles will be travelling at speed. You should help their progress by pulling over and allowing them to pass. Do so safely. Don't stop suddenly or in a dangerous position.

Question 2.24

Mark one answer

A flashing green beacon on a vehicle means

- police on non-urgent duties
- doctor on an emergency call
- road safety patrol operating
- gritting in progress

Answer

doctor on an emergency call

If you see such a vehicle in your mirrors, allow it to pass if you can. Be aware that someone's life could depend on the driver making good progress through traffic.

Question 2.25

Mark one answer

Diamond-shaped signs give instructions to

- tram drivers
- bus drivers
- lorry drivers
- taxi drivers

Answer

tram drivers

These signs apply to trams only. They are directed at tram drivers, but you should know their meaning so that you're aware of the priorities and are able to anticipate the actions of the driver.

Question 2.26

Mark one answer

Scooter riders should be especially careful when crossing tram lines because scooters have

- small engines
- wide panniers
- automatic gear boxes
- narrow tyres

Answer

narrow tyres

Tram rails can affect steering and braking, especially when wet. If you ride a small motorcycle with narrow tyres you can be affected more than riders on larger machines which have wider tyres.

Question 2.27

Mark one answer

On a road where trams operate, which of these vehicles will be most at risk from the tram rails?

- Cars
- Cycles
- Buses
- Lorries

Answer

Cycles

The narrow tyres of a cycle can become stuck in the tram rails. This could cause the cyclist to wobble or even lose balance altogether. The tram lines are also slippery, and this could cause a cyclist to slide or fall off.

Question 2.28

Mark one answer

A bus is stopped at a bus stop ahead of you. Its right-hand indicator is flashing. You should

- flash your headlights and slow down
- slow down and give way if it is safe to do so
- sound your horn and keep going
- slow down and then sound your horn

Answer

slow down and give way if it is safe to do so

Give way to buses whenever you can do so safely, especially when they signal to pull away from bus stops. Look out for people leaving the bus and crossing the road. Don't

- flash your headlights
- sound your horn
- give any other misleading signal.

Question 2.29

Mark one answer

A bus lane on your left shows no times of operation. This means it is

- not in operation at all
- only in operation at peak times
- in operation 24 hours a day
- only in operation in daylight hours

Answer

in operation 24 hours a day

Don't drive or park in a bus lane when it's in operation. This can cause disruption and spoil the efficiency of public transport.

Question 2.30

Mark one answer

You should ONLY flash your headlights to other road users

- to show that you are giving way
- to show that you are about to reverse
- to tell them that you have right of way
- to let them know that you are there

Answer

to let them know that you are there

You should only flash your headlamps to warn others of your presence. Don't use them to

- greet others
- show impatience
- give up your priority.

Question 2.31

Mark one answer

What should you use your horn for?

- To alert others to your presence
- To allow you right of way
- To greet other road users
- To signal your annoyance

Answer

To alert others to your presence

Don't use it to

- greet others
- show impatience
- give priority.

Your horn shouldn't be used between 11.30 pm and 7 am in a built-up area or when your vehicle is stationary – unless a moving vehicle poses a danger.

Question 2.32

Mark one answer

A vehicle pulls out in front of you at a junction. What should you do?

- Swerve past it and sound your horn
- Flash your headlights and drive up close behind
- Slow down and be ready to stop
- Accelerate past it immediately

Answer

Slow down and be ready to stop

Try to be ready for the unexpected. Plan ahead and learn to anticipate hazards. You'll then give yourself more time to react to any problems that might occur.

Be tolerant of the behaviour of other road users who don't behave correctly.

Question 2.33

Mark one answer

You are in a one-way street and want to turn right. You should position yourself

- in the right-hand lane
- in the left-hand lane
- in either lane, depending on the traffic
- just left of the centre line

Answer

in the right-hand lane

If you're travelling in a one-way street and wish to turn right you should take up a position in the right-hand lane. This will enable other road users not wishing to turn to proceed on the left. Indicate your intention and take up your position in good time.

Question 2.34

Mark one answer

You wish to turn right ahead. Why should you take up the correct position in good time?

- To allow other drivers to pull out in front of you
- To give a better view into the road that you're joining
- To help other road users know what you intend to do
- To allow drivers to pass you on the right

Answer

- **To help other road users know what you intend to do**

If you wish to turn right into a side road, take up your position in good time. Move to the centre of the road when it's safe to do so. This will allow vehicles to pass you on the left. Early planning will show other traffic what you intend to do.

Question 2.35

Mark two answers

You are driving along a country road. A horse and rider are approaching. What should you do?

- Increase your speed
- Sound your horn
- Flash your headlights
- Drive slowly past
- Give plenty of room
- Rev your engine

Answers

- **Drive slowly past**
- **Give plenty of room**

It's important that you reduce your speed. Passing too closely, at speed could startle the horse and unseat the rider.

Question 2.36

Mark one answer

A person herding sheep asks you to stop. You should

- ignore them as they have no authority
- stop and switch off your engine
- continue on but drive slowly
- try and get past quickly

Answer

- **stop and switch off your engine**

Allow the animals to clear the road before you proceed. Animals are unpredictable and startle easily; they could turn and run into your path.

Question 2.37

Mark one answer

When overtaking a horse and rider you should

- sound your horn as a warning
- go past as quickly as possible
- flash your headlights as a warning
- go past slowly and carefully

Answer

go past slowly and carefully

Horses can become startled by the sound of a car engine or the rush of air caused by passing too closely. Keep well back, and only pass when it is safe; leave them plenty of room. Consider that you may have to use the other side of the road to pass.

Question 2.38

Mark one answer

At a puffin crossing what colour follows the green signal?

- Steady red
- Flashing amber
- Steady amber
- Flashing green

Answer

Steady amber

Puffin crossings have infra-red sensors which detect when pedestrians are crossing and hold the red traffic signal until the crossing is clear. The use of a sensor means there is no flashing amber phase as there is with a pelican crossing.

Question 2.39

Mark one answer

You stop for pedestrians waiting to cross at a zebra crossing. They do not start to cross. What should you do?

- Be patient and wait
- Sound your horn
- Carry on
- Wave them to cross

Answer

Be patient and wait

If you stop for pedestrians and they don't start to cross don't

- wave them across
- sound your horn.This could be dangerous if another vehicle's approaching and hasn't seen or heard your signal.

Question 2.40

Mark one answer

You are riding on a country road. Two horses with riders are in the distance. You should

- continue at your normal speed
- change down the gears quickly
- slow down and be ready to stop
- flash your headlight to warn them

Answer

- **slow down and be ready to stop**

Animals are easily frightened by moving motor vehicles. If you're approaching horses keep your speed down and watch to see if the rider has any difficulty keeping control. Always be ready to stop if necessary.

Question 2.41

Mark one answer

You should never wave people across at pedestrian crossings because

- there may be another vehicle coming
- they may not be looking
- it is safer for you to carry on
- they may not be ready to cross

Answer

- **there may be another vehicle coming**

If it's safe you should always stop for pedestrians waiting at pedestrian crossings. Don't wave them to cross the road since another driver may not

- have seen them
- have seen your signal
- be able to stop safely.

Question 2.42

Mark one answer

At a pelican crossing the flashing amber light means you MUST

- stop and wait for the green light
- stop and wait for the red light
- give way to pedestrians waiting to cross
- give way to pedestrians already on the crossing

Answer

give way to pedestrians already on the crossing

Pelican crossings are light-controlled crossings where pedestrians use push-button controls to change the signals. Pelican crossings have no red-and-amber stage before green. Instead, they have a flashing amber light, which means you must give way to pedestrians on the crossing. If it's clear you may go on.

Question 2.43

Mark one answer

Following this vehicle too closely is unwise because

- your brakes will overheat
- your view ahead is increased
- your engine will overheat
- your view ahead is reduced

Answer

your view ahead is reduced

Staying back will increase your view of the road ahead. This will help you to see any hazards that might occur and allow you more time to react.

Question 2.44

Mark two answers

When riding a motorcycle your normal road position should allow

- other vehicles to overtake on your left
- the driver ahead to see you in the mirrors
- you to prevent following vehicles from overtaking
- you to be seen by traffic that is emerging from junctions ahead
- you to ride within half a metre (1 foot 8 inches) of the kerb

Answers

- **the driver ahead to see you in the mirrors**
- **you to be seen by traffic that is emerging from junctions ahead**

Keep clear of the centre of the road. You might

- obstruct overtaking traffic
- put yourself in danger from oncoming traffic
- encourage other traffic to overtake you on the left.

Question 2.45

Mark one answer

You are in a line of traffic. The driver behind you is following very closely. What action should you take?

- Ignore the following driver and continue to drive within the speed limit
- Slow down, gradually increasing the gap between you and the vehicle in front
- Signal left and wave the following driver past
- Move over to a position just left of the centre line of the road

Answer

- **Slow down, gradually increasing the gap between you and the vehicle in front**

It can be worrying to see that the car behind is following you too closely. If you ease back from the vehicle in front you'll give yourself a greater safety margin.

Question 2.46

Mark one answer

You are travelling at the legal speed limit. A vehicle comes up quickly behind, flashing its headlights. You should

- accelerate to make a gap behind you
- touch the brakes sharply to show your brake lights
- maintain your speed to prevent the vehicle from overtaking
- allow the vehicle to overtake

Answer

- **allow the vehicle to overtake**

Don't enforce the speed limit by blocking another vehicle's progress. This will only lead to the other driver becoming more frustrated. Allow the other vehicle to pass when you can do so safely.

Question 2.47

Mark three answers

Which of the following vehicles will use blue flashing beacons?

- Motorway maintenance
- Bomb disposal
- Blood transfusion
- Police patrol
- Breakdown recovery

Answers

- **Bomb disposal**
- **Blood transfusion**
- **Police patrol**

Try to move out of the way of emergency vehicles with blue flashing beacons. Do so safely and without delay.

Question 2.48

Mark one answer

When being followed by an ambulance showing a flashing blue beacon you should

- pull over as soon as safely possible to let it pass
- accelerate hard to get away from it
- maintain your speed and course
- brake harshly and immediately stop in the road

Answer

- **pull over as soon as safely possible to let it pass**

Pull over where the ambulance can pass safely. Check that there are no bollards or obstructions in the road that will prevent it doing so.

Question 2.49

Mark one answer

What type of emergency vehicle is fitted with a green flashing beacon?

- Fire engine
- Road gritter
- Ambulance
- Doctor's car

Answer

Doctor's car

A green flashing beacon on a vehicle means the driver or passenger is a doctor on an emergency call. Give way to them if it's safe to do so. Be aware that the vehicle may be travelling quickly or may stop in a hurry.

Question 2.50

Mark one answer

A vehicle has a flashing green beacon. What does this mean?

- A doctor is answering an emergency call
- The vehicle is slow-moving
- It is a motorway police patrol vehicle
- A vehicle is carrying hazardous chemicals

Answer

A doctor is answering an emergency call

A doctor attending an emergency might show a green flashing beacon on his or her vehicle. Give way to them as they will need to reach their destination quickly. Be aware that they might pull over suddenly.

Question 2.51

Mark one answer

At which type of crossing are cyclists allowed to ride across with pedestrians?

- Toucan
- Puffin
- Pelican
- Zebra

Answer

Toucan

A Toucan crossing is designed to allow pedestrians and cyclists to cross at the same time. Be prepared and look out for fast-approaching cyclists.

SECTION 3 SAFETY AND YOUR VEHICLE

This section looks at safety and your vehicle.

The questions will ask you about

- **Fault detection**

  be able to detect minor faults on your vehicle.

- **Defects and their effects on safety**

  be aware that an unroadworthy vehicle might endanger your passengers or other road users.

- **Use of safety equipment**

  make sure you have any necessary training

- **Emissions**

  make sure your vehicle complies with correct emissions regulations.

- **Noise**

  be aware that vehicles are noisy. Prevent excessive noise, especially at night.

Question 3.1

Mark one answer

When riding a different motorcycle you should

- ask someone to ride with you for the first time
- ride as soon as possible as all controls and switches are the same
- leave your gloves behind so switches can be operated easier at first
- be sure you know where all controls and switches are

Answer

- **be sure you know where all controls and switches are**

Before you ride any motorcycle make sure you're familiar with the layout of all the controls and switches. While control layouts are generally similar, there may be differences in their feel and method of operation.

Question 3.2

Mark one answer

When should you especially check the engine oil level?

- Before a long journey
- When the engine is hot
- Early in the morning
- Every 6000 miles

Answer

- **Before a long journey**

Also make checks on

- fuel
- water
- tyres.

Question 3.3

Mark one answer

Which of these, if allowed to get low, could cause an accident?

- Antifreeze level
- Brake fluid level
- Battery water level
- Radiator coolant level

Answer

- **Brake fluid level**

In order to keep your vehicle in good working order you should carry out frequent checks. As a driver or rider you must ensure that you're using a safe vehicle or machine that won't endanger other road users.

Question 3.4

Mark four answers

Which FOUR of these MUST be in good working order for your car to be roadworthy?

- Temperature gauge
- Speedometer
- Windscreen washers
- Windscreen wiper
- Oil warning light
- Horn

Answers

- **Speedometer**
- **Windscreen washers**
- **Windscreen wiper**
- **Horn**

Also check the

- lights – get someone to help you check the brake lights
- indicators
- battery – this may be maintenance-free and not need topping up
- steering – check for 'play' in the steering
- oil
- water
- suspension.

Question 3.5

Mark one answer

A loose drive chain on a motorcycle could cause

- the front wheel to wobble
- the ignition to cut out
- the brakes to fail
- the rear wheel to lock

Answer

- **the rear wheel to lock**

Drive chains are subject to wear and require frequent adjustment and lubrication. If the chain is worn or slack it can jump off the sprocket and lock the rear wheel.

Question 3.6

Mark three answers

A wrongly adjusted drive chain can

- cause an accident
- make wheels wobble
- create a noisy rattle
- affect gear changing
- cause a suspension fault

Answers

- **cause an accident**
- **create a noisy rattle**
- **affect gear changing**

A motorcycle drive chain will stretch as it wears and needs adjusting to keep the tension correct. If the chain is wrongly adjusted it can

- jump off the sprocket and lock the rear wheel, causing loss of control
- rattle as it flaps loosely
- cause problems selecting gears.

Question 3.7

Mark three answers

Which THREE does the law require you to keep in good condition?

- Gears
- Transmission
- Headlights
- Windscreen
- Seat belts

Answers

- **Headlights**
- **Windscreen**
- **Seat belts**

Also check the

- lights – get someone to help you check the brake lights
- indicators
- battery – this may be maintenance-free and not need topping up
- steering – check for 'play' in the steering
- oil
- water
- suspension.

Whether driving or riding, check that the speedometer is working once you've moved off.

Question 3.8

Mark one answer

New petrol-engined cars must be fitted with catalytic converters. The reason for this is to

- control exhaust noise levels
- prolong the life of the exhaust system
- allow the exhaust system to be recycled
- reduce harmful exhaust emissions

Answer

- **reduce harmful exhaust emissions**

We should all be concerned by the effect traffic has on our environment. Fumes from vehicles are causing damage to the air around us. Catalytic converters act like a filter, removing some of the toxic waste.

Question 3.9

Mark two answers

Which TWO are badly affected if the tyres are under-inflated?

- Braking
- Steering
- Changing gear
- Parking

Answers

- **Braking**
- **Steering**

Your tyres are your only contact with the road and therefore very important to your safety. Incorrect tyre pressures will affect steering and braking, so it's very important that you take the time to attend to them. Correct tyre pressures can reduce the risk of skidding and will provide a more comfortable ride.

Question 3.10

Mark one answer

What can cause heavy steering?

- Driving on ice
- Badly worn brakes
- Over-inflated tyres
- Under-inflated tyres

Answer

- **Under-inflated tyres**

If your tyres don't have enough air in them they'll drag against the surface of the road. This makes the steering feel heavy.

Question 3.11

Mark one answer

What is the most important reason why you should keep your motorcycle regularly maintained?

- To accelerate faster than other traffic
- So the motorcycle can carry panniers
- To keep the machine roadworthy
- So the motorcycle can carry a passenger

Answer

- **To keep the machine roadworthy**

Whenever you use any vehicle on the road it must be in a roadworthy condition. Regular maintenance will help to identify any faults at an early stage and help avoid more serious problems.

Question 3.12

Mark one answer

It is essential that tyre pressures are checked regularly. When should this be done?

- After any lengthy journey
- After travelling at high speed
- When tyres are hot
- When tyres are cold

Answer

When tyres are cold

When you check the tyre pressures do so when the tyres are cold. This will give you a more accurate reading. The heat generated from a long journey will raise the pressure inside the tyre.

Question 3.13

Mark one answer

How often should motorcycle tyre pressures be checked?

- Only during each regular service
- After each long journey
- At least monthly
- At least weekly

Answer

At least weekly

As a motorcyclist your tyres are vital to your safety. Make sure that you check the pressure in your tyres at least once a week. Don't ride your machine if the tyres are incorrectly inflated.

Question 3.14

Mark two answers

Driving with under-inflated tyres can affect

- engine temperature
- fuel consumption
- braking
- oil pressure

Answers

- **fuel consumption**
- **braking**

Regular checks of tyre pressures can prevent these effects.

Question 3.15

Mark one answer

The legal minimum depth of tread for motorcycle tyres is

- 1 mm
- 1.6 mm
- 2.5 mm
- 4 mm

Answer

- **1 mm**

The entire original tread should be continuous. Don't ride a machine with worn tyres.

Your tyres are your only contact with the road so it's very important that you ensure they're in good condition.

Question 3.16

Mark one answer

Your motorcycle has tubed tyres fitted as standard. When replacing a tyre you should

- replace the tube if it is 6 months old
- replace the tube if it has covered 6.000 miles
- replace the tube only if replacing the rear tyre
- replace the tube with each change of tyre

Answer

- **replace the tube with each change of tyre**

It isn't worth taking risks to save money. Your life could depend on the condition of your machine.

Question 3.17

Mark four answers

You are riding a machine of more than 50 cc. Which FOUR would make a tyre illegal?

- Tread less than 1.6 mm deep
- Tread less than 1 mm deep
- A large bulge in the wall
- A recut tread
- Exposed ply or cord
- A stone wedged in the tread

Answers

- **Tread less than 1 mm deep**
- **A large bulge in the wall**
- **A recut tread**
- **Exposed ply or cord**

When checking tyres make sure there are no bulges or cuts in the side walls. Always buy your tyres from a reputable dealer to ensure quality and value for money.

Question 3.18

Mark one answer

It is illegal to drive with tyres that

- have been bought second-hand
- have a large deep cut in the side wall
- are of different makes
- are of different tread patterns

Answer

- **have a large deep cut in the side wall**

When checking your tyres for cuts and bulges in the side walls don't forget the inner walls (i.e., those facing each other under the vehicle).

Question 3.19

Mark one answer

The legal minimum depth of tread for car tyres over three-quarters of the breadth is

- 1 mm
- 1.6 mm
- 2.5 mm
- 4 mm

Answer

- **1.6 mm**

Tyres must have a good depth of tread. The legal limit for cars is a minimum of 1.6 mm. This depth should be throughout the central three-quarters of the breadth of the tyre and around the entire circumference.

Question 3.20

Mark one answer

How should you ride a motorcycle when NEW tyres have just been fitted?

- Carefully, until the shiny surface is worn off
- By braking hard especially into bends
- Through normal riding with higher air pressures
- By riding at faster than normal speeds

Answer

- **Carefully, until the shiny surface is worn off**

New tyres have a shiny finish which needs to be worn off before the tyre will give the best grip, especially if the roads are wet.

Question 3.21

Mark two answers

Excessive or uneven tyre wear can be caused by faults in the

- gearbox
- braking system
- suspension
- exhaust system

Answers

- **braking system**
- **suspension**

Uneven wear on your tyres can be caused by the condition of your vehicle. Have it serviced regularly so that the brakes, steering and wheel alignment are checked.

Question 3.22

Mark one answer

Your vehicle pulls to one side when braking. You should

- change the tyres around
- consult your garage as soon as possible
- pump the pedal when braking
- use your handbrake at the same time

Answer

- **consult your garage as soon as possible**

The brakes on your vehicle or machine must be effective and properly adjusted. If your vehicle pulls to one side when braking, take it to be checked by a qualified mechanic. Don't take risks.

Question 3.23

Mark one answer

The main cause of brake fade is

- the brakes overheating
- air in the brake fluid
- oil on the brakes
- the brakes out of adjustment

Answer

- **the brakes overheating**

If your vehicle is fitted with drum brakes they can get hot and may lose a lot of their effect. This happens when they're continually used, such as on a long, steep downhill stretch of road. Using a lower gear will assist the braking and prevent the vehicle gaining momentum.

Question 3.24

Mark one answer

Your anti-lock brakes warning light stays on. You should

- check the brake fluid level
- check the footbrake free play
- check that the handbrake is released
- have the brakes checked immediately

Answer

- **have the brakes checked immediately**

Only drive the vehicle to a garage if it is safe to do so.

Question 3.25

Mark two answers

You should maintain cable operated brakes

- by regular adjustment when necessary
- at normal service times only
- yearly, before taking the machine for its MoT
- by oiling cables and pivots regularly

Answers

- **by regular adjustment when necessary**
- **by oiling cables and pivots regularly**

Keeping your brakes in good working order is vital for road safety. With cable operated brakes the cables need

- adjustment because they will stretch with use
- lubrication to prevent friction and wear of the cables and pivots.

Question 3.26

Mark one answer

What does this instrument panel light mean when lit ?

- Gear lever in park
- Gear lever in neutral
- Handbrake on
- Handbrake off

Answer

Handbrake on

If you are not sure about any lights or switches, check the vehicle manual. You should be aware that a light on the instrument panel could be a warning about the condition of your vehicle.

Question 3.27

Mark one answer

When MUST you use dipped headlights during the day?

- All the time
- Along narrow streets
- In poor visibility
- When parking

Answer

In poor visibility

This will allow other road users to see you. You should use them in heavy rain, mist, or in foggy conditions.

Question 3.28

Mark one answer

Which instrument panel warning light would show that headlights are on full beam ?

Answer

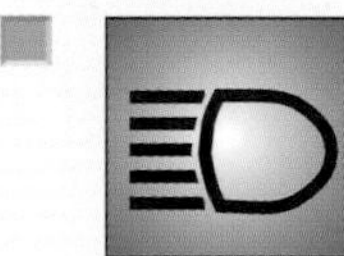

You should be aware of where all the warning lights and visual aids are on the vehicle you are driving. If you are driving a vehicle for the first time you should take time to check all the controls.

Question 3.29

Mark one answer

While driving, this warning light on your dashboard comes on. It means

- a fault in the braking system
- the engine oil is low
- a rear light has failed
- your seat belt is not fastened

Answer

a fault in the braking system

Don't ignore this warning light. It could have dangerous consequences.

Question 3.30

Mark one answer

You are driving on a motorway. The traffic ahead is braking sharply because of an accident. How could you warn following traffic?

- Briefly use the hazard warning lights
- Switch on the hazard warning lights continuously
- Briefly use the rear fog lights
- Switch on the headlights continuously

Answer

Briefly use the hazard warning lights

This situation (and on dual carriageways) is the only time you are permitted to use your hazard warning lights on the move. Only use them just long enough to ensure that your warning has been observed.

Question 3.31

Mark one answer

When may you use hazard warning lights?

- To park alongside another car
- To park on double yellow lines
- When you are being towed
- When you have broken down

Answer

When you have broken down

Hazard warning lights may be used to warn other road users when you

- have broken down and are causing an obstruction
- are on a motorway and want to warn the traffic behind you of a hazard ahead.

Don't use them when being towed.

Question 3.32

Mark one answer

Hazard warning lights should be used when vehicles are

- broken down and causing an obstruction
- faulty and moving slowly
- being towed along a road
- reversing into a side road

Answer

- **broken down and causing an obstruction**

Don't use hazard lights as an excuse for illegal parking. If you do use them, don't forget to switch them off when you move away. There must be a warning light on the control panel to show when the hazard lights are in operation.

Question 3.33

Mark one answer

It is important to wear suitable shoes when you are driving. Why is this?

- To prevent wear on the pedals
- To maintain control of the pedals
- To enable you to adjust your seat
- To enable you to walk for assistance if you break down

Answer

- **To maintain control of the pedals**

When you're driving or riding ensure that you're wearing comfortable clothing. Comfortable shoes will ensure that you have proper control of the pedals.

Question 3.34

Mark one answer

A properly adjusted head restraint will

- make you more comfortable
- help you to avoid neck injury
- help you to relax
- help you to maintain your driving position

Answer

- **help you to avoid neck injury**

The restraint should be adjusted so that it gives maximum protection to the head. This will help in the event of a rear-end collision.

Question 3.35

Mark one answer

What will reduce the risk of neck injury resulting from a collision?

- An air-sprung seat
- Anti-lock brakes
- A collapsible steering wheel
- A properly adjusted head restraint

Answer

- **A properly adjusted head restraint**

Head restraints will reduce the risk of neck injury if you're involved in a collision. They must be properly adjusted. Make sure they aren't positioned too low, as in an accident they could cause damage to the neck.

Question 3.36

Mark three answers

How can you, as a driver, help the environment?

- By reducing your speed
- By gentle acceleration
- By using leaded fuel
- By driving faster
- By harsh acceleration
- By servicing your vehicle properly

Answers

- **By reducing your speed**
- **By gentle acceleration**
- **By servicing your vehicle properly**

Plan ahead and watch the traffic flow. Constant late braking will mean that you have to accelerate again, when perhaps a gentle easing off the accelerator is all you need.

Cleaner oil means your engine is not only more efficient in it's power output, but it will produce fewer emissions and have a longer life.

Question 3.37

Mark three answers

To help the environment, you can avoid wasting fuel by

- having your vehicle properly serviced
- making sure your tyres are correctly inflated
- not over-revving in the lower gears
- driving at higher speeds where possible
- keeping an empty roof rack properly fitted
- servicing your vehicle less regularly

Answers

- **having your vehicle properly serviced**
- **making sure your tyres are correctly inflated**
- **not over-revving in the lower gears**

If you don't have your vehicle serviced regularly, the engine will not burn all the fuel efficiently. This will cause excess gases to be discharged into the atmosphere.

Question 3.38

Mark one answer

Why do MOT tests include a strict exhaust emission test?

- To recover the cost of expensive garage equipment
- To help protect the environment against pollution
- To discover which fuel supplier is used the most
- To make sure diesel and petrol engines emit the same fumes

Answer

- **To help protect the environment against pollution**

Emission tests are carried out to ensure your vehicle is not polluting the atmosphere. If your vehicle is not serviced regularly, it may fail the annual MOT test.

Question 3.39

Mark three answers

Which THREE things can you, as a road user, do to help the environment?

- Cycle when possible
- Drive on under-inflated tyres
- Use the choke for as long as possible on a cold engine
- Have your vehicle properly tuned and serviced
- Watch the traffic and plan ahead
- Brake as late as possible without skidding

Answers

- **Cycle when possible**
- **Have your vehicle properly tuned and serviced**
- **Watch the traffic and plan ahead**

The car is a very convenient mode of transport. We can travel directly from our homes, be dry and often with in-car entertainment. However, we all have an obligation to save the environment from excessive use of the combustion engine. Think about the journeys you take; often public transport can be even more convenient, quicker and less stressful.

Question 3.40

Mark three answers

As a driver you can cause MORE damage to the environment by

- choosing a fuel efficient vehicle
- making a lot of short journeys
- driving in as high a gear as possible
- accelerating as quickly as possible
- having your vehicle regularly serviced
- using leaded fuel

Answers

- **making a lot of short journeys**
- **accelerating as quickly as possible**
- **using leaded fuel**

For short journeys it may be quicker to walk, and is far better for your health too. In built-up areas just think about the time you are stationary in traffic with the engine running. This is damaging and expensive.

Question 3.41

Mark three answers

Motor vehicles can harm the environment. This has resulted in

- air pollution
- damage to buildings
- reduced health risks
- improved public transport
- less use of electrical vehicles
- using up natural resources

Answers

- **air pollution**
- **damage to buildings**
- **using up natural resources**

Exhaust emissions cause buildings to discolour and erode. Millions of pounds have been spent restoring old buildings to their original state. Constant vibration caused by heavy traffic also damages buildings.

Question 3.42

Mark three answers

To reduce the damage your vehicle causes to the environment you should

- use narrow side streets
- avoid harsh acceleration
- brake in good time
- anticipate well ahead
- use busy routes

Answers

- **avoid harsh acceleration**
- **brake in good time**
- **anticipate well ahead**

By looking well ahead and recognising hazards early you can avoid last minute harsh braking. Watch the traffic flow and judge your speed accordingly. Avoid over revving the engine and accelerating harshly

Question 3.43

Mark one answer

To help protect the environment you should NOT

- remove your roof rack when unloaded
- use your car for very short journeys
- walk, cycle, or use public transport
- empty the boot of unnecessary weight

Answer

- **use your car for very short journeys**

Try not to always use your car as a matter of routine, whatever the length of your journey. Consider walking or cycling; it is much better for both you and the environment.

Make use of the increasing number of cycle lanes.

Question 3.44

Mark one answer

You service your own vehicle. How should you get rid of the old engine oil?

- Take it to a local authority site
- Pour it down a drain
- Tip it into a hole in the ground
- Put it into your dustbin

Answer

- **Take it to a local authority site**

Never pour the oil down any drain. The oil is highly polluting and could harm wildlife. Confine it in a container and dispose of it sensibly at an authorised site.

Question 3.45

Mark one answer

Which of the following would NOT make you more visible in daylight?

- A black helmet
- A white helmet
- Switching on your dipped headlamp
- Wearing a fluorescent jacket

Answer

- **A black helmet**

Wearing bright or fluorescent clothes will help other road users to see you. Wearing a white helmet can also make you more visible.

Question 3.46

Mark one answer

When riding and wearing brightly-coloured clothing you will

- dazzle other motorists on the road
- be seen more easily by other motorists
- create a hazard by distracting other drivers
- be able to ride on unlit roads at night with sidelights

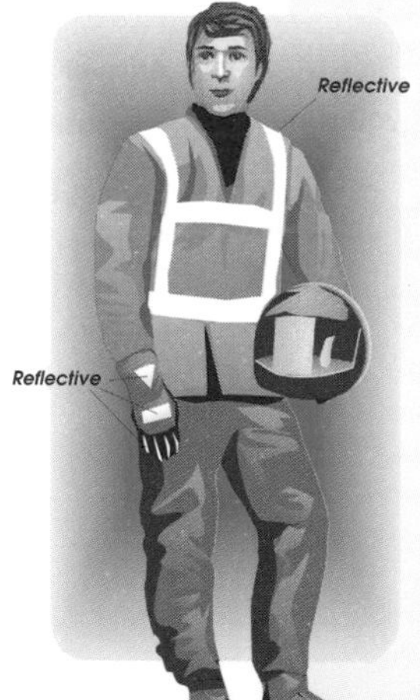

Answer

- **be seen more easily by other motorists**

For safety you want other road users to see you easily. One way of achieving this is to wear brightly-coloured or fluorescent clothing during daylight. At night reflective clothing is the best material to help others to see you.

Question 3.47

Mark one answer

You are riding a motorcycle in very hot weather. You should

- ride with your visor fully open
- continue to wear protective clothing
- wear trainers instead of boots
- slacken your helmet strap

Answer

continue to wear protective clothing

In very hot weather it's tempting to ride in light summer clothes. Don't do this. If you fall from your machine you'll have no protection from the hard road surface. Always wear your protective clothing, whatever the weather.

Question 3.48

Mark one answer

Why should you wear fluorescent clothing when riding in daylight?

- It reduces wind resistance
- It prevents injury if you come off the machine
- It helps other road users to see you
- It keeps you cool in hot weather

Answer

It helps other road users to see you

When riding a motorcycle it's very important that other road users are able to see you clearly. Fluorescent clothing will help towards this, reducing the risk of an accident. You must be visible from all sides.

Question 3.49

Mark one answer

Why should riders wear reflective clothing?

- To protect them from the cold
- To protect them from direct sunlight
- To be seen better in daylight
- To be seen better at night

Answer

To be seen better at night

Fluorescent clothing will help others to see you during the day. At night, however, you should wear clothing that reflects the light. This allows other road users to see you with their headlights. Ask your local motorcycle dealer about the correct clothing.

Question 3.50

Mark three answers

Which of the following make it easier for motorcyclists to be seen?

- Using a dipped headlight
- Wearing a fluorescent jacket
- Wearing a white helmet
- Wearing a grey helmet
- Wearing black leathers
- Using a tinted visor

Answers

- **Using a dipped headlight**
- **Wearing a fluorescent jacket**
- **Wearing a white helmet**

Many road accidents involving motorcyclists occur because another road user didn't see them. Using some form of visibility aid will help others to see you. Be aware that you're vulnerable and ride defensively.

Question 3.51

Mark one answer

You are carrying two 13-year-old children and their parents in your car. Who is responsible for seeing that the children wear seat belts?

- The children's parents
- You, the driver
- The front-seat passenger
- The children

Answer

- **You, the driver**

Seat belts save lives and reduce the risk of injury. You MUST wear a seat belt unless you're exempt. There are also legal requirements for your passengers. Make sure that you know the rules for wearing seat belts. Check the chart below.

Question 3.52

Mark one answer

You are driving a friend's children home from school. They are both under 14 years old. Who is responsible for making sure they wear a seat belt?

- An adult passenger
- The children
- You, the driver
- Your friend

Answer

- **You, the driver**

Children should always be secured and safe. They should be encouraged to fasten their seat belts themselves from an early age so that it becomes a matter of routine. As the driver you must check that the seat belts are fastened securely, it's your responsibility.

	FRONT SEAT	REAR SEAT	RESPONSIBILITY
Driver	Seat belt must be worn if fitted		Driver
Child under 3 years	Appropriate child restraint must be worn	Appropriate child restraint must be worn if fitted	Driver
Child aged 3 to 11 and under 1.5 metres (about 5 feet)	Appropriate child restraint must be worn if available. If not, an adult seat belt must be worn if fitted.	Appropriate child restraint must be worn if available. If not, an adult seat belt must be worn if fitted.	Driver
Child aged 12 or 13 or a younger child 1.5 metres in height (about 5 feet) or more	Adult seat belt must be worn if fitted	Adult seat belt must be worn if fitted	Driver
Adult passengers	Seat belt must be worn if fitted	Seat belt must be worn if fitted	Passenger

Question 3.53

Mark one answer

Car passengers MUST wear a seat belt if one is available, unless they are

- under 14 years old
- under 1.5 metres (5 feet) in height
- sitting in the rear seat
- exempt for medical reasons

Answer

- **exempt for medical reasons**

Although it's your adult passengers' responsibility for wearing a seat belt, remind them to put them on as they get into the car.

Question 3.54

Mark three answers

Excessive or uneven tyre wear can be caused by faults in which THREE?

- The gearbox
- The braking system
- The accelerator
- The exhaust system
- Wheel alignment
- The suspension

Answers

- **The braking system**
- **Wheel alignment**
- **The suspension**

Regular servicing will help to detect faults at an early stage and help prevent minor faults becoming serious or even dangerous.

Question 3.55

Mark one answer

Which of the following fairings would give you the best weather protection?

- Handlebar
- Sports
- Touring
- Windscreen

Answer

- **Touring**

Fairings give protection to the hands, legs and feet. They also make riding more comfortable by keeping you out of the wind.

Question 3.56

Mark one answer

It would be illegal to ride WITH a helmet on when

- the helmet is not fastened correctly
- the helmet is more than four years old
- you have borrowed someone else's helmet
- the helmet does not have chin protection

Answer

- **the helmet is not fastened correctly**

In an accident a motorcycle helmet which is incorrectly fastened is liable to come off and provide little or no protection. The law requires that when you ride on the road your helmet must be correctly fastened.

Question 3.57

Mark one answer

Your safety helmet has a small crack. You should

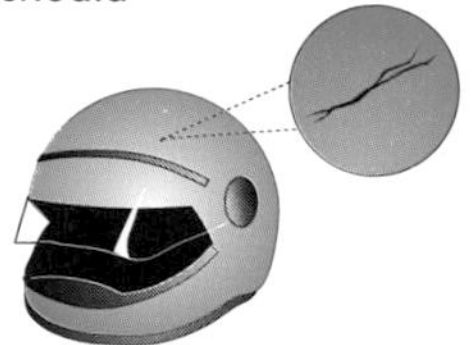

- get a new one before riding
- ride at low speeds only
- ask the police to inspect it
- have it repaired by an expert

Answer

- **get a new one before riding**

If you damage your motorcycle helmet, even slightly, buy a new one. The smallest damage can make a helmet unreliable. A little expense now may save your life later.

Buy a white helmet if possible. They're much more easily seen by other road users.

Question 3.58

Mark one answer

Your visor becomes badly scratched. You should

- polish it with a fine abrasive
- replace it
- wash it in soapy water
- clean it with petrol

Answer

- **replace it**

Your visor protects your eyes from wind, rain, insects and road dirt. It's therefore important to keep it clean and in good repair. A badly scratched visor might

- obscure your view
- cause dazzle from lights of oncoming vehicles.

Question 3.59

Mark two answers

You want to ride your motorcycle in the dark. What could you wear to be seen more easily?

- A black leather jacket
- Reflective clothing
- A white helmet
- A red helmet

Answers

- **Reflective clothing**
- **A white helmet**

When riding in the dark you will be more easy to see if you wear

- reflective clothing
- a white helmet

A white helmet contrasts starkly with the surrounding darkness, while reflective clothing reflects the light from other vehicles and makes the rider much more visible.

Question 3.60

Mark one answer

You are testing your suspension. You notice that your vehicle keeps bouncing when you press down on the front wing. What does this mean?

- Worn tyres
- Tyres under-inflated
- Steering wheel not located centrally
- Worn shock absorbers

Answer

- **Worn shock absorbers**

If you find that your vehicle bounces as you drive around a corner or bend the shock absorbers might be worn. Press down on the front wing, and if the vehicle continues to bounce take it to be checked by a qualified mechanic.

Question 3.61

Mark two answers

Which TWO of the following will improve fuel consumption?

- Reducing your road speed
- Planning well ahead
- Late and harsh braking
- Driving in lower gears
- Short journeys with a cold engine
- Rapid acceleration

Answers

- **Reducing your road speed**
- **Planning well ahead**

Harsh braking, constant gear changes and acceleration use more fuel. An engine will always use less fuel when travelling at a constant low speed. You need to look well ahead so you are able to anticipate hazards early. Easing off the accelerator and timing your approach could actually improve the miles per gallon of your vehicle.

Question 3.62

Mark three answers

Which THREE of the following are most likely to waste fuel?

- Reducing your speed
- Carrying unnecessary weight
- Using the wrong grade of fuel
- Under-inflated tyres
- Using different brands of fuel
- A fitted, empty roof rack

Answers

- **Carrying unnecessary weight**
- **Under-inflated tyres**
- **A fitted, empty roof rack**

Wasting fuel costs you, the driver, hard earned cash. It also causes unnecessary pollution to the atmosphere. Failing to carry out basic maintenance checks such as tyre pressures, can affect the handling of your vehicle. It is also an offence for which you can be prosecuted.

Question 3.63

Mark two answers

You have a loose filler cap on your diesel fuel tank. This will

- waste fuel and money
- make roads slippery for other road users
- improve your vehicles fuel consumption
- increase the level of exhaust emissions

Answers

- **waste fuel and money**
- **make roads slippery for other road users**

Diesel fuel is especially slippery if spilled on a wet road. At the end of a dry spell of weather you should be aware that the road surfaces may have a high level of diesel spillage that hasn't been washed away by rain.

Question 3.64

Mark one answer

To avoid spillage after refuelling, you should make sure that

- your tank is only 3/4 full
- you have used a locking filler cap
- you check your fuel gauge is working
- your filler cap is securely fastened

Answer

- **your filler cap is securely fastened**

As a learner driver it is sensible to practise filling your car with fuel. Ask your instructor if you can use a petrol station and fill the fuel tank yourself. You need to know where the filler cap is located on the car you are driving in order to park on the correct side of the pump. When filling the car, watch what you are doing to prevent overfilling and fuel spillage. Secure the filler cap as soon as you have replaced the fuel nozzle.

Question 3.65

Mark one answer

Extra care should be taken when refuelling, because diesel fuel when spilt is

- sticky
- odourless
- clear
- slippery

Answer

- **slippery**

If you are using diesel or are at a pump which has a diesel facility, be aware that the surface could be slippery. The fuel contamination on the soles of your shoes may cause them to slip when using the pedals.

Question 3.66

Mark one answer

You must NOT sound your horn

- between 10 pm and 6 am in a built-up area
- at any time in a built-up area
- between 11.30 pm and 7 am in a built-up area
- between 11.30 pm and 6 am on any road

Answer

between 11.30 pm and 7 am in a built-up area

Vehicles can be noisy. Every effort must be made to prevent excessive noise, especially in built-up areas at night. Don't

- rev the engine
- sound the horn between 11.30 pm and 7 am

Question 3.67

Mark one answer

When should you NOT use your horn in a built-up area?

- Between 8 pm and 8 am
- Between 9 pm and dawn
- Between dusk and 8 am
- Between 11.30 pm and 7 am

Answer

Between 11.30 pm and 7 am

Flash your headlights as an alternative. Only sound your horn to prevent an accident.

Question 3.68

Mark one answer

Why are mirrors often slightly curved (convex)?

- They give a wider field of vision
- They totally cover blind spots
- They make it easier to judge the speed of following traffic
- They make following traffic look bigger

Answer

They give a wider field of vision

Modern vehicles provide the driver with the equipment to help increase the field of vision. However, you should always be aware that even these mirrors might not reflect all that is around the vehicle. A check over the shoulder before you move off will be required.

Question 3.69

Mark one answer

You cannot see clearly behind when reversing. What should you do?

- Open your window to look behind
- Open the door and look behind
- Look in the nearside mirror
- Ask someone to guide you

Answer

- **Ask someone to guide you**

If you want to turn your car around try to find a place where you have good all-round vision. If this isn't possible and you're unable to see clearly, then get someone to guide you.

Question 3.70

Mark one answer

Why can it be helpful to have mirrors fitted on each side of your motorcycle?

- To judge the gap when filtering in traffic
- To give protection when riding in poor weather
- To make your machine appear larger to other drivers
- To give you the best view of the road behind

Answer

- **To give you the best view of the road behind**

When riding on the road you need to know as much about following traffic as you can. A mirror fitted on each side of your motorcycle will help give you the best view of the road behind.

Question 3.71

Mark one answer

When MUST you use a dipped headlight during the day?

- On country roads
- In poor visibility
- Along narrow streets
- When parking

Answer

- **In poor visibility**

It's important that other road users can see you clearly at all times. It will help other road users to see you if you use a dipped headlight during the day. If there's limited visibility you MUST use them.

Question 3.72

Mark one answer

Your side stand is not raised fully when you start to ride. What could this do?

- Alter the machine's centre of gravity
- Catch on your feet
- Dig into the ground when you are cornering
- Cause the machine to steer badly

Answer

- **Dig into the ground when you are cornering**

Make sure that your side stand's fully up before you move off. If it isn't up it could dig into the ground as you move away and might lead to an accident.

Question 3.73

Mark one answer

What is most likely to cause high fuel consumption?

- Poor steering control
- Accelerating around bends
- Staying in high gears
- Harsh braking and accelerating

Answer

- **Harsh braking and accelerating**

Look after your vehicle or machine. Have it regularly serviced and keep all the lights and windows (on a vehicle) clean. Driving or riding 'sympathetically' will help you to keep fuel consumption down. This practice is kinder to the environment and will also save you money.

Question 3.74

Mark two answers

A properly serviced vehicle will give

- lower insurance premiums
- you a refund on your road tax
- better fuel economy
- cleaner exhaust emissions

Answers

- **better fuel economy**
- **cleaner exhaust emissions**

When you purchase your vehicle, check at what intervals you should have it serviced. This can vary depending on model or manufacturer. Use the service manual and keep it up to date. The cleaner, the engine, the cleaner it's emissions.

Question 3.75

Mark one answer

Driving at 70 mph uses more fuel than driving at 50 mph by up to

- 10%
- 30%
- 75%
- 100%

Answer

- **30%**

Your vehicle will be cheaper to run if you avoid heavy acceleration. The higher the engine revs, the more fuel you will use.

Question 3.76

Mark one answer

When driving a car fitted with automatic transmission what would you use 'kick down' for?

- Cruise control
- Quick acceleration
- Slow braking
- Fuel economy

Answer

Quick acceleration

'Kick down' selects a lower gear, enabling the vehicle to accelerate faster.

Question 3.77

Mark one answer

When a roof rack is not in use it should be removed. Why is this?

- It will affect the suspension
- It is illegal
- It will affect your braking
- It will waste fuel

Answer

It will waste fuel

We are all responsible for the environment we live in. By each driver taking individual responsibility for conserving fuel, together it will make a difference.

Question 3.78

Mark one answer

A roof rack fitted to your car will

- reduce fuel consumption
- improve the road handling
- make your car go faster
- increase fuel consumption

Answer

increase fuel consumption

Make sure that any cover is securely fitted and does not flap about in the wind when driving. There are roof boxes available which will reduce wind resistance, and in turn, fuel consumption.

Question 3.79

Mark three answers

The pictured vehicle is 'environmentally friendly' because it

- reduces noise pollution
- uses diesel fuel
- uses electricity
- uses unleaded fuel
- reduces parking spaces
- reduces town traffic

Answers

- **reduces noise pollution**
- **uses electricity**
- **reduces town traffic**

The electric motors of trams don't emit dirty fumes which would add to those already emitted by the other town traffic. These types of motor are also much quieter than petrol or diesel engines.

Question 3.80

Mark one answer

Supertrams or Light Rapid Transit (LRT) systems are environmentally friendly because

- they use diesel power
- they use quieter roads
- they use electric power
- they do not operate during rush hour

Answer

- **they use electric power**

This means that they do not emit toxic fumes adding to city pollution problems. They are also a lot quieter and smoother to ride on.

Question 3.81

Mark one answer

'Red routes' in major cities have been introduced to

- raise the speed limits
- help the traffic flow
- provide better parking
- allow lorries to load more freely

Answer

- **help the traffic flow**

Traffic jams today are often caused by the volume of traffic. However, selfish parking can lead to the closure of an inside lane or traffic having to wait for oncoming vehicles, which may also cause delays. All the time the traffic is moving slowly, each engine is emitting toxic fumes.

Question 3.82

Mark three answers

To reduce the volume of traffic on the roads you could

- use public transport more often
- share a car when possible
- walk or cycle on short journeys
- travel by car at all times
- use a car with a smaller engine
- drive in a bus lane

Answers

- **use public transport more often**
- **share a car when possible**
- **walk or cycle on short journeys**

Travelling by public transport is an opportunity to get regular exercise by walking to the train or bus station. Exercise is good for everyone. Leave the car at home.

Question 3.83

Mark one answer

In some narrow residential streets you will find a speed limit of

- 20 mph
- 25 mph
- 35 mph
- 40 mph

Answer

- **20 mph**

There are numerous hazards to deal with in residential areas. These hazards can be unpredictable, hidden, static or moving. You need to allow yourself the time and space to deal with them. The safest way to do this is to reduce your speed.

Question 3.84

Mark one answer

Road humps, chicanes and narrowings are

- always at major road works
- used to increase traffic speed
- at toll-bridge approaches only
- traffic calming measures

Answer

- **traffic calming measures**

Remember that the car is a relatively late addition to our environment. Many areas, especially residential, were not built to allow for fast moving traffic. Drivers not considering the many dangers has resulted in measures being taken to slow the traffic down. It may be quicker to walk.

Question 3.85

Mark one answer

You enter a road where there are road humps. What should you do?

- Maintain a reduced speed throughout
- Accelerate quickly between each one
- Always keep to the maximum legal speed
- Drive slowly at school times only

Answer

Maintain a reduced speed throughout

The humps are there for a reason: to reduce the speed of the traffic. Don't accelerate harshly between them as this means you will only have to brake harshly to negotiate the next hump. Harsh braking and accelerating uses more fuel.

NI

Question 3.86

Mark three answers

A motorcyclist may only carry a pillion passenger when

- the rider has successfully completed CBT (Compulsory Basic Training)
- the rider holds a full licence for the category of machine
- the motorcycle is fitted with rear foot pegs
- the rider has a full car licence and is over 21
- there is a proper passenger seat fitted
- there is no sidecar fitted to the machine

Answers

the rider holds a full licence for the category of machine

the motorcycle is fitted with rear foot pegs

there is a proper passenger seat fitted

Before carrying a passenger on a motorcycle the rider must hold a full licence for the category being ridden and make sure that

- passenger footrests are fitted
- a proper passenger seat is fitted.

Question 3.87

Mark one answer

On your vehicle, where would you find a catalytic converter ?

- In the fuel tank
- In the air filter
- On the cooling system
- On the exhaust system

Answer

- **On the exhaust system**

Although carbon dioxide is still produced, it reduces the toxic and polluting gases by up to 90%. Unleaded fuel must be used in vehicles fitted with a catalytic converter.

Question 3.88

Mark two answers

For which TWO of these may you use hazard warning lights?

- When travelling on a motorway, to warn drivers behind of a hazard ahead
- When you are double parked on a two-way road
- When your direction indicators are not working
- When warning oncoming traffic that you intend to stop
- When your vehicle has broken down and is causing an obstruction

Answers

- **When travelling on a motorway, to warn drivers behind of a hazard ahead**
- **When your vehicle has broken down and is causing an obstruction**

Don't use them as an excuse to park illegally, such as when using a cash machine or postbox. They are an important safety feature and should only be used to warn other road users of a hazard.

Question 3.89

Mark one answer

Daytime visibility is poor but not seriously reduced. You should switch on

- headlights and fog lights
- front fog lights
- dipped headlights
- rear fog lights

Answer

- **dipped headlights**

Only use your fog lights when visibility is seriously reduced. Use dipped headlights in poor conditions.

Question 3.90

Mark one answer

Why are vehicles fitted with rear fog lights?

- To be seen when driving at high speed
- To use if broken down in a dangerous position
- To make them more visible in thick fog
- To warn drivers following closely to drop back

Answer

To make them more visible in thick fog

It makes it easier to spot a vehicle ahead in difficult conditions. Do not use other vehicle lights as a guide; it will give you a false sense of security.

Question 3.91

Mark one answer

Tyre pressures should be increased on your motorcycle when

- riding on a wet road
- carrying a pillion passenger
- travelling on an uneven surface
- riding on twisty roads

Answer

carrying a pillion passenger

Sometimes vehicle manufacturers advise you to increase your tyre pressures for high speed riding and when carrying extra weight. This information can be found in the vehicle handbook.

Question 3.92

Mark one answer

Your oil light comes on as you are riding. You should

- go to a dealer for an oil change
- go to the nearest garage for their advice
- ride slowly for a few miles to see if the light goes out
- stop as quickly as possible and try to find the cause

Answer

stop as quickly as possible and try to find the cause

If the oil pressure warning light comes on when the engine is running you may have a serious problem. Do NOT continue riding.

Question 3.93

Mark three answers

When may you have to increase the tyre pressures on your motorcycle?

- When carrying a pillion passenger
- After a long journey
- When carrying heavy loads
- When riding at high speeds
- When riding in hot weather

Answers

- **When carrying a pillion passenger**
- **When carrying heavy loads**
- **When riding at high speeds**

Read the manufacturer's handbook to see if they recommend increasing tyre pressures under certain conditions.

Question 3.94

Mark two answers

Which TWO of these items on a motorcycle MUST be kept clean?

- Number plate
- Wheels
- Engine
- Fairing
- Headlights

Answers

- **Number plate**
- **Headlights**

Maintenance is a vital part of road safety. Lights, indicators, reflectors and number plates MUST be kept clean and clear.

Question 3.95

Mark two answers

Motorcycle tyres MUST

- have the same tread pattern
- be correctly inflated
- be the same size, front and rear
- both be the same make
- have sufficient tread depth

Answers

- **be correctly inflated**
- **have sufficient tread depth**

Your safety and that of others may depend on the condition of your tyres. Before you ride you must check they are correctly inflated and have sufficient tread depth. Make sure these checks become part of a routine.

Question 3.96

Mark one answer

You are riding on a wet road. When braking you should

- apply the rear brake well before the front
- apply the front brake just before the rear
- avoid using the front brake at all
- avoid using the rear brake at all

Answer

- **apply the front brake just before the rear**

On wet roads you will have to be especially careful, brake earlier and more smoothly. Try to brake when the machine is upright.

Question 3.97

Mark one answer

You should use the engine cut-out switch on your motorcycle to

- save wear and tear on the battery
- stop the engine on short stops
- stop the engine in an emergency
- save wear and tear on the ignition

Answer

- **stop the engine in an emergency**

When stopping the engine normally, use the ignition switch.

Question 3.98

Mark one answer

Riding your motorcycle with a slack or worn drive chain may cause

- an engine misfire
- early tyre wear
- increased emissions
- a locked wheel

Answer

- **a locked wheel**

Check your drive chain regularly and adjust it if necessary (chains need frequent adjustment and lubrication). It needs to be adjusted until the free play is as specified in the handbook. Always use a special chain lubricant.

Question 3.99

Mark one answer

You have adjusted the drive chain tension. You should check the

- rear wheel alignment
- tyre pressures
- valve clearances
- sidelights

Answer

rear wheel alignment

Drive chains wear and need frequent adjustment and lubrication. If the drive chain is worn or slack it can jump off the sprocket and lock the rear wheel.

When you have adjusted the chain tension, you need to check the rear wheel alignment. Marks by the chain adjusters may be provided to make this easier.

Question 3.100

Mark one answer

As a driver you can help reduce pollution levels in town centres by

- driving more quickly
- using leaded fuel
- walking or cycling
- driving short journeys

Answer

walking or cycling

Using a vehicle for short journeys when the engine has not fully warmed up causes large amounts of pollution. Walking or cycling does not create pollution. It might have health benefits as well.

Question 3.101

Mark one answer

You will use more fuel if you drive your vehicle with tyres that are

- under-inflated
- of different makes
- over-inflated
- new and hardly used

Answer

under-inflated

Check your tyre pressures frequently – normally once a week. If pressures are lower than those recommended by the vehicle manufacturer, there will be more 'rolling resistance' and the engine will have to work harder to overcome this.

Question 3.102

Mark two answers

How should you dispose of a used vehicle battery?

- Take it to a local authority site
- Put it in the dustbin
- Break it up into pieces
- Leave it on waste land
- Take it to a garage
- Burn it on a fire

Answers

- **Take it to a local authority site**
- **Take it to a garage**

Old batteries contain acid and can cause pollution. They should be disposed of safely.

Question 3.103

Mark one answer

The purpose of a catalytic converter is to reduce

- fuel consumption
- the risk of fire
- toxic exhaust gases
- engine wear

Answer

- **toxic exhaust gases**

Catalytic converters are designed to reduce toxic emissions by up to 90%. They work more efficiently when the engine has reached its normal working temperature.

Question 3.104

Mark one answer

Which of these fuels should be used in a vehicle fitted with a catalytic converter?

- Leaded petrol
- Propane gas
- Butane gas
- Unleaded petrol

Answer

- **Unleaded petrol**

If used in a vehicle fitted with a catalytic converter, leaded petrol will damage the specially treated filter inside the unit.

Question 3.105

Mark one answer

Unbalanced wheels on a car may cause

- the steering to pull to one side
- the steering to vibrate
- the brakes to fail
- the tyres to deflate

Answer

- **the steering to vibrate**

If your wheels are out of balance it will cause the steering to vibrate at certain speeds. It is not a fault that will rectify itself. You will have to consult a garage or tyre fitting firm as this is specialist work.

Question 3.106

Mark two answers

Turning the steering wheel while your car is stationary can cause damage to the

- gearbox
- engine
- brakes
- steering
- tyres

Answers

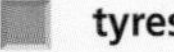

- **steering**
- **tyres**

Turning the steering wheel when the car is not moving can cause unnecessary wear to the tyres and steering mechanism. This is known as 'dry steering'.

Question 3.107

Mark one answer

Your vehicle has a catalytic converter. Its purpose is to reduce

- exhaust noise
- fuel consumption
- exhaust emissions
- engine noise

Answer

- **exhaust emissions**

Catalytic converters reduce the harmful gases given out by the engine. These gases are changed by a chemical process as they pass through a specially treated honeycombed filter.

Question 3.108

Mark one answer

Catalytic converters are fitted to make the

- engine produce more power
- exhaust system easier to replace
- engine run quietly
- exhaust fumes cleaner

Answer

- **exhaust fumes cleaner**

Harmful gases in the exhaust system pollute the atmosphere. These gases are reduced by up to 90% if a catalytic converter is fitted. These converters can be especially beneficial to those of us who live and work near congested roads.

This section looks at safety margins and how they can be affected by conditions.

The questions will ask you about

- **Stopping distances**

  leave enough room to stop in all conditions.

- **Road surfaces**

  be aware of uneven or slippery surfaces.

- **Skidding**

  be aware that preventing a skid is most important, but you should also know how to react should you lose control of your vehicle.

- **Weather conditions**

  be aware that weather conditions will have an effect on how your vehicle behaves.

NI

Question 4.1

Mark one answer

Your vehicle is fitted with anti-lock brakes. To stop quickly in an emergency you should

- brake firmly and pump the brake pedal on and off
- brake rapidly and firmly without releasing the brake pedal
- brake gently and pump the brake pedal on and off
- brake rapidly once, and immediately release the brake pedal

Answer

- **brake rapidly and firmly without releasing the brake pedal**

Once you have applied the brake keep your foot firmly on the pedal. Releasing the brake and re-applying it will disable the anti-lock brake system.

NI

Question 4.2

Mark one answer

Your car is fitted with anti-lock brakes. You need to stop in an emergency. You should

- brake normally and avoid turning the steering wheel
- press the brake pedal rapidly and firmly until you have stopped
- keep pushing and releasing the foot brake quickly to prevent skidding
- apply the handbrake to reduce the stopping distance

Answer

- **press the brake pedal rapidly and firmly until you have stopped**

Keep pressure on the brake pedal until you have come to a stop. You need to prevent the car from stalling; do this by depressing the clutch pedal.

NI

Question 4.3

Mark one answer

You are driving a vehicle fitted with anti-lock brakes. You need to stop in an emergency. You should apply the footbrake

- slowly and gently
- slowly but firmly
- rapidly and gently
- rapidly and firmly

Answer

- **rapidly and firmly**

Look well ahead down the road as you drive. You will be given clues about the hazards ahead such as road signs or brake lights. Give yourself time and space to react safely. You may have to stop in an emergency. This may be due to a misjudgement by another driver or a hazard that has given you little time to react, such as a child running out into the road. In this case, if your vehicle has anti-lock brakes you should apply the brakes immediately and keep them applied until you stop.

Question 4.4

Mark one answer

Anti-lock brakes reduce the chances of a skid occurring particularly when

- driving down steep hills
- braking during normal driving
- braking in an emergency
- driving on good road surfaces

Answer

- **braking in an emergency**

The anti-lock braking system will operate when the brakes have been applied harshly. It will reduce the chances of your car skidding, but you must be aware that on wet or icy roads it is not a miracle cure for careless driving.

Question 4.5

Mark two answers

Your vehicle has anti-lock brakes, but they may not always prevent skidding. This is most likely to happen when driving

- in foggy conditions
- on surface water
- on loose road surfaces
- on dry tarmac
- at night on unlit roads

Answers

- **on surface water**
- **on loose road surfaces**

In very wet weather water can build up between the tyre and the road surface. As a result your vehicle actually rides on a thin film of water and your tyres will not grip the road. Gravel or shingle road surfaces also offer less grip and can present problems when braking.

Question 4.6

Mark one answer

Anti-lock brakes prevent wheels from locking. This means the tyres are less likely to

- aquaplane
- skid
- puncture
- wear

Answer

- **skid**

Electronic sensors detect when the wheels are about to lock, then repeats the process in a very short space of time, reducing the risk of skidding.

Question 4.7

Mark one answer

Anti-lock brakes are most effective when you

- keep pumping the foot brake to prevent skidding
- brake normally, but grip the steering wheel tightly
- brake rapidly and firmly until you have slowed down
- apply the handbrake to reduce the stopping distance

Answer

- **brake rapidly and firmly until you have slowed down**

Releasing the brake before you have slowed right down will disable the system. If you have to brake in an emergency, ensure that you keep your foot firmly on the brake pedal until the vehicle has stopped.

Question 4.8

Mark one answer

Vehicles fitted with anti-lock brakes

- are impossible to skid
- can be steered while you are braking
- accelerate much faster
- are not fitted with a handbrake

Answer

- **can be steered while you are braking**

Preventing the wheels from locking means that the vehicle's steering and stability can be maintained, leading to safer stopping. However, you must ensure that the engine does not stall, as this could disable the power steering. When stopping in an emergency, and braking harshly, depress the clutch pedal as you brake.

Question 4.9

Mark two answers

Anti-lock brakes may not work as effectively if the road surface is

- dry
- loose
- wet
- good
- firm

Answers

- **loose**
- **wet**

Poor contact with the road surface could cause one or more of the tyres to lose grip on the road. Be especially aware when driving in poor weather conditions, when the road surface is uneven or has loose chippings.

Question 4.10

Mark one answer

Anti-lock brakes are of most use when you are

- braking gently
- driving on worn tyres
- braking excessively
- driving normally

Answer

braking excessively

Anti-lock brakes will not be required when braking normally. Looking well down the road and anticipating possible hazards could prevent you having to brake late and harshly. Knowing you have anti-lock brakes should not encourage you to drive less carefully.

Question 4.11

Mark one answer

Driving a vehicle fitted with anti-lock brakes allows you to

- brake harder because it is impossible to skid
- drive at higher speeds
- steer and brake at the same time
- pay less attention to the road ahead

Answer

steer and brake at the same time

Anti-lock brakes will help you continue to steer when braking, but in poor weather conditions this will be less effective. Depress the clutch pedal to prevent the car stalling. The power steering system uses an engine-driven pump and will only operate when the engine is running.

Question 4.12

Mark one answer

When would an anti-lock braking system start to work?

- After the parking brake has been applied
- Whenever pressure on the brake pedal is applied
- Just as the wheels are about to lock
- When the normal braking system fails to operate

Answer

Just as the wheels are about to lock

Electronic sensors detect when the wheels are about to lock, releases the brakes enough to to allow the wheels to revolve and grip, then repeats the process in a very short space of time.

Question 4.13

Mark one answer

Anti-lock brakes will take effect when

- you do not brake quickly enough
- excessive brake pressure has been applied
- you have not seen a hazard ahead
- speeding on slippery road surfaces

Answer

excessive brake pressure has been applied

If your car is fitted with anti-lock brakes, they will take effect when you use them harshly in an emergency. The system will only activate when it senses the wheels are about to lock.

Question 4.14

Mark one answer

Anti-lock brakes can greatly assist with

- a higher cruising speed
- steering control when braking
- control when accelerating
- motorway driving

Answer

steering control when braking

If the wheels of your vehicle lock they will not grip the road. This will have a severe affect on your steering control. In good conditions the anti-lock system will allow you to retain some steering control.

Question 4.15

Mark one answer

You are on a good, dry road surface and your vehicle has good brakes and tyres. What is the overall stopping distance at 40 mph?

- 23 metres (75 feet)
- 36 metres (120 feet)
- 53 metres (175 feet)
- 96 metres (315 feet)

Answer

36 metres (120 feet)

Factors that affect how long it takes you to stop include

- how fast you're going
- whether you're travelling on the level, uphill or downhill
- the weather and road conditions
- the condition of tyres, brakes and suspension
- your reaction times.

Question 4.16

Mark one answer

You are on a good, dry road surface. Your vehicle has good brakes and tyres. What is the braking distance at 50 mph?

- 38 metres (125 feet)
- 14 metres (46 feet)
- 24 metres (79 feet)
- 55 metres (180 feet)

Answer

38 metres (125 feet)

The braking distance is how far you travel from the moment you first apply the brakes to the point where you stop. Stopping distance can be divided into

- thinking distance
- braking distance.

The thinking distance is how far you travel from the moment you see the need to brake to the moment you apply the brakes.

Question 4.17

Mark one answer

Your overall stopping distance will be longer when riding

- at night
- in the fog
- with a passenger
- up a hill

Answer

with a passenger

When carrying a passenger on a motorcycle the overall weight will be much more than when riding alone. This additional weight will make it harder for you to stop in an emergency.

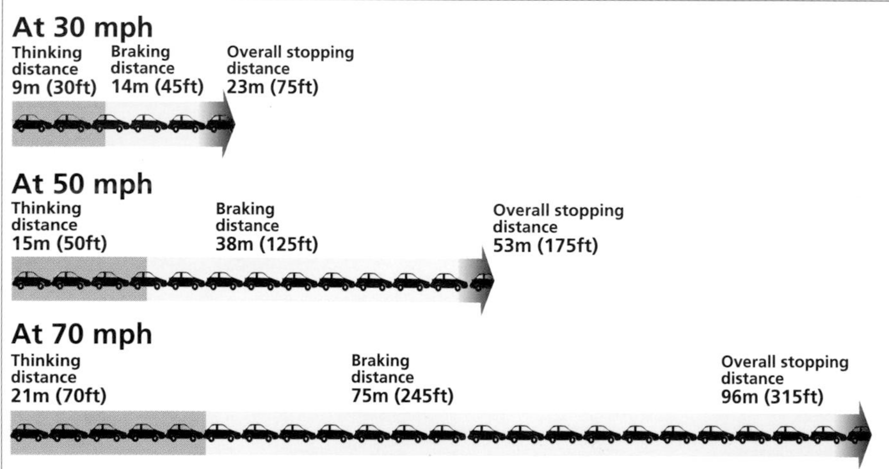

Question 4.18

Mark one answer

You are riding a motorcycle in good road conditions. The most effective way to use the brakes is to

- apply both brakes with greater pressure on the rear
- apply both brakes with equal pressure
- apply the rear brake first and the front just before you stop
- apply both brakes with greater pressure on the front

Answer

- **apply both brakes with greater pressure on the front**

This technique gives the best stopping power in good conditions because

- the combined weight of the machine and rider is thrown forward
- the front tyre is pressed more firmly on the road, giving a better grip.

Question 4.19

Mark one answer

What is the shortest stopping distance at 70 mph?

- 53 metres (175 feet)
- 60 metres (197 feet)
- 73 metres (240 feet)
- 96 metres (315 feet)

Answer

- **96 metres (315 feet)**

Note that this is the *shortest* distance. It will take at least this distance to think, brake and stop.

Question 4.20

Mark one answer

You are travelling at 50 mph on a good, dry road. What is your shortest overall stopping distance?

- 36 metres (120 feet)
- 53 metres (175 feet)
- 75 metres (245 feet)
- 96 metres (315 feet)

Answer

- **53 metres (175 feet)**

Even in good conditions it will take you further than you think for your car to stop. Don't just learn the figures – understand how far the distance is.

Question 4.21

Mark one answer

What is the shortest overall stopping distance on a dry road from 60 mph?

- 53 metres (175 feet)
- 58 metres (190 feet)
- 73 metres (240 feet)
- 96 metres (315 feet)

Answer

- **73 metres (240 feet)**

Pace out 73 metres and then look back. It's probably further than you think.

Question 4.22

Mark three answers

When driving in fog, which of the following are correct?

- Use dipped headlights
- Use headlights on full beam
- Allow more time for your journey
- Keep close to the car in front
- Slow down
- Use sidelights only

Answers

- **Use dipped headlights**
- **Allow more time for your journey**
- **Slow down**

If your journey is not necessary, don't venture out. You will be taking unnecessary risks. If you have to travel and someone is expecting you the other end, let them know that you will be taking longer than usual for your journey. This will stop them worrying if you don't turn up on time.

Question 4.23

Mark one answer

'Only a fool breaks the Two-Second Rule' refers to

- the time recommended when using the choke
- the separation distance when riding in good conditions
- restarting a stalled engine in busy traffic
- the time you should keep your foot down at a junction

Answer

- **the separation distance when riding in good conditions**

It is very important that you always leave a safe gap between yourself and any vehicle you're following. In good conditions you need to leave

- at least one metre for every mile per hour of your speed or
- a two-second time interval.

Question 4.24

Mark one answer

You are on a fast, open road in good conditions. For safety, the distance between you and the vehicle in front should be

- a two-second time gap
- one car length
- 2 metres (6 feet 6 inches)
- two car lengths

Answer

a two-second time gap

One useful method of checking that you've allowed enough room between you and the vehicle in front is the 'Two-Second Rule'. You should allow a two-second time gap as a safe separation distance.

Begin by saying 'Only a fool breaks the Two-Second Rule' when the vehicle in front passes a fixed point. You shouldn't reach that point before you finish saying it. If you do, you're travelling too close and should drop back.

Question 4.25

Mark one answer

Your overall stopping distance will be much longer when travelling

- in the rain
- in fog
- at night
- in strong winds

Answer

in the rain

Extra care should be taken in wet weather. Wet roads will affect the time it takes you to stop. Your stopping distance could be at least doubled.

Question 4.26

Mark one answer

On a wet road what is the safest way to stop?

- Change gear without braking
- Use the back brake only
- Use the front brake only
- Use both brakes

Answer

Use both brakes

Motorcyclists need to take extra care when stopping on wet road surfaces. Plan well ahead so that you're able to brake in good time. You should

- ensure your machine is upright
- brake when travelling in a straight line.

Question 4.27

Mark one answer

The road surface is very important to motorcyclists because

- there can be many areas where road markings are poor
- some roads are tarmac and others concrete
- as traffic increases there is less room for riders
- only a small part of the tyre touches the road

Answer

- **only a small part of the tyre touches the road**

A motorcyclist needs to be aware of the affect road conditions have on stability, steering and braking. Only a small part of the tyre is in contact with the road at any time which means that any change to the road surface can affect the grip on the road.

Question 4.28

Mark four answers

Road surface is very important to motorcyclists. Which FOUR of these are more likely to reduce the stability of your machine?

- Potholes
- Drain covers
- Concrete
- Oil patches
- Tarmac
- Loose gravel

Answers

- **Potholes**
- **Drain covers**
- **Oil patches**
- **Loose gravel**

Apart from the weather conditions, the road surface and any changes in it can affect the stability of your motorcycle. Be on the lookout for poor road surfaces.

Question 4.29

Mark one answer

You are riding in town at night. The roads are wet after rain. The reflections from wet surfaces will

- affect your stopping distance
- affect your road holding
- make it easy to see unlit objects
- make it hard to see unlit objects

Answer

make it hard to see unlit objects

If you can't see clearly, slow down and stop. Make sure that your visor or goggles are clean.

Be extra cautious in these conditions.

Question 4.30

Mark one answer

What is the most common cause of skidding?

- Worn tyres
- Driver error
- Other vehicles
- Pedestrians

Answer

Driver error

Skids don't just happen. They're caused by a driver asking too much of the vehicle for the amount of grip the tyres have on the road at the time.

Question 4.31

Mark one answer

You are driving in heavy rain. Your steering suddenly becomes very light. You should

- steer towards the side of the road
- apply gentle acceleration
- brake firmly to reduce speed
- ease off the accelerator

Answer

ease off the accelerator

Braking harshly in this situation could cause the tyres to lift off the road surface and the wheels to lock, which will result in loss of control. If your vehicle's fitted with an anti-lock braking system (ABS) and it starts to slide on the wet road surface, apply and maintain maximum force to the brake pedal.

Question 4.32

Mark one answer

You are riding in heavy rain when your rear wheel skids as you accelerate. To get control again you must

- change down to a lower gear
- ease off the throttle
- brake to reduce speed
- put your feet down

Answer

- **ease off the throttle**

If you feel your back wheel beginning to skid as you pull away, ease off the throttle. This will give your rear tyre the chance to grip the road and stop the skid.

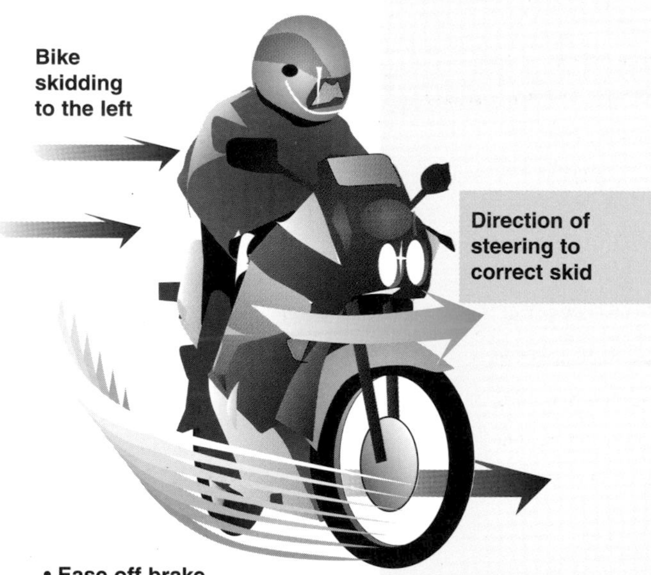

Question 4.33

Mark one answer

You have driven through a flood. What is the first thing you should do?

- Stop and check the tyres
- Stop and dry the brakes
- Check your exhaust
- Test your brakes

Answer

Test your brakes

After passing through a flood or ford test your brakes. Before you do so, make sure that you check behind for following traffic. Don't brake sharply. The vehicle behind may not be able to stop quickly. If necessary, signal your intentions.

Question 4.34

Mark one answer

You are driving along a country road. You see this sign. AFTER dealing safely with the hazard you should always

- check your tyre pressures
- switch on your hazard warning lights
- accelerate briskly
- test your brakes

Answer

test your brakes

Deep water can affect your brakes, so you should check that they're working properly before you build up speed again. Check your mirrors and consider what's behind you before you do this.

Question 4.35

Mark one answer

Braking distances on ice can be

- twice the normal distance
- five times the normal distance
- seven times the normal distance
- ten times the normal distance

Answer

ten times the normal distance

Braking and stopping distances will also be affected by icy and snowy weather. You need to take extra care and expect your stopping distance to increase by up to ten times the normal distance.

Question 4.36

Mark one answer

Freezing conditions will affect the distance it takes you to come to a stop. You should expect stopping distances to increase by up to

- two times
- three times
- five times
- ten times

Answer

- **ten times**

You must take the road and weather conditions into account when driving. It will take considerably longer to stop in bad weather.

Question 4.37

Mark one answer

You are driving on an icy road. How can you avoid wheelspin?

- Drive at a slow speed in as high a gear as possible
- Use the handbrake if the wheels start to slip
- Brake gently and repeatedly
- Drive in a low gear at all times

Answer

- **Drive at a slow speed in as high a gear as possible**

If you're travelling on an icy road extra caution will be required to avoid any loss of control. You can reduce wheelspin by driving

- at a slow speed
- in as high a gear as possible.

Question 4.38

Mark one answer

Skidding is mainly caused by

- the weather
- the driver
- the vehicle
- the road

Answer

- **the driver**

You should always consider the conditions and drive accordingly.

Question 4.39

Mark one answer

It is snowing. Before starting your journey you should

- think if you need to ride at all
- try to avoid taking a passenger
- plan a route avoiding towns
- take a hot drink before setting out

Answer

- **think if you need to ride at all**

Snow is one weather condition when it's better not to ride at all. If you must go out, try and keep to main roads which are the most likely to be clear and well gritted.

Question 4.40

Mark two answers

You are driving in freezing conditions. What should you do when approaching a sharp bend?

- Slow down before you reach the bend
- Gently apply your handbrake
- Firmly use your footbrake
- Coast into the bend
- Avoid sudden steering movements

Answers

- **Slow down before you reach the bend**
- **Avoid sudden steering movements**

Avoid steering and braking at the same time. In icy conditions it's very important that you constantly assess what's ahead.

Question 4.41

Mark one answer

When riding in extremely cold conditions what can you do to keep warm?

- Stay close to the vehicles in front
- Wear suitable clothing
- Lie flat on the tank
- Put one hand on the exhaust pipe

Answer

Wear suitable clothing

Motorcyclists are exposed to the elements and can become very cold when riding in wintry conditions. It's important to keep warm or concentration could be affected.

The only way to stay warm is to wear suitable clothing. If you do find yourself getting cold then stop at a suitable place to warm up.

Question 4.42

Mark one answer

You are turning left on a slippery road. The back of your vehicle slides to the right. You should

- brake firmly and not turn the steering wheel
- steer carefully to the left
- steer carefully to the right
- brake firmly and steer to the left

Answer

steer carefully to the right

This should stop the sliding and allow you to regain control. Don't

- use the accelerator
- use the brakes
- use the clutch.

Question 4.43

Mark one answer

You are braking on a wet road. Your vehicle begins to skid. Your vehicle does not have anti-lock brakes. What is the FIRST thing you should do?

- Quickly pull up the handbrake
- Release the footbrake fully
- Push harder on the brake pedal
- Gently use the accelerator

Answer

Release the footbrake fully

If the skid has been caused by braking too hard for the conditions, release the brake. This will allow the wheels to turn and so limit the skid.

Skids are much easier to get into than they are to get out of. Prevention is better than cure. Stay alert to the road and weather conditions. Never drive so fast that you can't stop within the distance that you can see to be clear.

Question 4.44

Mark one answer

How can you tell when you are driving over black ice?

- It is easier to brake
- The noise from your tyres sounds louder
- You see black ice on the road
- Your steering feels light

Answer

- **Your steering feels light**

Sometimes you may not be able to see that the road is icy. Black ice makes a road look damp. The signs that you're travelling on black ice can be

- the steering feels light
- the noise from your tyres suddenly goes quiet.

Question 4.45

Mark one answer

Coasting the vehicle

- improves the driver's control
- makes steering easier
- reduces the driver's control
- uses more fuel

Answer

- **reduces the driver's control**

'Coasting' is the term used when the clutch is held down and the vehicle is freewheeling. This reduces the driver's control of the vehicle. When you coast, the engine can't drive the wheels to pull you through a corner. Coasting also prevents the engine braking from holding the car back.

Question 4.46

Mark four answers

Before starting a journey in freezing weather you should clear ice and snow from your vehicle's

- aerial
- windows
- bumper
- lights
- mirrors
- number plates

Answers

- **windows**
- **lights**
- **mirrors**
- **number plates**

Don't travel unless you really have to. Making unnecessary journeys will increase the risk of an accident. It is important that any snow or ice is not covering lights, mirrors, number plates or windows.

Question 4.47

Mark one answer

You are driving in falling snow. Your wipers are not clearing the windscreen. You should

- set the windscreen demister to cool
- be prepared to clear the windscreen by hand
- use the windscreen washers
- partly open the front windows

Answer

be prepared to clear the windscreen by hand

Before you set off you should ensure that you can see clearly through all the windows. Don't be lazy and just rely on the wipers to clear the front and rear, as this will leave dangerous blind spots. If you need to, pull up safely and clear the windows by hand.

Question 4.48

Mark one answer

You are trying to move off on snow. You should use

- the lowest gear you can
- the highest gear you can
- a high engine speed
- the handbrake and footbrake together

Answer

the highest gear you can

If you attempt to move in a low gear such as first (1) the engine will rev at a higher speed. This could cause the wheels to spin and dig into the snow further.

Question 4.49

Mark one answer

When driving in falling snow you should

- brake firmly and quickly
- be ready to steer sharply
- use sidelights only
- brake gently in plenty of time

Answer

brake gently in plenty of time

Braking on snow can be extremely dangerous. Be gentle with both the accelerator and brake to prevent wheelspin.

Question 4.50

Mark one answer

The MAIN benefit of having four-wheel drive is to improve

- road holding
- fuel consumption
- stopping distances
- passenger comfort

Answer

road holding

This does not replace the skills you need to drive safely. The extra grip the drive on the wheels provide help when travelling in slippery or uneven roads.

Question 4.51

Mark one answer

When driving in fog in daylight you should use

- sidelights
- full beam headlights
- hazard lights
- dipped headlights

Answer

dipped headlights

Don't drive in fog unless you really have to. Use dipped headlights during daylight. If the visibility is below 100 metres (328 feet) use fog lights and high-intensity rear lights. Let other road users know that you're there.

Question 4.52

Mark one answer

Why should you ride with a dipped headlight on in the daytime?

- It helps other road users to see you
- It means that you can ride faster
- Other vehicles will get out of the way
- So that it is already on when it gets dark

Answer

It helps other road users to see you

Your life could depend on being seen clearly.

Question 4.53

Mark one answer

Motorcyclists are only allowed to use high-intensity rear fog lights when

- a pillion passenger is being carried
- they ride a large touring machine
- visibility is 100 metres (328 feet) or less
- they are riding on the road for the first time

Answer

visibility is 100 metres (328 feet) or less

If your motorcycle is fitted with high-intensity rear fog lamps you should only use them when visibility is 100 metres (328 feet) or less. This rule applies to all other motor vehicles using these lamps

Question 4.54

Mark two answers

In very hot weather the road surface can get soft. Which TWO of the following will be affected most?

- The suspension
- The steering
- The braking
- The exhaust

Answers

- **The steering**
- **The braking**

Take care when braking or cornering. Tyres don't grip well on soft tarmac.

Question 4.55

Mark two answers

In very hot weather the road surface can get soft. Which TWO of the following will be affected most?

- The suspension
- The grip of the tyres
- The braking
- The exhaust

Answers

- **The grip of the tyres**
- **The braking**

Only a small part of your vehicle's tyres are in contact with the road. This is why you must consider and respect the surface you're on.

Question 4.56

Mark two answers

You are riding in very hot weather. What are TWO effects that melting tar has on the control of your machine?

- It can make the surface slippery
- It can reduce tyre grip
- It can reduce stopping distances
- It can improve braking efficiency

Answers

- **It can make the surface slippery**
- **It can reduce tyre grip**

In hot weather never be tempted to ride without protective clothing. If you fall from your machine you'll have no protection from the road surface.

Question 4.57

Mark one answer

Where are you most likely to be affected by a sidewind?

- On a narrow country lane
- On an open stretch of road
- On a busy stretch of road
- On a long, straight road

Answer

On an open stretch of road

In windy conditions care must be taken on exposed roads. A strong gust of wind can blow you off course. Watch out for other road users, who may be affected more than you, such as

- cyclists
- motorcyclists
- high-sided lorries
- vehicles towing trailers.

Question 4.58

Mark one answer

In windy conditions you need to take extra care when

- using the brakes
- making a hill start
- turning into a narrow road
- passing pedal cyclists

Answer

passing pedal cyclists

You should always give cyclists plenty of room when overtaking. When it's windy a sudden gust could blow them off course.

Question 4.59

Mark one answer

Your indicators may be difficult to see in bright sunlight. What should you do?

- Put your indicator on earlier
- Give an arm signal as well as using your indicator
- Touch the brake several times to show the stop lights
- Turn as quickly as you can

Answer

Give an arm signal as well as using your indicator

You should always ensure that other road users are aware of your intentions. If you feel your indicator might not be seen then give an arm signal as well.

Question 4.60

Mark two answers

You are riding at night. To be seen more easily you should

- ride with your headlight on dipped beam
- wear reflective clothing
- keep the motorcycle clean
- stay well out to the right
- wear waterproof clothing

Answers

- **ride with your headlight on dipped beam**
- **wear reflective clothing**

Reflective clothing works by reflecting light from the headlights of the other vehicles. This will make it easier for you to be seen. Fluorescent clothing, although effective during the day, won't show up as well as reflective clothing at night.

Question 4.61

Mark two answers

When riding at night you should

- ride with your headlight on dipped beam
- wear reflective clothing
- wear a tinted visor
- ride in the centre of the road
- give arm signals

Answers

- **ride with your headlight on dipped beam**
- **wear reflective clothing**

Fluorescent clothing shows up in daylight, but at night you should wear reflective clothing. This could be a tabard or reflective body strap.

Question 4.62

Mark three answers

You MUST use your headlight

- when riding in a group
- at night when street lighting is poor
- when carrying a passenger
- on motorways during darkness
- at times of poor visibility
- when parked on an unlit road

Answers

- **at night when street lighting is poor**
- **on motorways during darkness**
- **at times of poor visibility**

Your headlight is to help you see in the dark and to help other road users to see you. You must use your headlight at all times when visibility is seriously reduced, or at night

- on all roads where street lighting is more than 183 metres (600 feet) apart
- on all motorways.

Question 4.63

Mark one answer

You are about to go down a steep hill. To control the speed of your vehicle you should

- select a high gear and use the brakes carefully
- select a high gear and use the brakes firmly
- select a low gear and use the brakes carefully
- select a low gear and avoid using the brakes

Answer

- **select a low gear and use the brakes carefully**

When travelling down a steep hill your vehicle will tend to increase speed. This will also make it more difficult for you to stop. To maintain control and prevent the vehicle running away

- select a lower gear – the engine will then help to control your speed
- use the brakes carefully.

Question 4.64

Mark one answer

You are on a long, downhill slope. What should you do to help control the speed of your vehicle?

- Select neutral
- Select a lower gear
- Grip the handbrake firmly
- Apply the parking brake gently

Answer

- **Select a lower gear**

Selecting a low gear when travelling downhill will help you to control your speed. The engine will assist the brakes and prevent your vehicle gathering speed.

Question 4.65

Mark one answer

How can you use the engine of your vehicle as a brake ?

- By changing to a lower gear
- By selecting reverse gear
- By changing to a higher gear
- By selecting neutral gear

Answer

- **By changing to a lower gear**

You should do this for downhill stretches of road. This will prevent excess use of the brakes which could lessen their effectiveness.

Question 4.66

Mark two answers

You wish to park facing DOWNHILL. Which TWO of the following should you do?

- Turn the steering wheel towards the kerb
- Park close to the bumper of another car
- Park with two wheels on the kerb
- Put the handbrake on firmly
- Turn the steering wheel away from the kerb

Answers

- **Turn the steering wheel towards the kerb**
- **Put the handbrake on firmly**

The kerb will help stop any forward movement of the vehicle.

Question 4.67

Mark one answer

You are driving in a built-up area. You approach a speed hump. You should

- move across to the left-hand side of the road
- wait for any pedestrians to cross
- slow your vehicle right down
- stop and check both pavements

Answer

- **slow your vehicle right down**

Many towns have speed humps to slow down traffic. They're often where there are pedestrians, so

- slow right down when driving over them
- look out for pedestrians.

Speed humps might affect your steering and suspension if you drive too fast.

Question 4.68

Mark one answer

When approaching a right-hand bend you should keep well to the left. Why is this?

- To improve your view of the road
- To overcome the effect of the road's slope
- To let faster traffic from behind overtake
- To be positioned safely if the vehicle skids

Answer

- **To improve your view of the road**

Don't

- move over to the right to try and straighten the bend. You could endanger yourself by getting too close to oncoming traffic.
- cross or straddle unbroken white lines along the centre of the road
- drive so fast that you can't stop within your range of vision.

Question 4.69

Mark three answers

You should not overtake when

- intending to turn left shortly afterwards
- in a one-way street
- approaching a junction
- driving up a long hill
- the view ahead is blocked

Answers

- **intending to turn left shortly afterwards**
- **approaching a junction**
- **the view ahead is blocked**

Before you overtake you should ask yourself if it's really necessary. Getting there safely is more important than taking unnecessary risks.

Question 4.70

Mark two answers

You are riding through a flood. Which TWO should you do?

- Keep in a high gear and stand up on the footrests
- Keep the engine running fast to keep water out of the exhaust
- Ride slowly and test your brakes when you are out of the water
- Turn your headlight off to avoid any electrical damage

Answers

- **Keep the engine running fast to keep water out of the exhaust**
- **Ride slowly and test your brakes when you are out of the water**

Take extra care when riding through flood water or fords. Ride through with high engine revs whilst partly slipping the clutch, to prevent water entering the exhaust system.

Try your brakes as soon as you are clear.

Question 4.71

Mark one answer

You have just ridden through a flood. When clear of the water you should test your

- starter motor
- headlight
- steering
- brakes

Answer

- **brakes**

If you have ridden through deep water your brakes may be less effective. Ride slowly whilst gently applying both brakes until normal braking is restored.

Question 4.72

Mark one answer

When going through flood water you should ride

- quickly in a high gear
- slowly in a high gear
- quickly in a low gear
- slowly in a low gear

Answer

- **slowly in a low gear**

If you have to go through a flood ride slowly in a low gear. Keep the engine running fast enough to keep water out of the exhaust. You may need to slip the clutch to do this.

Question 4.73

Mark two answers

You have to ride in foggy weather. You should

- stay close to the centre of the road
- switch only your sidelights on
- switch on your dipped headlights
- be aware of others not using their headlights
- always ride in the gutter to see the kerb

Answers

- **switch on your dipped headlights**
- **be aware of others not using their headlights**

Only travel in fog if your journey is absolutely necessary. Fog is often patchy and visibility can suddenly reduce without warning.

Question 4.74

Mark one answer

When riding at night you should NOT

- switch on full beam headlights
- overtake slower vehicles in front
- use dipped beam headlights
- use tinted glasses, lenses or visors

Answer

- **use tinted glasses, lenses or visors**

Do not use tinted glasses, lenses or visors at night because they reduce the amount of available light reaching your eyes. It's very important to keep your visor or goggles clean to give a clear view of the road at all times.

Question 4.75

Mark one answer

At a mini roundabout it is important that a motorcyclist should avoid

- turning right
- using signals
- taking lifesavers
- the painted area

Answer

- **the painted area**

Avoid riding over the painted area because these areas become very slippery, especially when wet. Even on dry roads only a small part of the motorcycle's tyre makes contact with the road. Any reduction of grip can, therefore, affect the stability of your machine.

Question 4.76

Mark two answers

Which of the following should you do when riding in fog?

- Keep close to the vehicle in front
- Use your dipped headlight
- Ride close to the centre of the road
- Keep your visor or goggles clear
- Keep the vehicle in front in view

Answers

- **Use your dipped headlight**
- **Keep your visor or goggles clear**

Riding in fog presents extra risks. Make yourself visible and keep a sharp lookout for other road users.

Question 4.77

Mark two answers

You are riding on a motorway in a crosswind. You should take extra care when

- approaching service areas
- overtaking a large vehicle
- riding in slow moving traffic
- approaching an exit
- riding in exposed places

Answers

- **overtaking a large vehicle**
- **riding in exposed places**

Take extra care when overtaking large vehicles or riding in exposed places on windy days. Strong crosswinds can suddenly blow you off course. They can also affect the stability of other road others.

Question 4.78

Mark one answer

The roads are icy. You should drive slowly

- in the highest gear possible
- in the lowest gear possible
- with the handbrake partly on
- with your left foot on the brake

Answer

- **in the highest gear possible**

Driving at a slow speed in a high gear will help your vehicle maintain the best possible grip.

Question 4.79

Mark one answer

You are driving along a wet road. How can you tell if your vehicle is aquaplaning?

- The engine will stall
- The engine noise will increase
- The steering will feel very heavy
- The steering will feel very light

Answer

- **The steering will feel very light**

If you drive at speed in very wet conditions your steering may suddenly feel 'light'. This means that the tyres have lifted off the surface of the road and are skating on the surface of the water. This is known as aquaplaning. Reduce speed but don't brake until your steering returns to a normal 'feel'.

Question 4.80

Mark one answer

You have just gone through deep water. To dry off the brakes you should

- accelerate and keep to a high speed for a short time
- drive or ride slowly while pressing the brake pedal
- avoid using the brakes at all for a few miles
- stop for at least an hour to allow them time to dry

Answer

- **drive or ride slowly while pressing the brake pedal**

Water on the brake linings acts as a lubricant, causing the brakes to work less efficiently. Using the brakes lightly as you go along will dry them out.

Question 4.81

Mark two answers

How can you tell if you are driving on ice?

- The tyres make a rumbling noise
- The tyres make hardly any noise
- The steering becomes heavier
- The steering becomes lighter

Answers

- **The tyres make hardly any noise**
- **The steering becomes lighter**

Drive extremely carefully when the roads are icy. When travelling on ice, tyres make virtually no noise. If the steering feels unresponsive you may be driving over ice.

SECTION 5 HAZARD AWARENESS

This section looks at judgement and hazard perception.

The questions will ask you about

- **Anticipation**

  plan ahead to prevent last-second reactions.

- **Hazard awareness**

  recognise a hazard ahead and preparing yourself for it.

- **Attention**

  look out for problems ahead when you're driving or riding.

- **Speed and distance**

  be aware of the correct speed for the situation, leaving enough space to react.

- **Reaction time**

  be aware that you need time to react.

- **The effects of alcohol and drugs**

  understand how these will affect your reaction time.

- **Tiredness**

  don't drive or ride if you're tired. You need to be alert at all times.

Question 5.1

Mark one answer

You see this sign on the rear of a slow-moving lorry that you want to pass. It is travelling in the middle lane of a three-lane motorway. You should

- cautiously approach the lorry then pass on either side
- follow the lorry until you can leave the motorway
- wait on the hard shoulder until the lorry has stopped
- approach with care and keep to the left of the lorry

Answer

- **approach with care and keep to the left of the lorry**

This sign indicates that you should keep to the left of the vehicle. If you wish to overtake then you should do so on the left. Be aware that there might be workmen in the area.

Question 5.2

Mark two answers

Where would you expect to see these markers?

- On a motorway sign
- At the entrance to a narrow bridge
- On a large goods vehicle
- On a builder's skip placed on the road

Answers

- **On a large goods vehicle**
- **On a builder's skip placed on the road**

These markers are reflective so that they show up at night. If you see them ahead then you should be aware that there might be a stationary, slow or long vehicle.

Question 5.3

Mark one answer

What does this signal from a police officer, mean to oncoming traffic?

- Go ahead
- Stop
- Turn left
- Turn right

Answer

Stop

Police officers might be found at a point where there's heavy traffic or a breakdown of traffic lights. Check your up-to-date copy of *The Highway Code* for the signals that they use.

Question 5.4

Mark one answer

What is the main hazard shown in this picture?

- Vehicles turning right
- Vehicles doing U-turns
- The cyclist crossing the road
- Parked cars around the corner

Answer

The cyclist crossing the road

Look at the picture carefully and try to imagine you are there. The cyclist in this picture isn't crossing the road in the correct place. You must be able to deal with the unexpected, especially when you're planning your approach to a hazardous junction. There will be several things to think about on your approach so look well ahead to give yourself time to deal with them.

Question 5.5

Mark one answer

Which road user has caused a hazard?

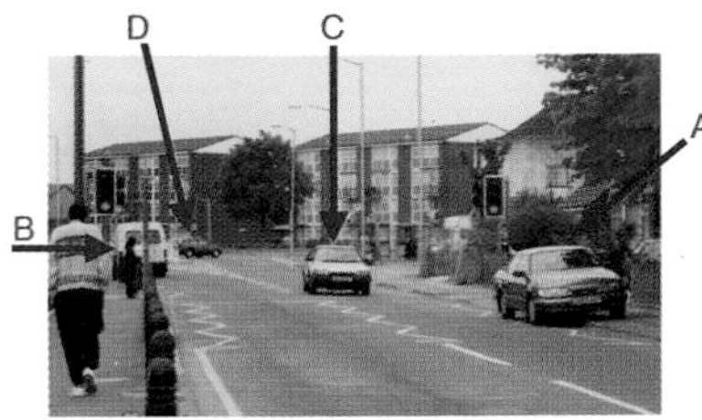

- The parked car (arrowed A)
- The pedestrian waiting to cross (arrowed B)
- The moving car (arrowed C)
- The car turning (arrowed D)

Answer

- **The parked car (arrowed A)**

The car has parked on the approach to a pedestrian crossing. The road is marked with white zigzag lines. Don't park on these – they're there for a reason. Parking here will

- block the view for pedestrians wishing to cross the road
- restrict the view of the crossing for traffic approaching.

Question 5.6

Mark one answer

What should the driver of the car approaching the crossing do?

- Continue at the same speed
- Sound the horn
- Drive through quickly
- Slow down and get ready to stop

Answer

- **Slow down and get ready to stop**

Look well ahead to see if any hazards are developing. This will give you more time to deal with them in the correct way. The man in the picture is clearly intending to cross the road. You should be travelling at a speed that allows you to check your mirror, slow down and stop in good time. You shouldn't have to brake harshly.

Question 5.7

Mark one answer

What should the driver of the red car do?

- Wave the pedestrians who are waiting to cross
- Wait for the pedestrian in the road to cross
- Quickly drive behind the pedestrian in the road
- Tell the pedestrian in the road she should not have crossed

Answer

- **Wait for the pedestrian in the road to cross**

Some people might take longer to cross the road. They may be elderly or have a disability. Be patient and don't hurry them by showing your impatience. They might have poor eyesight or not be able to hear traffic approaching.

Don't signal or wave the pedestrian to cross the road. Other road users may not have seen your signal and this could lead the pedestrian into a hazardous situation.

Question 5.8

Mark three answers

What THREE things should the driver of the grey car (arrowed) be especially aware of?

- Pedestrians stepping out between cars
- Other cars behind the grey car
- Doors opening on parked cars
- The bumpy road surface
- Cars leaving parking spaces
- Empty parking spaces

Answers

- **Pedestrians stepping out between cars**
- **Doors opening on parked cars**
- **Cars leaving parking spaces**

Your awareness in hazardous situations is very important. In a busy street like the one in the picture there are many potential dangers. You might not be able to see a pedestrian crossing from between the parked vehicles. A driver or passenger of a parked car might open a door.

Drive or ride at a speed that will allow you to stop in good time if a hazard suddenly appears. It could happen at any time.

Question 5.9

Mark one answer

What should the driver of the red car (arrowed) do?

- Sound the horn to tell other drivers where he is
- Squeeze through the gap
- Wave the driver of the white car to go on
- Wait until the car blocking the way has moved

Answer

Wait until the car blocking the way has moved

If you're moving in slow-moving traffic think ahead so that you don't block junctions or stop others' progress. Don't

- force others to give way to you
- sound the horn to gain priority
- flash your lights to gain or give priority
- give any other misleading signal.

Question 5.10

Mark one answer

What should the driver of the grey car (arrowed) do?

- Cross if the way is clear
- Reverse out of the box junction
- Wait in the same place until the lights are green
- Wait until the lights are red then cross

Answer

Cross if the way is clear

Yellow markings are marked on the road to prevent busy junctions becoming blocked with traffic. Don't enter the box unless your exit road is clear.

When turning right you can wait in the box if your exit road is clear but you can't proceed due to the oncoming traffic.

Question 5.11

Mark one answer

The red lights are flashing. What should you do when coming up to this level crossing?

- Go through quickly
- Go through carefully
- Stop before the barrier
- Switch on hazard warning lights

Answer

- **Stop before the barrier**

Approach and cross level crossings with care. If you need to stop, wait patiently. In this picture there's a junction on the left, before the crossing; keep clear of the defined road markings. Don't

- try to beat the barrier by driving through
- drive or ride onto the crossing unless the road is clear on the other side
- drive or ride nose-to-tail over it
- stop on or just over the crossing.

Question 5.12

Mark two answers

What are TWO main hazards you should be aware of when going along this street?

- Glare from the sun
- Car doors opening suddenly
- Lack of road markings
- The headlights on parked cars being switched on
- Large goods vehicles
- Children running out from between vehicles

Answers

- **Car doors opening suddenly**
- **Children running out from between vehicles**

When driving or riding on roads where there are many parked vehicles you must take extra care. Always be ready for the unexpected and drive or ride accordingly.

Children are small and you might not be able to see them about to emerge from between cars. Drivers may be getting in and out of their vehicles, providing another potential hazard. If the road is narrow, as it is in this picture, you'll also need to look well down the road. This will help you to deal with any oncoming traffic safely.

Question 5.13

Mark one answer

What is the main hazard you should be aware of when following this cyclist?

- The cyclist may move into the left and dismount
- The cyclist may swerve out into the road
- The contents of the cyclist's carrier may fall onto the road
- The cyclist may wish to turn right at the end of the road

Answer

The cyclist may swerve out into the road

When following a cyclist be aware that they also have to deal with the hazards around them. They may wobble or swerve to avoid a pot-hole in the road. They might see a potential hazard and change direction suddenly. Don't drive or ride very close to them or rev your engine impatiently. This will only add to their perception of a hazard and may rush them into a dangerous decision.

Question 5.14

Mark one answer

The driver of which car has caused a hazard?

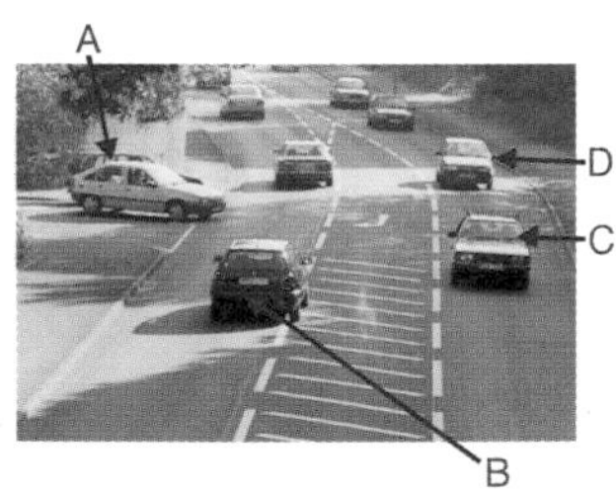

- Car A
- Car B
- Car C
- Car D

Answer

Car A

The driver of car A has forced the approaching vehicle to the right onto the hatch-marked area of the road. It has also blocked the view of the other vehicle trying to emerge.

When dealing with busy junctions consider the other road users around you. Your actions must not put any other driver or rider at risk.

Question 5.15

Mark one answer

You think the driver of the vehicle in front has forgotten to cancel the right indicator. You should

- flash your lights to alert the driver
- sound your horn before overtaking
- overtake on the left if there is room
- stay behind and not overtake

Answer

stay behind and not overtake

The driver may be unsure of the location of a junction and suddenly turn. Be cautious.

Question 5.16

Mark one answer

What is the main hazard the driver of the red car (arrowed) should be most aware of?

- Glare from the sun may affect the driver's vision
- The black car may stop suddenly
- The bus may move out into the road
- Oncoming vehicles will assume the driver is turning right

Answer

The bus may move out into the road

You should try to anticipate the actions of the other road users around you. The driver of the red car should have made a mental note that the bus was at the bus stop. If you do this you'll be prepared for the bus pulling out. Look and see how many more passengers are waiting to board. If the last one has just got on, the bus is likely to move off.

Question 5.17

Mark one answer

In heavy motorway traffic you are being followed closely by the vehicle behind. How can you lower the risk of an accident?

- Increase your distance from the vehicle in front
- Tap your foot on the brake pedal sharply
- Switch on your hazard lights
- Move onto the hard shoulder and stop

Answer

- **Increase your distance from the vehicle in front**

On a busy motorway, traffic might still travel at high speeds although the weight of traffic means the vehicles are close together. Don't follow too close to the vehicle in front. If a driver behind seems to be 'pushing' you, increase your distance from the car in front by easing off the accelerator. This will lessen the risk of an accident involving several vehicles.

Question 5.18

Mark one answer

You are travelling on this dual carriageway. Why may you need to slow down?

- There is a broken white line in the centre
- There are solid white lines either side
- There are roadworks ahead of you
- There are no footpaths

Answer

- **There are roadworks ahead of you**

Look well ahead and read any road signs as you drive. They are there to inform you of what is ahead. In this case you may need to slow right down and change direction. Make sure you are well prepared for the hazard.

Question 5.19

Mark one answer

What does the solid white line at the side of the road indicate?

- Traffic lights ahead
- Edge of the carriageway
- Footpath on the left
- Cycle path

Answer

Edge of the carriageway

This road marking gives you a warning. This is especially useful in bad weather when visibility is restricted.

Question 5.20

Mark one answer

You see this sign ahead. You should expect the road to

- go steeply uphill
- go steeply downhill
- bend sharply to the left
- bend sharply to the right

Answer

bend sharply to the left

Adjust your speed in good time so that you are able to select the correct gear for the bend. Driving too fast into the bend will lead to lack of control.

Question 5.21

Mark one answer

You are approaching this cyclist. You should

- overtake before the cyclist gets to the junction
- flash your headlights at the cyclist
- slow down and allow the cyclist to turn
- overtake the cyclist on the left-hand side

Answer

- **slow down and allow the cyclist to turn**

Keep well back and allow the cyclist room to take up the correct position for the turn. Don't drive up close behind or try to squeeze past through a narrow gap.

Question 5.22

Mark one answer

You have just been overtaken by this motorcyclist who is cutting in sharply. You should

- sound the horn
- brake firmly
- keep a safe gap
- flash your lights

Answer

- **keep a safe gap**

If you need to, take your foot off the accelerator and drop back to allow a safe separation distance. Try not to react by braking sharply as you could lose control. Any vehicles behind you will have to react in the same way, and it could lead to an accident.

Question 5.23

Mark one answer

Why must you take extra care when turning right at this junction?

- Road surface is poor
- Footpaths are narrow
- Road markings are faint
- There is reduced visibility

Answer

There is reduced visibility

You may have to pull forward slowly until you can see down the road. Be aware that the traffic approaching the junction can't see you either. If you don't know that it's clear, don't go.

Question 5.24

Mark one answer

What is the main hazard in this picture?

- The pedestrian
- The parked cars
- The junction on the left
- The driveway on the left

Answer

The pedestrian

As you drive make a mental note of pedestrians on the pavement. They could suddenly decide to cross the road or step off the kerb.

Question 5.25

Mark one answer

This yellow sign on a vehicle indicates this is

- a vehicle broken down
- a school bus
- an ice cream van
- a private ambulance

Answer

a school bus

Buses which carry children to and from school stop at places other than scheduled bus stops. Be aware that they might pull over to allow children to get on or off. This will normally be in rush hours when traffic is heavy.

Question 5.26

Mark one answer

You are driving towards this level crossing. What would be the first warning of an approaching train?

- Both half barriers down
- A steady amber light
- One half barrier down
- Twin flashing red lights

Answer

A steady amber light

This will be followed by a twin flashing red light which gives you a further warning. There is also a sound alarm to alert you. You must obey the lights. Stop.

Question 5.27

Mark two answers

You are driving along this motorway. It is raining. When following this lorry you should

- allow at least a two-second gap
- move left and drive on the hard shoulder
- allow at least a four-second gap
- be aware of spray reducing your vision
- move right and stay in the right hand lane

Answers

- **allow at least a four-second gap**
- **be aware of spray reducing your vision**

The two-second time gap will increase to four seconds when the roads are wet. If you stay well back you will increase your

- vision around the vehicle
- visibility through the windscreen
- degree of safety.

Question 5.28

Mark one answer

You are behind this cyclist. When the traffic lights change, what should you do?

- Try to move off before the cyclist
- Allow the cyclist time and room
- Turn right but give the cyclist room
- Tap your horn and drive through first

Answer

- **Allow the cyclist time and room**

Hold back and allow the cyclist to move off. In some towns, junctions have special areas across the front of the traffic lane to allow cyclists to wait for the lights to change.

Question 5.29

Mark one answer

You are driving towards this left hand bend. What dangers should you be aware of?

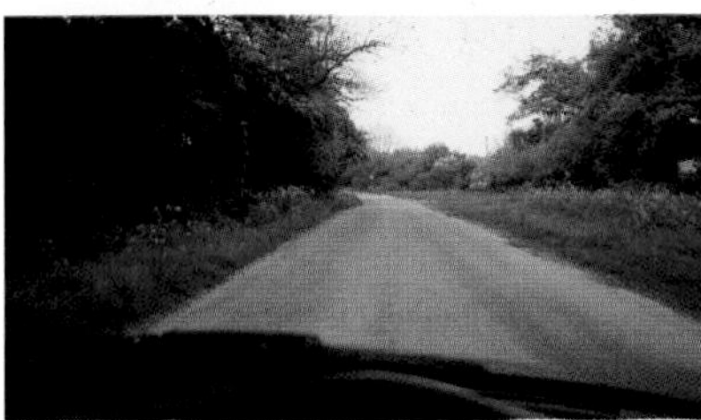

- A vehicle overtaking you
- No white lines in the centre of the road
- No sign to warn you of the bend
- Pedestrians walking towards you

Answer

Pedestrians walking towards you

Pedestrians walking on a road with no pavement will walk against the direction of the traffic. You can't see around this bend; there may be hidden dangers. Always consider this so you give yourself time to react to them.

Question 5.30

Mark one answer

When approaching this bridge you should give way to

- bicycles
- buses
- motorcycles
- cars

Answer

buses

A double-decker bus will have to take up a position in the centre of the road so that it can clear the bridge. There is normally a sign to indicate this. Look well down the road, through the bridge and consider that you may have to stop and give way to any bus approaching.

Question 5.31

Mark one answer

What type of vehicle could you expect to meet in the middle of the road?

- Lorry
- Bicycle
- Car
- Motorcycle

Answer

- **Lorry**

A large vehicle might have to take up all the road to allow the top of the vehicle to clear the bridge. The arch of the bridge is at its highest point in the centre.

Question 5.32

Mark two answers

When approaching this hazard why should you slow down?

- Because of the bend
- Because its hard to see to the right
- Because of approaching traffic
- Because of animals crossing
- Because of the level crossing

Answers

- **Because of the bend**
- **Because of the level crossing**

There are two hazards clearly signed in this picture. You should be preparing for the bend by slowing down and selecting the correct gear. You might also have to stop for the level crossing, so be alert and be prepared.

Question 5.33

Mark one answer

While driving, you see this sign ahead. You should

- stop at the sign
- slow, but continue around the bend
- slow to a crawl and continue
- stop and look for open farm gates

Answer

slow, but continue around the bend

Drive around the bend at a steady speed in the correct gear. Be aware that you might have to stop for approaching trains.

Question 5.34

Mark one answer

Why should the junction on the left be kept clear?

- To allow vehicles to enter and emerge
- To allow the bus to reverse
- To allow vehicles to make a 'U' turn
- To allow vehicles to park

Answer

To allow vehicles to enter and emerge

If you are waiting in traffic look well down the queue. Judge stopping so that you are able to leave a gap allowing traffic to flow in and out of the junction.

Question 5.35

Mark one answer

When the traffic lights change to green the white car should

- wait for the cyclist to pull away
- move off quickly and turn in front of the cyclist
- move close up to the cyclist to beat the lights
- sound the horn to warn the cyclist

Answer

wait for the cyclist to pull away

Before you move away check all around; cyclists often filter along the nearside of waiting traffic. Allow the cyclist to move off safely.

Question 5.36

Mark one answer

You intend to turn left at the traffic lights. Just before turning you should

- check your right mirror
- move close up to the white car
- straddle the lanes
- check for bicycles on your left

Answer

check for bicycles on your left

This is especially important if you have been stationary and are about to move off. Cyclists do often try to filter past vehicles in this way. You should always check your nearside.

Question 5.37

Mark one answer

You should reduce your speed when driving along this road because

- there is a staggered junction ahead
- there is a low bridge ahead
- there is a change in the road surface
- the road ahead narrows

Answer

there is a staggered junction ahead

Traffic could be turning off to the left or right ahead of you. They will be slowing right down or stopping to allow oncoming traffic to clear. Be prepared for this situation as you might have to slow down or stop behind them.

Question 5.38

Mark one answer

You are driving at 60 mph. As you approach this hazard you should

- maintain your speed
- reduce your speed
- take the next right turn
- take the next left turn

Answer

reduce your speed

There could be stationary traffic ahead, waiting to turn right. Other traffic could be emerging and they will take time to gather speed.

Question 5.39

Mark two answers

The traffic ahead of you in the left lane is slowing. You should

- be wary of cars on your right cutting in
- accelerate past the vehicles in the left lane
- pull up on the left hand verge
- move across and continue in the right hand lane
- slow down keeping a safe separation distance

Answers

- **be wary of cars on your right cutting in**
- **slow down keeping a safe separation distance**

Allow the traffic to merge into the nearside lane. Leave enough room so that your separation distance is not shortened drastically if a vehicle pulls into the left hand lane ahead of you.

Question 5.40

Mark one answer

What might you expect to happen in this situation?

- Traffic will move into the right-hand lane
- Traffic speed will increase
- Traffic will move into the left-hand lane
- Traffic will not need to change position

Answer

- **Traffic will move into the left-hand lane**

Be courteous and allow the traffic to merge into the left-hand lane. Try not to cut the vehicle off so that the driver has to steer sharply at the end of the lane.

Question 5.41

Mark one answer

You are driving on a road with several lanes. You see these signs above the lanes. What do they mean?

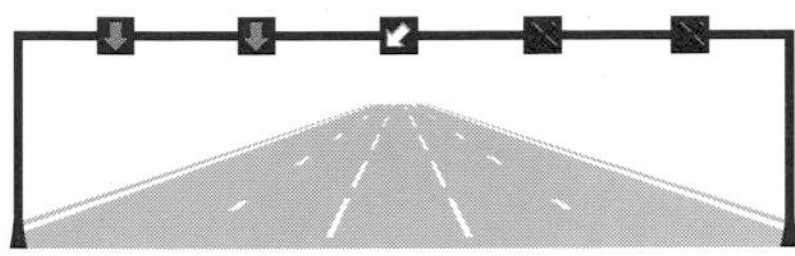

- The two right lanes are open
- The two left lanes are open
- Traffic in the left lanes should stop
- Traffic in the right lanes should stop

Answer

- **The two left lanes are open**

If you see a red cross above your lane it means that there is an obstruction ahead. You will have to move into the lane which is showing the green light. If all the lanes are showing a red cross, then you must stop.

Question 5.42

Mark one answer

At this blind junction you must stop

- behind the line, then edge forward to see clearly
- beyond the line at a point where you can see clearly
- only if there is traffic on the main road
- only if you are turning to the right

Answer

- **behind the line, then edge forward to see clearly**

The stop sign has been put here because it is a dangerous junction. You must stop. It will not be possible to assess the situation on the move, however slowly.

Question 5.43

Mark two answers

As a provisional licence holder, you must not drive a motor car

- at more than 50 mph
- on your own
- on the motorway
- under the age of 18 years of age at night
- with passengers in the rear seats

Answers

- **on your own**
- **on the motorway**

When you have passed your practical test you will be able to drive on a motorway. It is recommended that you have instruction on motorway driving before you venture out on your own. Ask your instructor about this.

Question 5.44

Mark one answer

To drive or ride you MUST be able to read a number plate from what distance?

- 10 metres (32 feet)
- 15 metres (50 feet)
- 20.5 metres (67 feet)
- 25.5 metres (84 feet)

Answer

- **20.5 metres (67 feet)**

When you take your practical test your examiner will ask you to read a number plate from a distance of 20.5 metres (67 feet). This is a legal requirement to ensure that you see situations around you on the road.

Question 5.45

Mark one answer

You are about to travel home. You cannot find the glasses you need to wear. You should

- go home slowly, keeping to quiet roads
- borrow a friend's glasses and use those
- go home at night, so that the lights will help you
- find a way of getting home without driving or riding

Answer

- **find a way of getting home without driving or riding**

Don't be tempted to drive if you've lost or forgotten your glasses. It's obvious that you must be able to see clearly when driving.

Question 5.46

Mark one answer

You MUST wear glasses or contact lenses when driving on public roads if

- you are the holder of an orange badge
- you cannot read a vehicle number plate from a distance of 36 metres (120 feet) without them
- there is an eyesight problem in your family
- you cannot read a vehicle number plate from a distance of 20.5 metres (67 feet) without them

Answer

- **you cannot read a vehicle number plate from a distance of 20.5 metres (67 feet) without them**

When you take your practical test your examiner will test your eyesight. You can wear glasses or contact lenses to do this, but then you must wear them every time you drive.

Question 5.47

Mark one answer

As a driver you find that your eyesight has become very poor. Your optician says he cannot help you. The law says that you should tell

- the licensing authority
- your own doctor
- the local police station
- another optician

Answer

- **the licensing authority**

This will have a serious affect on your judgement and concentration. The Driver and Vehicle Licensing Agency can be contacted by telephoning 01792 772 151

Question 5.48

Mark one answer

You find that you need glasses to read vehicle number plates at the required distance. When MUST you wear them?

- Only in bad weather conditions
- At all times when driving or riding
- Only when you think it necessary
- Only in bad light or at night time

Answer

- **At all times when driving or riding**

Have your eyesight tested before you start your practical training. Then, throughout your driving life, have periodical checks to ensure that your eyes haven't deteriorated.

Question 5.49

Mark one answer

After passing your driving test, you suffer from ill health. This affects your driving. You MUST

- inform your local police station
- get on as best you can
- not inform anyone as you hold a full licence
- inform the licensing authority

Answer

- **inform the licensing authority**

The licensing authority won't automatically take away your licence without investigation. Contact the Driver and Vehicle Licensing Agency for advice.

Question 5.50

Mark three answers

Which THREE result from drinking alcohol?

- Less control
- A false sense of confidence
- Faster reactions
- Poor judgement of speed
- Greater awareness of danger

Answers

- **Less control**
- **A false sense of confidence**
- **Poor judgement of speed**

You must understand the dangers of mixing alcohol with driving or riding. One drink is too many if you're going to drive or ride. Alcohol will reduce your ability to drive or ride safely.

Question 5.51

Mark three answers

Which THREE of these are likely effects of drinking alcohol?

- Reduced co-ordination
- Increased confidence
- Poor judgement
- Increased concentration
- Faster reactions
- Colour blindness

Answers

- **Reduced co-ordination**
- **Increased confidence**
- **Poor judgement**

Alcohol can increase confidence to a point where a driver or rider's behaviour might become 'out of character'. Someone who normally behaves sensibly suddenly takes risks and enjoys it. Never let yourself or your friends get into this situation.

Question 5.52

Mark three answers

Drinking any amount of alcohol is likely to

- slow down your reactions to hazards
- increase the speed of your reactions
- worsen your judgement of speed
- improve your awareness of danger
- give a false sense of confidence

Answers

- **slow down your reactions to hazards**
- **worsen your judgement of speed**
- **give a false sense of confidence**

Never drink if you are going to drive. It's always the safest option not to drink at all. Don't be tempted, it's not worth it.

Question 5.53

Mark one answer

You are invited to a pub lunch. You know that you will have to drive in the evening. What is your best course of action?

- Avoid mixing your alcoholic drinks
- Not drink any alcohol at all
- Have some milk before drinking alcohol
- Eat a hot meal with your alcoholic drinks

Answer

- **Not drink any alcohol at all**

Alcohol will stay in the body for this length of time. Drinking during the day will affect your performance at work or study. Avoid drinking at all even if you have not planned to drive in the evening.

Question 5.54

Mark three answers

What else can seriously affect your concentration, other than alcoholic drinks?

- Drugs
- Tiredness
- Tinted windows
- Contact lenses
- Loud music

Answers

- **Drugs**
- **Tiredness**
- **Loud music**

The least distraction can allow your concentration to drift. Think about your driving, and that only, to stay in full control of your vehicle.

Question 5.55

Mark one answer

How does alcohol affect you?

- It speeds up your reactions
- It increases your awareness
- It improves your co-ordination
- It reduces your concentration

Answer

- **It reduces your concentration**

Concentration and good judgement at all times are needed to be a good, safe driver.

Question 5.56

Mark one answer

You have been convicted of driving whilst unfit through drink or drugs. You will find this is likely to cause the cost of one of the following to rise considerably. Which one?

- Road fund licence
- Insurance premiums
- Vehicle test certificate
- Driving licence

Answer

- **Insurance premiums**

You have proved yourself to be a risk to yourself and others on the road. For this reason insurance companies may charge you a high premium.

Question 5.57

Mark one answer

What advice should you give to a driver who has had a few alcoholic drinks at a party?

- Have a strong cup of coffee and then drive home
- Drive home carefully and slowly
- Go home by public transport
- Wait a short while and then drive home

Answer

- **Go home by public transport**

Drinking black coffee or waiting a few hours won't make any difference. Alcohol takes time to leave the body. You might even be unfit to drive or ride the following morning.

Question 5.58

Mark one answer

You go to a social event and need to drive a short time after. What precaution should you take?

- Avoid drinking alcohol on an empty stomach
- Drink plenty of coffee after drinking alcohol
- Avoid drinking alcohol completely
- Drink plenty of milk before drinking alcohol

Answer

- **Avoid drinking alcohol completely**

This is always going to be the safest option. One drink could be too many.

Question 5.59

Mark one answer

Your doctor has given you a course of medicine. Why should you ask how it will affect you?

- Drugs make you a better driver or rider by quickening your reactions
- You will have to let your insurance company know about the medicine
- Some types of medicine can cause your reactions to slow down
- The medicine you take may affect your hearing

Answer

Some types of medicine can cause your reactions to slow down

Always check the label of any medication container. The contents might affect your driving. If you aren't sure, ask your doctor or pharmacist.

Question 5.60

Mark one answer

You have been taking medicine for a few days which made you feel drowsy. Today you feel better but still need to take the medicine. You should only drive

- if your journey is necessary
- at night on quiet roads
- if someone goes with you
- after checking with your doctor

Answer

after checking with your doctor

Take care, it's not worth taking risks. Always check to be really sure. The medicine may have an affect on you later in the day.

Question 5.61

Mark one answer

You are about to return home from holiday when you become ill. A doctor prescribes drugs which are likely to affect your driving. You should

- drive only if someone is with you
- avoid driving on motorways
- not drive yourself
- never drive at more than 30 mph

Answer

not drive yourself

Find another way to get home. This may be very inconvenient, but it isn't worth the risk to other road users, your passengers or yourself.

Question 5.62

Mark two answers

During periods of illness your ability to drive may be impaired. You MUST

- see your doctor each time before you drive
- only take smaller doses of any medicines
- be medically fit to drive
- not drive after taking certain medicines
- take all your medicines with you when you drive

Answers

- **be medically fit to drive**
- **not drive after taking certain medicines**

Medication can affect your concentration and your judgement when dealing with hazards. This, of course, is highly dangerous; be responsible.

Question 5.63

Mark two answers

You are not sure if your cough medicine will affect you. What TWO things could you do?

- Ask your doctor
- Check the medicine label
- Drive or ride if you feel alright
- Ask a friend or relative for advice

Answers

- **Ask your doctor**
- **Check the medicine label**

If you're taking medicine or drugs prescribed by your doctor, check to ensure that they won't make you drowsy. If you forget to ask at the time of your visit to the surgery, check with your pharmacist.

Question 5.64

Mark one answer

You take some cough medicine given to you by a friend. What should you do before driving?

- Ask your friend if taking the medicine affected their driving
- Drink some strong coffee one hour before driving
- Check the label to see if the medicine will affect your driving
- Drive a short distance to see if the medicine is affecting your driving

Answer

- **Check the label to see if the medicine will affect your driving**

Never drive or ride having taken drugs you don't know about. They might affect your judgement and perception, and therefore endanger lives.

Question 5.65

Mark two answers

You feel drowsy when driving. You should

- stop and rest as soon as possible
- turn the heater up to keep you warm and comfortable
- make sure you have a good supply of fresh air
- continue with your journey but drive more slowly
- close the car windows to help you concentrate

Answers

- **stop and rest as soon as possible**
- **make sure you have a good supply of fresh air**

You will be putting other road users at risk if you continue to drive. Pull over and stop in a safe place. If you are driving a long distance, think about finding some accommodation in order to get some sleep before continuing your journey.

Question 5.66

Mark two answers

You are driving along a motorway and become tired. You should

- stop at the next service area and rest
- leave the motorway at the next exit and rest
- increase your speed and turn up the radio volume
- close all your windows and set heating to warm
- pull up on the hard shoulder and change drivers

Answers

- **stop at the next service area and rest**
- **leave the motorway at the next exit and rest**

If you have planned your journey properly, to include rest stops, you will arrive at your destination in good time.

Question 5.67

Mark one answer

You are taking drugs that are likely to affect your driving. What should you do?

- Seek medical advice before driving
- Limit your driving to essential journeys
- Only drive if accompanied by a full licence-holder
- Drive only for short distances

Answer

- **Seek medical advice before driving**

Check with your doctor or pharmacist if you think that the drugs you're taking are likely to make you feel drowsy.

Question 5.68

Mark one answer

You are about to drive home. You feel very tired and have a severe headache. You should

- wait until you are fit and well before driving
- drive home, but take a tablet for headaches
- drive home if you can stay awake for the journey
- wait for a short time, then drive home slowly

Answer

wait until you are fit and well before driving

All your concentration should be on your driving. Any pain you feel will distract you. Change your plans and be safe.

Question 5.69

Mark one answer

If you are feeling tired it is best to stop as soon as you can. Until then you should

- increase your speed to find a stopping place quickly
- ensure a supply of fresh air
- gently tap the steering wheel
- keep changing speed to improve concentration

Answer

ensure a supply of fresh air

If you're travelling on a long journey, plan your route before you leave. This will help you to

- be decisive at intersections and junctions
- plan your rest stops
- know approximately how long the journey will take.

Make sure that the vehicle you're travelling in is well ventilated. A warm, stuffy atmosphere can make you drowsy, which will impair your judgement and perception.

Question 5.70

Mark one answer

You are on a motorway. You feel tired. You should

- carry on but go slowly
- leave the motorway at the next exit
- complete your journey as quickly as possible
- stop on the hard shoulder

Answer

leave the motorway at the next exit

If you do feel tired and there's no service station for many miles, leave the motorway at the next exit. Find a road off the motorway where you can pull up and stop safely.

Question 5.71

Mark one answer

If your motorway journey seems boring and you feel drowsy whilst driving you should

- open a window and drive to the next service area
- stop on the hard shoulder for a sleep
- speed up to arrive at your destination sooner
- slow down and let other drivers overtake

Answer

- **open a window and drive to the next service area**

Never stop on the hard shoulder to rest. If there is not a service station for several miles, then leave the motorway at the next exit.

Question 5.72

Mark one answer

You are planning a long journey. Do you need to plan rest stops?

- Yes, you should plan to stop every half an hour
- Yes, regular stops help concentration
- No, you will be less tired if you get there as soon as possible
- No, only fuel stops will be needed

Answer

- **Yes, regular stops help concentration**

Try to plan your journey so that you can take two rest stops. You will need to stop for something to eat within this six hours in order to keep up your energy level. If this is allowed to drop you will become tired and lose concentration.

Question 5.73

Mark three answers

Driving long distances can be tiring. You can prevent this by

- stopping every so often for a walk
- opening a window for some fresh air
- ensuring plenty of refreshment breaks
- completing the journey without stopping
- eating a large meal before driving

Answers

- **stopping every so often for a walk**
- **opening a window for some fresh air**
- **ensuring plenty of refreshment breaks**

A stuffy, warm vehicle will cause you to feel tired. Playing loud music could prevent you hearing the approach of an emergency vehicle.

Question 5.74

Mark two answers

Which TWO things would help to keep you alert during a long journey?

- Finishing your journey as fast as you can
- Keeping off the motorways and using country roads
- Making sure that you get plenty of fresh air
- Making regular stops for refreshments

Answers

- **Making sure that you get plenty of fresh air**
- **Making regular stops for refreshments**

Make sure that the vehicle you're driving is well ventilated. A warm, stuffy atmosphere will make you feel drowsy. Open a window or turn down the heating.

Question 5.75

Mark three answers

Which THREE are likely to make you lose concentration while driving?

- Looking at road maps
- Listening to loud music
- Using your windscreen washers
- Looking in your wing mirror
- Using a mobile phone

Answers

- **Looking at road maps**
- **Listening to loud music**
- **Using a mobile phone**

Looking at road maps while driving is very dangerous. If you aren't sure of your route, stop in a safe place and check the map. You must not allow anything to take your attention away from the road.

If you need to use a mobile phone, stop in a safe place before doing so.

Question 5.76

Mark two answers

You get cold and wet when riding. Which TWO are likely to happen?

- You may lose concentration
- You may slide off the seat
- Your visor may freeze up
- Your reaction times may be slower
- Your helmet may loosen

Answers

- **You may lose concentration**
- **Your reaction times may be slower**

If you're riding a motorcycle you should ensure that you're wearing suitable clothing. If you become cold and uncomfortable this could cause you to lose concentration.

Question 5.77

Mark one answer

A driver pulls out of a side road in front of you. You have to brake hard. You should

- ignore the error and stay calm
- flash your lights to show your annoyance
- sound your horn to show your annoyance
- overtake as soon as possible

Answer

ignore the error and stay calm

If you're driving or riding where there are a number of side roads, be alert. Drivers approaching or emerging from the side road might not be able to see you. Be especially careful if there are a lot of parked vehicles.

If a vehicle does emerge and you have to stop quickly

- try to be tolerant
- learn from the experience.

Question 5.78

Mark one answer

Another driver does something that upsets you. You should

- try not to react
- let them know how you feel
- flash your headlights several times
- sound your horn

Answer

try not to react

There are occasions when other drivers or riders make a misjudgement or a mistake. If this happens try not to let it worry you. Don't react by showing anger. Sounding the horn, flashing the headlamps or shouting at the other driver won't help the situation. Good anticipation will help to prevent these incidents becoming accidents.

Question 5.79

Mark one answer

Another driver's behaviour has upset you. It may help if you

- stop and take a break
- shout abusive language
- gesture to them with your hand
- follow their car, flashing the headlights

Answer

stop and take a break

Tiredness may make you more irritable than you would be normally. You might react differently to situations because of it. If you feel yourself becoming tense, take a break.

Question 5.80

Mark one answer

An elderly person's driving ability could be affected because they may be unable to

- obtain car insurance
- understand road signs
- react very quickly
- give signals correctly

Answer

react very quickly

Poor eyesight and hearing could affect their judgement of speed and distances. This may cause them to be more hesitant. Be tolerant of other drivers on the road and allow them time and room.

Question 5.81

Mark one answer

You take the wrong route and find you are on a one-way street. You should

- reverse out of the road
- turn round in a side road
- continue to the end of the road
- reverse into a driveway

Answer

continue to the end of the road

Never reverse or turn your vehicle around in a one-way street. This is highly dangerous. Carry on and find another route checking the direction signs as you drive.

If you need to check a map, stop in a safe place.

Question 5.82

Mark one answer

Why should you check over your shoulder before turning right into a side road?

- To make sure the road is clear
- To check for emerging traffic
- To check for overtaking vehicles
- To confirm your intention to turn

Answer

To check for overtaking vehicles

Take a last check over your shoulder before committing yourself to a manoeuvre. This is especially important when turning right.

Question 5.83

Mark one answer

What could happen if you do not keep to the left on right-hand bends?

- You may not be able to see overtaking vehicles
- You may not be able to judge the sharpness of the bend
- Your head may cross over the centre line
- You may not be able to see vehicles to the rear

Answer

Your head may cross over the centre line

Do not ride too close to the centre line on right-hand bends. It might mean that as you lean into the bend you put yourself in danger from oncoming vehicles.

Question 5.84

Mark one answer

You are riding up to a zebra crossing. You intend to stop for waiting pedestrians. How could you let them know you are stopping?

- By signalling with your left arm
- By waving them across
- By flashing your headlight
- By signalling with your right arm

Answer

By signalling with your right arm

Giving an arm signal would also indicate to any approaching vehicles as well as the pedestrians that you are stopping at the pedestrian crossing.

Question 5.85

Mark one answer

You have just passed these warning lights. What hazard would you expect to see next?

- A level crossing with no barrier
- An ambulance station
- A school crossing patrol
- An opening bridge

Answer

A school crossing patrol

These lights warn of children crossing the road to a nearby school. Great care must be taken when the lights are operating.

Question 5.86

Mark one answer

You are driving along this road. The driver on the left is reversing from a driveway. You should

- move to the opposite side of the road
- drive through as you have priority
- sound your horn and be prepared to stop
- speed up and drive through quickly

Answer

- **sound your horn and be prepared to stop**

White lights at the rear of a car show that it is about to reverse. Sound your horn as a warning and reduce your speed as a precaution.

Question 5.87

Mark one answer

Which of the following types of glasses should not be worn when driving or riding at night?

- Half-moon
- Round
- Bi-focal
- Tinted

Answer

- **Tinted**

If you are driving or riding at night or in poor visibility, tinted lenses will reduce the efficiency of your vision, by reducing the amount of available light reaching your eyes.

Question 5.88

Mark two answers

Why should you be especially cautious when going past this bus?

- There is traffic approaching in the distance
- The driver may open the door
- It may suddenly move off
- People may cross the road in front of it
- There are bicycles parked on the pavement

Answers

- **It may suddenly move off**
- **People may cross the road in front of it**

A stationary bus at a bus stop can hide pedestrians just in front of it who might be about to cross the road. Only drive past at a speed that will enable you to stop safely if you need to.

Question 5.89

Mark one answer

You have been involved in an argument before starting your journey. This has made you feel angry. You should

- start to drive, but open a window
- drive slower than normal and turn your radio on
- have an alcoholic drink to help you relax before driving
- calm down before you start to drive

Answer

- **calm down before you start to drive**

If you are feeling irritated or angry you should wait until you have calmed down before setting out on a journey.

SECTION 6 VULNERABLE ROAD USERS

This section looks at the risks when dealing with vulnerable road users.

The questions will ask you about

- **Pedestrians**

  be aware of their actions as they cross the road.

- **Children**

  be aware that they are particularly unpredictable on and around roads.

- **Elderly drivers**

  be aware that they may be slower to make decisions.

- **Disabled people**

  be aware that they might not be able to react to danger as quickly or easily as the able-bodied.

- **Cyclists**

  be aware that they may swerve to avoid obstructions and are often affected by weather conditions.

- **Motorcyclists**

  be aware of their presence on the road.

- **Animals**

  be aware that animals can be unpredictable and may move slowly.

- **New drivers**

  be aware that they may be more hesitant, allow for this and be patient. They lack experience and are, therefore, more vulnerable.

Question 6.1

Mark one answer

You should not ride too closely behind a lorry because

- you will breathe in the lorry's exhaust fumes
- wind from the lorry will slow you down
- drivers behind you may not be able to see you
- it will reduce your view ahead

Answer

- **it will reduce your view ahead**

If you're following a large vehicle your view beyond it will be restricted. Drop back. This will help you to see more of the road ahead.

Question 6.2

Mark one answer

You are riding in fast-flowing traffic. The vehicle behind is following too closely. You should

- slow down gradually to increase the gap in front of you
- slow down as quickly as possible by braking
- accelerate to get away from the vehicle behind you
- apply the brakes sharply to warn the driver behind

Answer

- **slow down gradually to increase the gap in front of you**

Vehicles travelling too close together are dangerous. Increase the safety margin by dropping back.

Question 6.3

Mark one answer

You are riding along a main road with many side roads. Why should you be particularly careful?

- Gusts of wind from the side roads may push you off course
- Drivers coming out from side roads may not see you
- The road will be more slippery where cars have been turning
- Drivers will be travelling slowly when they approach a junction

Answer

- **Drivers coming out from side roads may not see you**

If you're riding along a main road where there are many side roads, be alert. Drivers approaching or emerging from side roads may not be able to see you. Be especially careful if there are a lot of parked vehicles.

Always drive at a speed that will enable you to slow down and stop in good time. If you look well ahead and anticipate the actions of other road users you'll avoid having to brake suddenly or harshly.

Question 6.4

Mark one answer

You are on a country road. What should you expect to see coming towards you on YOUR side of the road?

- Motorcycles
- Bicycles
- Pedestrians
- Horse riders

Answer

- **Pedestrians**

On a quiet country road always be aware that there may be a hazard just around the next bend, such as a slow-moving vehicle or pedestrians. There might not be a pavement and people may be walking on your side of the road.

Question 6.5

Mark one answer

Which sign means that there may be people walking along the road?

Answer

Always check the road signs as you drive. They'll keep you informed of hazards ahead and help you to anticipate any problems.

There are different types of signs showing pedestrians. Learn the meaning of each one. This will help you to be aware of the hazard ahead.

Question 6.6

Mark one answer

You are turning left into a side road. Pedestrians are crossing the road near the junction. You must

- wave them on
- sound your horn
- switch on your hazard lights
- wait for them to cross

Answer

- **wait for them to cross**

Before you turn into a junction, check that it's clear. Check the pavement in each direction. If there are pedestrians crossing, let them cross in their own time.

Question 6.7

Mark one answer

You are turning left at a junction. Pedestrians have started to cross the road. You should

- go on, giving them plenty of room
- stop and wave at them to cross
- blow your horn and proceed
- give way to them

Answer

give way to them

If you're turning into a side road you should give way to pedestrians already crossing. They have priority. Don't

- wave them across the road
- sound your horn
- flash your lights
- give any other misleading signal – other road users may misinterpret your signal and you might lead the pedestrian into a dangerous situation.

If a pedestrian is slow or indecisive be patient and wait. Don't hurry them across by revving the engine.

Question 6.8

Mark one answer

You are turning left from a main road into a side road. People are already crossing the road into which you are turning. You should

- continue, as it is your right of way
- signal to them to continue crossing
- wait and allow them to cross
- sound your horn to warn them of your presence

Answer

wait and allow them to cross

Always check the road you're turning into. Approaching at the correct speed will allow you enough time to observe and react.

Question 6.9

Mark one answer

You are at a road junction, turning into a minor road. There are pedestrians crossing the minor road. You should

- stop and wave the pedestrians across
- sound your horn to let the pedestrians know that you are there
- give way to the pedestrians who are already crossing
- carry on; the pedestrians should give way to you

Answer

- **give way to the pedestrians who are already crossing**

Always look into the road you're turning into. If there are pedestrians crossing, be considerate, but don't wave or signal to them to cross. Signal your intention to turn as you approach.

Question 6.10

Mark one answer

You are turning left into a side road. What hazards should you be especially aware of?

- One way street
- Pedestrians
- Traffic congestion
- Parked vehicles

Answer

- **Pedestrians**

Make sure that you have reduced your speed and are in the correct gear for the turn. Look into the road before you turn and always give way to any pedestrians who are crossing.

Question 6.11

Mark one answer

You want to reverse into a side road. You are not sure that the area behind your car is clear. What should you do?

- Look through the rear window only
- Get out and check
- Check the mirrors only
- Carry on, assuming it is clear

Answer

- **Get out and check**

It's always safer to be sure. You may not be able to see a small child close behind your car. The shape and size of your vehicle can restrict visibility.

Question 6.12

Mark one answer

You are about to reverse into a side road. A pedestrian wishes to cross behind you. You should

- wave to the pedestrian to stop
- give way to the pedestrian
- wave to the pedestrian to cross
- reverse before the pedestrian starts to cross

Answer

give way to the pedestrian

If you need to reverse into a side road, try to find a place that's free from traffic and pedestrians.

Look all around before and during the manoeuvre. Always stop and give way to any pedestrians who wish to cross behind you. Don't

- wave them across the road
- sound the horn
- flash your lights
- give any other misleading signal – other road users may not have seen your signal and you might lead the pedestrian into a dangerous situation.

Question 6.13

Mark one answer

Who is especially in danger of not being seen as you reverse your car?

- Motorcyclists
- Car drivers
- Cyclists
- Children

Answer

Children

As you look through the rear of your vehicle you will not be able to see a small child. Be aware of this before you reverse. If there are children about, get out and check if it is clear.

Question 6.14

Mark one answer

You are reversing around a corner when you notice a pedestrian walking behind you. What should you do?

- Slow down and wave the pedestrian across
- Continue reversing and steer round the pedestrian
- Stop and give way
- Continue reversing and sound your horn

Answer

- **Stop and give way**

Wait until the pedestrian has passed, then look around again before you start to reverse. Don't forget that you may not be able to see a small child directly behind your vehicle. Be aware of the possibility of hidden dangers.

Question 6.15

Mark one answer

You intend to turn right into a side road. Just before turning you should check for motorcyclists who might be

- overtaking on your left
- following you closely
- emerging from the side road
- overtaking on your right

Answer

- **overtaking on your right**

Never attempt to change direction to the right without checking your right-hand mirror. A motorcyclist might not have seen your signal, it could be hidden by the car behind you. This action should become a matter of routine.

Question 6.16

Mark one answer

You want to turn right from a junction but your view is restricted by parked vehicles. What should you do?

- Move out quickly, but be prepared to stop
- Sound your horn and pull out if there is no reply
- Stop, then move slowly forward until you have a clear view
- Stop, get out and look along the main road to check

Answer

- **Stop, then move slowly forward until you have a clear view**

If you want to turn right from a junction and your view is restricted STOP. Ease forward until you can see – there might be something approaching.

IF YOU DON'T KNOW, DON'T GO.

Question 6.17

Mark one answer

You are at the front of a queue of traffic waiting to turn right into a side road. Why is it important to check your right mirror just before turning?

- To look for pedestrians about to cross
- To check for overtaking vehicles
- To make sure the side road is clear
- To check for emerging traffic

Answer

- **To check for overtaking vehicles**

There could be a motorcyclist riding along the outside of the queue. Always check your mirror, situations behind you can change in the time you have been waiting to turn.

Question 6.18

Mark three answers

In which THREE places would parking your vehicle cause danger or obstruction to other road users?

- In front of a property entrance
- At or near a bus stop
- On your driveway
- In a marked parking space
- On the approach to a level crossing

Answers

- **In front of a property entrance**
- **At or near a bus stop**
- **On the approach to a level crossing**

Don't park your vehicle where parking restrictions apply. Think carefully before you slow down and stop. Look at road markings and signs to ensure that you aren't parking illegally.

Question 6.19

Mark three answers

In which THREE places would parking cause an obstruction to others?

- Near the brow of a hill
- In a lay-by
- Where the kerb is raised
- Where the kerb has been lowered for wheelchairs
- At or near a bus stop

Answers

- **Near the brow of a hill**
- **Where the kerb has been lowered for wheelchairs**
- **At or near a bus stop**

Think about the affect your parking will have on other road users. Don't forget that not all vehicles are the size of a car. Large vehicles will need more room to pass and might need more time to do so. Leaving the traffic unsighted, as before the brow of a hill, causes unnecessary risks. Think before you park your car.

Question 6.20

Mark one answer

What must a driver do at a pelican crossing when the amber light is flashing?

- Signal the pedestrian to cross
- Always wait for the green light before proceeding
- Give way to any pedestrians on the crossing
- Wait for the red-and-amber light before proceeding

Answer

- **Give way to any pedestrians on the crossing**

The flashing amber light allows pedestrians already on the crossing to get to the other side before a green light shows to the traffic. Let them do this at their own pace.

Question 6.21

Mark two answers

You have stopped at a pelican crossing. A disabled person is crossing slowly in front of you. The lights have now changed to green. You should

- allow the person to cross
- drive in front of the person
- drive behind the person
- sound your horn
- be patient
- edge forward slowly

Answers

- **allow the person to cross**
- **be patient**

At a pelican crossing the green light means you may proceed as long as the crossing is clear. If someone hasn't finished crossing, be patient and wait for them.

Question 6.22

Mark one answer

As you approach a pelican crossing the lights change to green. Elderly people are halfway across. You should

- wave them to cross as quickly as they can
- rev your engine to make them hurry
- flash your lights in case they have not heard you
- wait because they will take longer to cross

Answer

- **wait because they will take longer to cross**

Even if the lights turn to green, wait for them to clear the crossing. Allow them to cross the road in their own time.

Question 6.23

Mark one answer

A toucan crossing is different from other crossings because

- moped riders can use it
- it is controlled by a traffic warden
- it is controlled by two flashing lights
- cyclists can use it

Answer

- **cyclists can use it**

Pedestrians and cyclists are shown the green light together. The signals are push-button operated and there is no flashing amber phase.

Question 6.24

Mark two answers

At toucan crossings

- there is no flashing amber light
- cyclists are not permitted
- there is a continuously flashing amber beacon
- pedestrians and cyclists may cross
- you only stop if someone is waiting to cross

Answers

- **there is no flashing amber light**
- **pedestrians and cyclists may cross**

There are some crossings where cycle routes lead the cyclists to cross at the same place as pedestrians. Always look out for cyclists, as they're likely to be approaching faster than pedestrians.

Question 6.25

Mark one answer

You are driving past parked cars. You notice a wheel of a bicycle sticking out between them. What should you do?

- Accelerate past quickly and sound your horn
- Slow down and wave the cyclist across
- Brake sharply and flash your headlights
- Slow down and be prepared to stop for a cyclist

Answer

- **Slow down and be prepared to stop for a cyclist**

Scan the road as you drive. Try to anticipate hazards by being aware of the places where they are likely to occur. You'll then be able to react in good time, if necessary.

Question 6.26

Mark one answer

You are driving past a line of parked cars. You notice a ball bouncing out into the road ahead. What should you do?

- Continue driving at the same speed and sound your horn
- Continue driving at the same speed and flash your headlights
- Slow down and be prepared to stop for children
- Stop and wave the children across to fetch their ball

Answer

Slow down and be prepared to stop for children

Beware of children playing in the street and running out into the road. If a ball bounces out from the pavement slow down and stop. Don't encourage anyone to retrieve it. Other road users may not see your signal and you might lead a child into a dangerous situation.

Question 6.27

Mark one answer

What does this sign tell you?

- No cycling
- Cycle route ahead
- Route for cycles only
- End of cycle route

Answer

Cycle route ahead

With people's concern today for the environment, cycle routes are being created in our towns and cities. These can be defined by road markings and signs. Don't straddle or drive in them. Respect the presence of cyclists on the road and give them plenty of room if you need to pass.

Question 6.28

Mark one answer

How will a school crossing patrol signal you to stop?

- By pointing to children on the opposite pavement
- By displaying a red light
- By displaying a stop sign
- By giving you an arm signal

Answer

By displaying a stop sign

If someone steps out into the road with a school crossing sign you must stop. Don't

- wave anyone across the road
- get impatient or rev your engine.

Question 6.29

Mark one answer

Where would you see this sign?

- In the window of a car taking children to school
- At the side of the road
- At playground areas
- On the rear of a school bus or coach

Answer

On the rear of a school bus or coach

Vehicles that are used to carry children to and from school will be travelling at busy times of the day. If you're following a vehicle with this sign be prepared for it to make frequent stops. It might pick up or set down passengers in places other than normal bus stops.

Question 6.30

Mark one answer

Where would you see this sign?

- Near a school crossing
- At a playground entrance
- On a school bus
- At a 'pedestrians only' area

Answer

On a school bus

Watch out for children crossing the road from the other side of the bus.

Question 6.31

Mark one answer

You are parking your vehicle in the street. The car parked in front of you is displaying an orange badge. You should

- park close to it to save road space
- allow room for a wheelchair
- wait until the orange-badge holder returns
- park with two wheels on the pavement

Answer

allow room for a wheelchair

Think about the room that's needed to open the rear of the vehicle and lift a chair in. Room might be needed to manoeuvre a chair between the two cars.

Question 6.32

Mark one answer

You are following a car driven by an elderly driver. You should

- expect the driver to drive badly
- flash your lights and overtake
- be aware that the driver's reactions may not be as fast as yours
- stay very close behind but be careful

Answer

be aware that the driver's reactions may not be as fast as yours

You must show consideration to other road users. Their reactions may be slower and they might need more time to deal with a situation. Be tolerant and don't lose patience or show your annoyance.

Question 6.33

Mark one answer

Which sign tells you that pedestrians may be walking in the road as there is no pavement?

Answer

If you have to pass pedestrians who are walking at the side of the road, you must give them plenty of room. The draught caused by your vehicle could unsteady them, or they could turn around when they hear your car engine and step sideways into the road.

Question 6.34

Mark one answer

What does this sign mean?

- No route for pedestrians and cyclists
- A route for pedestrians only
- A route for cyclists only
- A route for pedestrians and cyclists

Answer

A route for pedestrians and cyclists

This shared route is for pedestrians and cyclists only. Be aware that when it ends the cyclists will be rejoining the main road.

Question 6.35

Mark one answer

You see a pedestrian with a white stick and red band. This means that the person is

- physically disabled
- deaf only
- blind only
- deaf and blind

Answer

deaf and blind

If the person is deaf as well as blind the stick will have a red reflective band. You can't tell if a pedestrian is deaf. Don't assume everyone can hear you approaching.

Question 6.36

Mark one answer

You are driving towards a zebra crossing. Waiting to cross is a person in a wheelchair. You should

- continue on your way
- wave to the person to cross
- wave to the person to wait
- be prepared to stop

Answer

be prepared to stop

As you would with an able-bodied pedestrian, you should prepare to slow down and stop. Don't wave the pedestrian across as they, due to their seated position, might not be able to see traffic beyond in a right-hand lane. There might be a motorcyclist on your offside.

Question 6.37

Mark one answer

What action would you take when elderly people are crossing the road?

- Wave them across so they know that you have seen them
- Be patient and allow them to cross in their own time
- Rev the engine to let them know that you are waiting
- Tap the horn in case they are hard of hearing

Answer

- **Be patient and allow them to cross in their own time**

Don't hurry elderly people across the road by driving up close to them or revving the engine. Be aware that they might take longer to cross. They might also be hard of hearing and not able to hear your approach.

Question 6.38

Mark one answer

You see two elderly pedestrians about to cross the road ahead. You should

- expect them to wait for you to pass
- speed up to get past them quickly
- stop and wave them across the road
- be careful, they may misjudge your speed

Answer

- **be careful, they may misjudge your speed**

Their concentration, judgement, hearing and/or vision could be impaired. Be aware that if they proceed to cross they will take more time to do so.

Question 6.39

Mark one answer

You are following a motorcyclist on an uneven road. You should

- allow less room so you can be seen in their mirrors
- overtake immediately
- allow extra room in case they swerve to avoid pot-holes
- allow the same room as normal because road surfaces do not affect motorcyclists

Answer

- **allow extra room in case they swerve to avoid pot-holes**

Pot-holes in the road can unsteady a motorcyclist. For this reason the rider might swerve to avoid an uneven road surface. Watch out at places where this is likely to occur.

Question 6.40

Mark one answer

What does this sign mean?

- Contra-flow pedal cycle lane
- With-flow pedal cycle lane
- Pedal cycles and buses only
- No pedal cycles or buses

Answer

- **With-flow pedal cycle lane**

This will be marked on the road, sometimes with a different colour surface. Leave these clear for cyclists and don't pass too closely when you overtake.

Question 6.41

Mark one answer

You should NEVER attempt to overtake a cyclist

- just before you turn left
- just before you turn right
- on a one-way street
- on a dual carriageway

Answer

- **just before you turn left**

If you want to turn left and there's a cyclist in front of you, hold back. Wait until the cyclist has passed the junction and then turn left behind them.

Question 6.42

Mark one answer

You are following a cyclist. You wish to turn left just ahead. You should

- overtake the cyclist before the junction
- pull alongside the cyclist and stay level until after the junction
- hold back until the cyclist has passed the junction
- go around the cyclist on the junction

Answer

- **hold back until the cyclist has passed the junction**

When driving or riding make allowances for cyclists. Allow them plenty of room. If you're following a cyclist, be aware that they also have to deal with hazards around them. They might swerve or change direction suddenly to avoid an uneven road surface.

Question 6.43

Mark one answer

You are coming up to a roundabout. A cyclist is signalling to turn right. What should you do?

- Overtake on the right
- Give a horn warning
- Signal the cyclist to move across
- Give the cyclist plenty of room

Answer

- **Give the cyclist plenty of room**

If you're following a cyclist who's signalling to turn right at a roundabout, leave plenty of room. Give them space and time to get into the correct lane.

Question 6.44

Mark one answer

You are following two cyclists. They approach a roundabout in the left-hand lane. In which direction should you expect the cyclists to go?

- Left
- Right
- Any direction
- Straight ahead

Answer

Any direction

If you're following a cyclist into a roundabout, be aware of them as they might not be taking the exit you anticipate. Cyclists approaching in the left-hand lane may be turning right but may not have been able to get into the correct lane due to heavy traffic. Give them room.

Question 6.45

Mark one answer

You are approaching this roundabout and see the cyclist signal right. Why is the cyclist keeping to the left?

- It is a quicker route for the cyclist
- The cyclist is going to turn left instead
- The cyclist thinks *The Highway Code* does not apply to bicycles
- The cyclist is slower and more vulnerable

Answer

The cyclist is slower and more vulnerable

Cycling in today's heavy traffic can be hazardous. Some cyclists may not feel happy about crossing the path of traffic to take up a position in an outside lane. Be aware of this and understand that, although in the left-hand lane, the cyclist might be turning right.

Question 6.46

Mark one answer

When you are overtaking a cyclist you should leave as much room as you would give to a car. What is the main reason for this?

- The cyclist might change lanes
- The cyclist might get off the bike
- The cyclist might swerve
- The cyclist might have to make a right turn

Answer

- **The cyclist might swerve**

If you intend to overtake a cyclist, look at the road ahead. Check if the cyclist needs to change direction for a parked vehicle or an uneven road surface. When you have a safe place to overtake leave as much room as you would for a car. Don't cut in sharply or pass too closely.

Question 6.47

Mark two answers

Which TWO should you allow extra room when overtaking?

- Motorcycles
- Tractors
- Bicycles
- Road-sweeping vehicles

Answers

- **Motorcycles**
- **Bicycles**

Don't pass riders too closely as this may cause them to lose balance. Always leave as much room as you would for a car, and don't cut in.

Question 6.48

Mark one answer

Why should you allow extra room when overtaking a motorcyclist on a windy day?

- The rider may turn off suddenly to get out of the wind
- The rider may be blown across in front of you
- The rider may stop suddenly
- The rider may be travelling faster than normal

Answer

- **The rider may be blown across in front of you**

A motorcyclist's position on the road can be affected by high winds. If you're driving or riding on a windy day, be aware that the conditions might force a motorcyclist to swerve or wobble. Take this into consideration if you're following or wish to overtake.

Question 6.49

Mark one answer

Why should you look particularly for motorcyclists and cyclists at junctions?

- They may want to turn into the side road
- They may slow down to let you turn
- They are harder to see
- They might not see you turn

Answer

They are harder to see

These road users could be hazards that are hidden from your view. Parked cars could cause you to lose sight of them. Consider that cyclists may need more time to make a turn.

Question 6.50

Mark one answer

You are waiting to come out of a side road. Why should you watch carefully for motorcycles?

- Motorcycles are usually faster than cars
- Police patrols often use motorcycles
- Motorcycles are small and hard to see
- Motorcycles have right of way

Answer

Motorcycles are small and hard to see

If you're waiting to emerge from a side road, watch out for motorcyclists. They're smaller and more difficult to see. Be especially careful if there are parked vehicles restricting your view. There might be a motorcyclist approaching.

IF YOU DON'T KNOW, DON'T GO.

Question 6.51

Mark one answer

Where should you take particular care to look out for motorcyclists and cyclists?

- On dual carriageways
- At junctions
- At zebra crossings
- On one-way streets

Answer

At junctions

Motorcyclists and cyclists may be more difficult to see on the road. This is especially the case at junctions. You may not be able to see a motorcyclist approaching a junction if your view's blocked by other traffic. Be aware of the possibility. A motorcycle may be travelling as fast as a car, or faster. Make sure that you judge speeds correctly before you emerge.

Question 6.52

Mark one answer

In daylight, an approaching motorcyclist is using a dipped headlight. Why?

- So that the rider can be seen more easily
- To stop the battery overcharging
- To improve the rider's vision
- The rider is inviting you to proceed

Answer

- **So that the rider can be seen more easily**

A motorcycle can be lost out of sight behind another vehicle. The use of the headlight helps to make it more conspicuous and therefore more easily seen.

Question 6.53

Mark one answer

Where in particular should you look out for motorcyclists?

- In a filling station
- At a road junction
- Near a service area
- When entering a car park

Answer

- **At a road junction**

Always look ahead and try to make use of the information you see. This will enable you to anticipate possible hazards, and give you more time to deal with them as they occur.

Question 6.54

Mark one answer

Motorcyclists should wear bright clothing mainly because

- they must do so by law
- it helps keep them cool in summer
- the colours are popular
- drivers often do not see them

Answer

- **drivers often do not see them**

Although they're advised to wear clothing that's bright or reflective, motorcyclists often wear black. This means that they're difficult to see. Look out for them.

Question 6.55

Mark one answer

There is a slow-moving motorcyclist ahead of you. You are unsure what the rider is going to do. You should

- pass on the left
- pass on the right
- stay behind
- move closer

Answer

- **stay behind**

Be patient. The motorcyclist might be turning right or changing direction.

Question 6.56

Mark one answer

You are travelling behind a moped. You want to turn left just ahead. You should

- overtake the moped before the junction
- pull alongside the moped and stay level until just before the junction
- sound your horn as a warning and pull in front of the moped
- stay behind until the moped has passed the junction

Answer

- **stay behind until the moped has passed the junction**

Passing the moped and turning into the junction could mean that you cut across the front of it. This might force the rider to slow down, stop or even lose control.

Question 6.57

Mark one answer

Motorcyclists will often look round over their right shoulder just before turning right. This is because

- they need to listen for following traffic
- motorcycles do not have mirrors
- looking around helps them balance as they turn
- they need to check for traffic in their blind area

Answer

- **they need to check for traffic in their blind area**

If you're behind a motorcyclist who makes a quick glance over their shoulder, expect them to be changing direction. They should do this before turning. By observing this you'll get an early signal of their intention.

Question 6.58

Mark three answers

At road junctions which of the following are most vulnerable?

- Cyclists
- Motorcyclists
- Pedestrians
- Car drivers
- Lorry drivers

Answers

- **Cyclists**
- **Motorcyclists**
- **Pedestrians**

Good effective observation, coupled with appropriate action, can save lives.

Question 6.59

Mark one answer

You want to turn right from a main road into a side road. Just before turning you should

- cancel your right-turn signal
- select first gear
- check for traffic overtaking on your right
- stop and set the handbrake

Answer

- **check for traffic overtaking on your right**

Motorcyclists often overtake queues of vehicles. Always make that last check in the mirror to avoid turning across their path.

Question 6.60

Mark one answer

Motorcyclists are particularly vulnerable

- when moving off
- on dual carriageways
- when approaching junctions
- on motorways

Answer

- **when approaching junctions**

Another road user failing to see a motorcyclist at a junction is a major cause of collision accidents. Wherever streams of traffic join or cross there's the potential for this type of accident to occur. Ride defensively and make yourself easy to see by wearing bright clothing.

Question 6.61

Mark three answers

Which THREE of the following are hazards motorcyclists present in queues of traffic?

- Cutting in just in front of you
- Riding in single file
- Passing very close to you
- Riding with their headlight on dipped beam
- Filtering between the lanes

Answers

- **Cutting in just in front of you**
- **Passing very close to you**
- **Filtering between the lanes**

Where there's more than one lane of queuing traffic motorcyclists use the opportunity to make progress by riding between the lanes. Be aware that they may be passing on either side. Check your mirrors before you move off.

Question 6.62

Mark one answer

You are driving on a main road. You intend to turn right into a side road. Just before turning you should

- adjust your interior mirror
- flash your headlamps
- steer over to the left
- check for traffic overtaking on your right

Answer

- **check for traffic overtaking on your right**

A last check in the offside mirror will allow you sight of any cyclist or motorcyclist passing on your offside.

Question 6.63

Mark one answer

Ahead of you there is a vehicle with a flashing amber beacon. This means it is

- slow moving
- broken down
- a doctor's car
- a school crossing patrol

Answer

- **slow moving**

As you approach the vehicle assess the situation. Due to it's slow progress you will need to judge whether it is safe to overtake.

Question 6.64

Mark one answer

You are driving in slow-moving queues of traffic. Just before changing lane you should

- sound the horn
- look for motorcyclists filtering through the traffic
- give a 'slowing down' arm signal
- change down to first gear

Answer

- **look for motorcyclists filtering through the traffic**

In this situation motorcyclists could be passing you on either side. Always check before you change lanes or change direction.

Question 6.65

Mark one answer

An injured motorcyclist is lying unconscious in the road. You should

- remove the safety helmet
- seek medical assistance
- move the person off the road
- remove the leather jacket

Answer

- **seek medical assistance**

In an injury situation the earlier proper medical attention is given the better. Either send someone to phone for help or go yourself. Only move an injured person if further danger is threatened.

Do not remove the safety helmet.

Question 6.66

Mark three answers

You are riding on a country lane. You see cattle on the road. You should

- slow down
- stop if necessary
- give plenty of room
- rev your engine
- sound your horn
- ride up close behind them

Answers

- **slow down**
- **stop if necessary**
- **give plenty of room**

Try not to startle the animals. They can be easily frightened by noise or by traffic passing too closely.

Question 6.67

Mark one answer

You are driving in town. There is a bus at the bus stop on the other side of the road. Why should you be careful?

- The bus may have broken down
- Pedestrians may come from behind the bus
- The bus may move off suddenly
- The bus may remain stationary

Answer

- **Pedestrians may come from behind the bus**

If you see a bus ahead watch out for pedestrians. They may not be able to see you if they're crossing behind the bus.

Question 6.68

Mark two answers

You are about to overtake horse riders. Which TWO of the following could scare the horses?

- Sounding your horn
- Giving arm signals
- Riding slowly
- Revving your engine

Answers

- **Sounding your horn**
- **Revving your engine**

When passing horses allow plenty of space and slow down. Animals can become frightened by sudden or loud noises, so don't sound your horn or rev the engine.

Question 6.69

Mark one answer

How should you overtake horse riders?

- Drive up close and overtake as soon as possible
- Speed is not important but allow plenty of room
- Use your horn just once to warn them
- Drive slowly and leave plenty of room

Answer

Drive slowly and leave plenty of room

If you're driving or riding on a country road then take extra care. Be ready for

- farm animals
- horses
- pedestrians
- farm vehicles.

Always be prepared to slow down or stop.

Question 6.70

Mark one answer

You notice horse riders in front. What should you do FIRST?

- Pull out to the middle of the road
- Be prepared to slow down
- Accelerate around them
- Signal right

Answer

Be prepared to slow down

When you're driving or riding you must always look well ahead and be ready to deal with hazards as they occur.

Question 6.71

Mark one answer

You are on a narrow country road. Where would you find it most difficult to see horses and riders ahead of you?

- On left-hand bends
- When travelling downhill
- When travelling uphill
- On right-hand bends

Answer

On left-hand bends

You're more likely to come across horses on country roads. These roads can be narrow, so extra care must be taken when approaching left-hand bends, as your view of the road ahead will be restricted.

Question 6.72

Mark one answer

A horse rider is in the left-hand lane approaching a roundabout. You should expect the rider to

- go in any direction
- turn right
- turn left
- go ahead

Answer

- **go in any direction**

Horses and their riders will move more slowly than other road users. They might not have time to cut across busy traffic to take up positions in the offside lane. For this reason a horse and rider may approach a roundabout in the left-hand lane, even though they're turning right.

Question 6.73

Mark two answers

You are approaching a roundabout. There are horses just ahead of you. You should

- be prepared to stop
- treat them like any other vehicle
- give them plenty of room
- accelerate past as quickly as possible
- sound your horn as a warning

Answers

- **be prepared to stop**
- **give them plenty of room**

Horse riders often keep to the outside of the roundabout even if they are turning right. Give them room in case they have to cross lanes of traffic.

Question 6.74

Mark one answer

You see a horse rider as you approach a roundabout. They are signalling right but keeping well to the left. You should

- proceed as normal
- keep close to them
- cut in front of them
- stay well back

Answer

- **stay well back**

Allow the riders to enter and exit the roundabout in their own time. Don't drive up close behind or alongside them, as this could disturb the horses .

Question 6.75

Mark three answers

Which THREE should you do when passing sheep on a road?

- Allow plenty of room
- Go very slowly
- Pass quickly but quietly
- Be ready to stop
- Briefly sound your horn

Answers

- **Allow plenty of room**
- **Go very slowly**
- **Be ready to stop**

If you see animals in the road ahead, slow down and be ready to stop. Animals are easily frightened by

- noise
- vehicles passing too close to them.

Stop if signalled to do so by the person in charge. Switch off your engine if the animals are taking a long time to clear the road.

Question 6.76

Mark one answer

You have a collision whilst your car is moving. What is the first thing you must do?

- Stop only if there are injured people
- Call the emergency services
- Stop at the scene of the accident
- Call your insurance company

Answer

- **Stop at the scene of the accident**

It is the law. Apart from taking responsibility for any mistake you have made, the incident will have shaken you. You will need time to take stock before you drive on.

Question 6.77

Mark one answer

Riders are more likely to have a serious accident if they

- wear glasses or contact lenses
- have recently passed their test
- are carrying pillion passengers
- have not taken a theory test

Answer

- **have recently passed their test**

It takes time to experience different situations on the road. Develop safe habits and a responsible attitude from the start. This will help you to become a better rider.

Question 6.78

Mark one answer

How would you react to drivers who appear to be inexperienced?

- Sound your horn to warn them of your presence
- Be patient and prepare for them to react more slowly
- Flash your headlights to indicate that it is safe for them to proceed
- Overtake them as soon as possible

Answer

- **Be patient and prepare for them to react more slowly**

Learners might not have confidence when they first start to drive. Allow them plenty of room and don't react adversely to their hesitation. We all learn from experience, but new drivers will have had less practice in dealing with all the situations that might occur.

Question 6.79

Mark one answer

You have just passed your test. How can you decrease your risk of accidents on the motorway?

- By keeping up with the car in front
- By never going over 40 mph
- By staying only in the left-hand lane
- By taking further training

Answer

- **By taking further training**

You're more likely to have an accident in the first year after taking your test. Lack of experience means that you might not react to hazards as quickly as a more experienced driver or rider. Further training will help you to become safer on the roads.

If you're a motorcyclist ask your Compulsory Basic Training (CBT) instructor about this.

Question 6.80

Mark one answer

Which age group is most likely to be involved in a road accident?

- 36 to 45-year-olds
- 55-year-olds and over
- 46 to 55-year-olds
- 17 to 25-year-olds

Answer

- **17 to 25-year-olds**

Statistics show that if you're between the ages of 17 and 25 you're more likely to be involved in a road accident. There are several reasons contributing to this, but in most cases accidents are due to driver or rider error.

Question 6.81

Mark one answer

You are following a learner driver who stalls at a junction. You should

- be patient as you expect them to make mistakes
- stay very close behind and flash your headlights
- start to rev your engine if they take too long to restart
- immediately steer around them and drive on

Answer

- **be patient as you expect them to make mistakes**

Learning is a process of practice and experience. Try to understand this and tolerate others who are at the beginning of this process.

Question 6.82

Mark one answer

A learner driver has begun to emerge into your path from a side road on the left. You should

- be ready to slow down and stop
- let them emerge then ride close behind
- turn into the side road
- brake hard, then wave them out

Answer

- **be ready to slow down and stop**

If you see another vehicle begin to emerge into your path you should ride defensively. Always be ready to slow down or stop if necessary.

Question 6.83

Mark one answer

The vehicle ahead is being driven by a learner. You should

- keep calm and be patient
- ride up close behind
- put your headlight on full beam
- sound your horn and overtake

Answer

- **keep calm and be patient**

Learners might take longer to react to traffic situations. Don't unnerve them by riding up close behind.

Question 6.84

Mark one answer

A friend wants to teach you to drive a car. They must

- be over 21 and have held a full licence for at least two years
- be over 18 and hold an advanced driver's certificate
- be over 18 and have fully comprehensive insurance
- be over 21 and have held a full licence for at least three years

Answer

be over 21 and have held a full licence for at least three years

Teaching someone to drive is a responsible task. You're advised to contact a qualified Approved Driving Instructor (ADI) about learning to drive. This will ensure that you're taught the correct procedures from the start.

Question 6.85

Mark one answer

At night you see a pedestrian wearing reflective clothing and carrying a bright red light. What does this mean?

- You are approaching roadworks
- You are approaching an organised walk
- You are approaching a slow-moving vehicle
- You are approaching an accident black spot

Answer

You are approaching an organised walk

The people involved in the march should be keeping to the left, but this can't be assumed. Pass slowly, ensuring that you have the time to do so safely. Be aware that the pedestrians have their backs to you and might not know that you're there.

Question 6.86

Mark one answer

You are dazzled at night by a vehicle behind you. You should

- set your mirror to anti dazzle
- set your mirror to dazzle the other driver
- brake sharply to a stop
- switch your rear lights on and off

Answer

set your mirror to anti dazzle

Most modern vehicles have this facility. The interior mirror of your vehicle can be set to the anti-dazzle position. This prevents distraction from the lights of traffic behind you. You will still be able to see the lights, but the dazzle will be greatly reduced.

Question 6.87

Mark one answer

There are flashing amber lights under a school warning sign. What action should you take?

- Reduce speed until you are clear of the area
- Keep up your speed and sound the horn
- Increase your speed to clear the area quickly
- Wait at the lights until they change to green

Answer

- **Reduce speed until you are clear of the area**

The flashing amber lights are switched on to warn drivers that children may be crossing near a school.

Question 6.88

Mark one answer

Why is it vital for a rider to make a lifesaver check before turning right?

- To check for any overtaking traffic
- To confirm that they are about to turn
- To make sure the side road is clear
- To check that the rear indicator is flashing

Answer

- **To check for any overtaking traffic**

The lifesaver glance is what it says. This action makes you aware of what is happening behind and alongside before you alter your course. This glance must be timed so that you still have time to react if it isn't safe to carry out your manoeuvre.

Question 6.89

Mark one answer

Which of the following types of crossing can detect when people are on them?

- Pelican
- Toucan
- Zebra
- Puffin

Answer

- **Puffin**

'Puffin' is an acronym for **p**edestrian **u**ser **f**riendly **in**telligent crossing. Sensors detect when people are crossing and will hold the waiting traffic on a red signal until the pedestrians are clear.

Question 6.90

Mark one answer

The road outside this school is marked with yellow zigzag lines. What do these lines mean?

- You may park on the lines when dropping off school children
- You may park on the lines when picking school children up
- You must not wait or park your vehicle here at all
- You must stay with your vehicle if you park here

Answer

- **You must not wait or park your vehicle here at all**

Parking here will block the view of the school gates. Doing this will endanger the lives of children on their way to and from school.

Question 6.91

Mark one answer

You are approaching this crossing. You should

- prepare to slow down and stop
- stop and wave the pedestrians across
- speed up and pass by quickly
- drive on unless the pedestrians step out

Answer

- **prepare to slow down and stop**

Be courteous and prepare to stop. Do not wave people across as this could be dangerous if another vehicle is approaching the crossing.

Question 6.92

Mark one answer

You see a pedestrian with a dog. The dog has a bright orange lead and collar. This especially warns you that the pedestrian is

- elderly
- dog training
- colour blind
- deaf

Answer

 **deaf**

Take extra care as the pedestrian is more vulnerable. Always be aware that this pedestrian may not hear you.

SECTION 7 OTHER TYPES OF VEHICLE

This section looks at the risks when dealing with different types of vehicle.

The questions will ask you about

- **Motorcycles**

  be aware that they may need as much room as a car.

- **Lorries**

  are larger and need more room on the road.

- **Buses**

  are usually large and might make frequent stops.

Question 7.1

Mark one answer

The road is wet. Why might a motorcyclist steer round drain covers on a bend?

- To avoid puncturing the tyres on the edge of the drain covers
- To prevent the motorcycle sliding on the metal drain covers
- To help judge the bend using the drain covers as marker points
- To avoid splashing pedestrians on the pavement

Answer

- **To prevent the motorcycle sliding on the metal drain covers**

The actions other drivers take may be due to the size or characteristics of their vehicle. If you understand this it will help you to anticipate their actions.

Motorcyclists will be checking the road ahead for uneven or slippery surfaces, especially in wet weather. They may need to move across their lane to avoid road surface hazards.

Question 7.2

Mark one answer

It is very windy. You are behind a motorcyclist who is overtaking a high-sided vehicle. What should you do?

- Overtake the motorcyclist immediately
- Keep well back
- Stay level with the motorcyclist
- Keep close to the motorcyclist

Answer

- **Keep well back**

Motorcyclists are affected more by windy weather than other vehicles. Keep well back as they could be blown off course.

Question 7.3

Mark one answer

It is very windy. You are about to overtake a motorcyclist. You should

- overtake slowly
- allow extra room
- sound your horn
- keep close as you pass

Answer

- **allow extra room**

Side winds can blow a cyclist across the lane. Passing too close could also cause a draught, unsteadying the rider.

Question 7.4

Mark one answer

You are about to overtake a slow-moving motorcyclist. Which one of these signs would make you take special care?

Answer

In windy weather watch out for motorcyclists, as they can be blown sideways and veer into your path. Pass them leaving plenty of room and check your mirror as you pass and pull back in.

Question 7.5

Mark one answer

You are waiting to emerge left from a minor road. A large vehicle is approaching from the right. You have time to turn, but you should wait. Why?

- The large vehicle can easily hide an overtaking vehicle
- The large vehicle can turn suddenly
- The large vehicle is difficult to steer in a straight line
- The large vehicle can easily hide vehicles from the left

Answer

- **The large vehicle can easily hide an overtaking vehicle**

Don't only consider the hazards you can see. The hidden, possible hazards are the most dangerous as they are often unexpected. By considering the possible dangers when emerging, you can lessen the risk.

Question 7.6

Mark one answer

You are following a large articulated vehicle. It is going to turn left into a narrow road. What action should you take?

- Move out and overtake on the right
- Pass on the left as the vehicle moves out
- Be prepared to stop behind
- Overtake quickly before the lorry moves out

Answer

- **Be prepared to stop behind**

Lorries are larger and longer than other vehicles. This will affect their position when approaching junctions – especially when turning left. They need more room so that they don't cut in and mount the kerb when turning.

Question 7.7

Mark one answer

You are following a long vehicle. It approaches a crossroads and signals left, but moves out to the right. You should

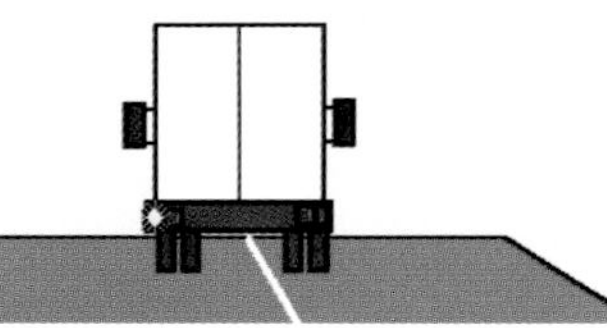

- get closer in order to pass it quickly
- stay well back and give it room
- assume the signal is wrong and it is really turning right
- overtake as it starts to slow down

Answer

- **stay well back and give it room**

Approaching a left turn a lorry may swing out to the right. This is to allow the rear wheels to clear the kerb as it turns. If you see a gap on the nearside don't try to filter through.

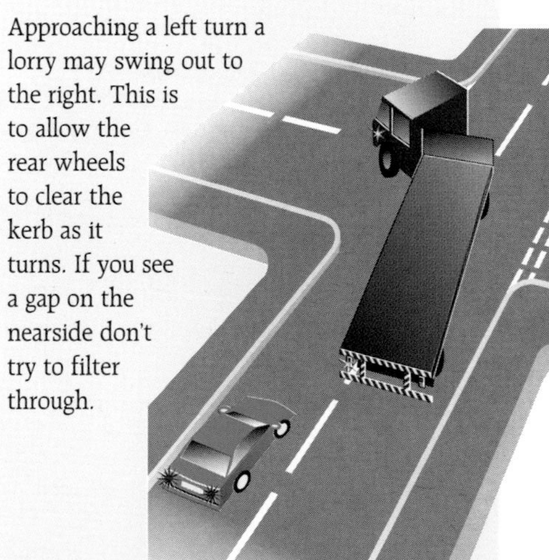

Question 7.8

Mark one answer

You are riding behind a long vehicle. There is a mini-roundabout ahead. The vehicle is signalling left, but positioned to the right. You should

- sound your horn
- overtake on the left
- keep well back
- flash your headlights

Answer

keep well back

The long vehicle needs more room to make the left turn. Don't overtake on the left. Staying well back will also give you a better view around the vehicle.

Question 7.9

Mark one answer

You are following a long vehicle approaching a crossroads. The driver signals right but moves close to the left-hand kerb. What should you do?

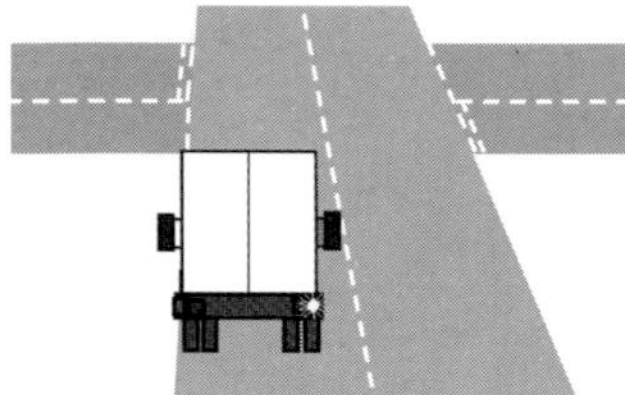

- Warn the driver of the wrong signal
- Wait behind the long vehicle
- Report the driver to the police
- Overtake on the right-hand side

Answer

Wait behind the long vehicle

When a long vehicle is going to turn right it may need to keep close to the left-hand kerb. This is to prevent the rear end of the trailer cutting the corner. You need to be aware of how long vehicles behave in such situations. Don't overtake the lorry because it could turn as you're alongside. Stay behind and give plenty of room.

Question 7.10

Mark one answer

You are approaching a mini-roundabout. The long vehicle in front is signalling left, but positioned over to the right. You should

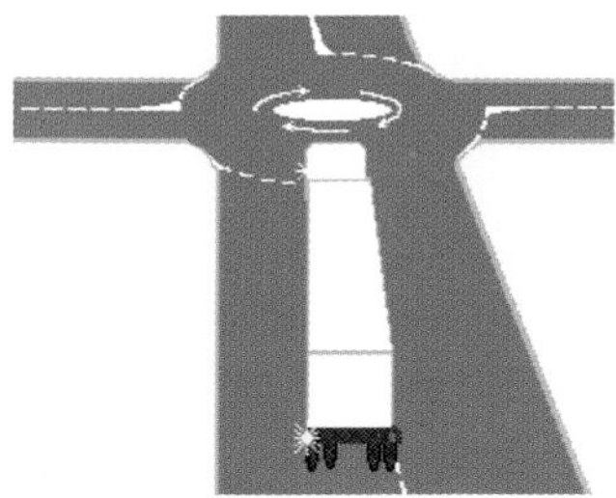

- sound your horn
- overtake on the left
- follow the same course as the lorry
- keep well back

Answer

keep well back

At mini-roundabouts there isn't much room for a long vehicle to manoeuvre. It will have to swing out wide so that it can complete the turn safely. Keep well back and allow plenty of room. Don't drive or ride along its nearside.

Question 7.11

Mark one answer

You are following a large vehicle. Side and end markers are being displayed. This means the load

- is higher than normal
- may be flammable
- is in two parts
- overhangs at the rear

Answer

overhangs at the rear

Always keep a safe distance from the vehicle in front. In this case you should judge your separation distance from the extreme rear of the load the vehicle is carrying.

Question 7.12

Mark one answer

You are towing a caravan. Which is the safest type of rear view mirror to use?

- Interior wide-angle-view mirror
- Extended-arm side mirrors
- Ordinary door mirrors
- Ordinary interior mirror

Answer

- **Extended-arm side mirrors**

Towing a large trailer or caravan can greatly reduce your view of the road. The correct equipment will help you to get a better view behind and around the unit.

Question 7.13

Mark one answer

You keep well back while waiting to overtake a large vehicle. A car fills the gap. You should

- sound your horn
- drop back further
- flash your headlights
- start to overtake

Answer

- **drop back further**

It's very frustrating when your separation distance is shortened by another car. React positively and consider your own and your passengers' safety.

Question 7.14

Mark one answer

Before overtaking a large vehicle you should keep well back. Why is this?

- To give acceleration space to overtake quickly on blind bends
- To get the best view of the road ahead
- To leave a gap in case the vehicle stops and rolls back
- To offer other drivers a safe gap if they want to overtake you

Answer

- **To get the best view of the road ahead**

When following a large vehicle keep well back. If you're too close

- you won't be able to see the road ahead
- the driver of the long vehicle might not be able to see you in his mirrors.

Question 7.15

Mark one answer

You wish to overtake a long, slow-moving vehicle on a busy road. You should

- follow it closely and keep moving out to see the road ahead
- flash your headlights for the oncoming traffic to give way
- stay behind until the driver waves you past
- keep well back until you can see that it is clear

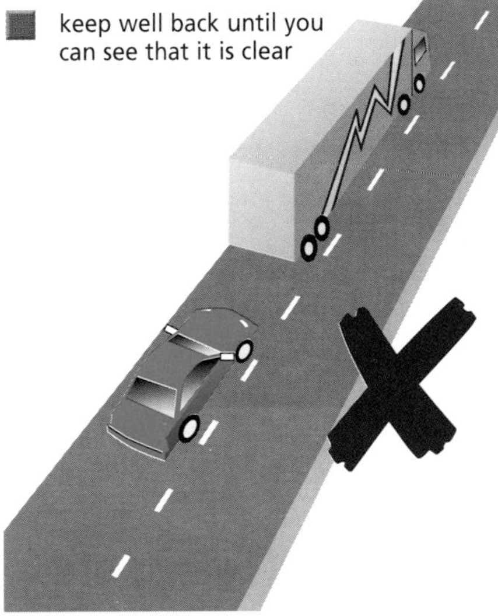

Answer

- **keep well back until you can see that it is clear**

If you wish to overtake a long vehicle, stay well back so that you can see the road ahead. Don't

- get up close to the vehicle – this will restrict your view of the road ahead
- get impatient – overtaking on a busy road calls for sound judgement
- take a gamble – only overtake when you can see that you can safely complete the manoeuvre
- flash your headlights – this could confuse and mislead other traffic
- sound your horn.

Question 7.16

Mark one answer

You are driving downhill. There is a car parked on the other side of the road. Large, slow lorries are coming towards you. You should

- keep going because you have the right of way
- slow down and give way
- speed up and get past quickly
- pull over on the right behind the parked car

Answer

- **slow down and give way**

Large vehicles need several gear changes to build up speed, and this takes time, especially on an uphill gradient. You should keep this in mind and give way so that they can maintain momentum up the hill.

Question 7.17

Mark one answer

Why is passing a lorry more risky than passing a car?

- Lorries are longer than cars
- Lorries may suddenly pull up
- The brakes of lorries are not as good
- Lorries climb hills more slowly

Answer

- **Lorries are longer than cars**

Hazards to watch for include

- oncoming traffic
- junctions
- bends or dips, which could restrict your view
- any signs or road markings prohibiting overtaking.

Never begin to overtake unless you can see that it's safe to complete the manoeuvre.

Question 7.18

Mark two answers

As a driver, why should you be more careful where trams operate?

- Because they do not have a horn
- Because they do not stop for cars
- Because they are silent
- Because they cannot steer to avoid you
- Because they do not have lights

Answers

- **Because they are silent**
- **Because they cannot steer to avoid you**

You should take extra care when you first encounter trams. You will have to get used to dealing with a different traffic system. As well as being silent, they can travel very quickly.

Question 7.19

Mark one answer

You are driving along a road and you see this signal. It means

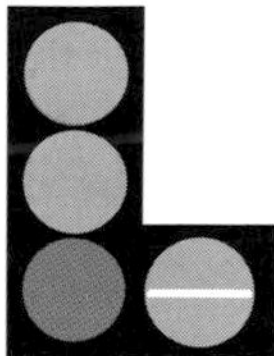

- cars must stop
- trams must stop
- both trams and cars must stop
- both trams and cars can continue

Answer

- **trams must stop**

Trams are popular in some cities, not least because they don't create fumes so they're cleaner. You may not live in an area that has trams, but you should still learn the signs. You never know when you might drive through a town that has them.

Question 7.20

Mark two answers

You are travelling behind a bus that pulls up at a bus stop. What should you do?

- Accelerate past the bus sounding your horn
- Watch carefully for pedestrians
- Be ready to give way to the bus
- Pull in closely behind the bus

Answers

- **Watch carefully for pedestrians**
- **Be ready to give way to the bus**

There might be pedestrians crossing from in front of the bus. Look out for them if you intend to pass. Consider staying back and waiting.

How many people are waiting to get on the bus? Check the queue if you can. The bus might be moving off straight away.

Question 7.21

Mark two answers

You are driving in town. Ahead of you a bus is at a bus stop. Which TWO of the following should you do?

- Be prepared to give way if the bus suddenly moves off
- Continue at the same speed but sound your horn as a warning
- Watch carefully for the sudden appearance of pedestrians
- Pass the bus as quickly as you possibly can

Answers

- **Be prepared to give way if the bus suddenly moves off**
- **Watch carefully for the sudden appearance of pedestrians**

As you approach, look out for any signal the driver might make. If you pass the vehicle, watch out for pedestrians attempting to cross the road from the other side of the bus. They will be hidden from view until the last moment.

Question 7.22

Mark one answer

When you approach a bus signalling to move off from a bus stop you should

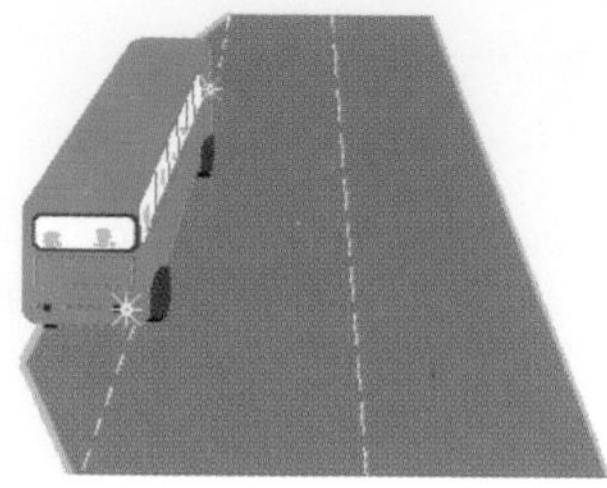

- get past before it moves
- allow it to pull away, if it is safe to do so
- flash your headlights as you approach
- signal left and wave the bus on

Answer

allow it to pull away, if it is safe to do so

Give way to buses whenever you can do so safely, especially when they signal to pull away from bus stops. Look out for people who've got off the bus and may try to cross the road. Don't

- try to accelerate past before it moves away
- flash your lights – other road users may be misled by this signal.

Question 7.23

Mark one answer

Which of these vehicles is LEAST likely to be affected by crosswinds?

- Cyclists
- Motorcyclists
- High-sided vehicles
- Cars

Answer

Cars

Crosswinds can take you by surprise

- after overtaking a large vehicle
- when passing gaps between hedges or buildings
- on exposed sections of road.

Question 7.24

Mark one answer

You are following a large lorry on a wet road. Spray makes it difficult to see. You should

- drop back until you can see better
- put your headlights on full beam
- keep close to the lorry, away from the spray
- speed up and overtake quickly

Answer

- **drop back until you can see better**

In the wet, large vehicles may throw up a lot of spray. This will make it difficult to see ahead. Dropping back further will

- move you out of the spray and so allow you to see further
- increase your separation distance.

It takes longer to stop in the wet and you need to allow more room. Don't

- get up close behind
- overtake, unless you can see the way ahead is clear.

Question 7.25

Mark one answer

You are on a wet motorway with surface spray. You should use

- hazard flashers
- dipped headlights
- rear fog lights
- sidelights

Answer

- **dipped headlights**

When surface spray reduces visibility, switch on your dipped headlights. This will help other road users to see you.

Question 7.26

Mark two answers

You are driving in heavy traffic on a wet road. Spray makes it difficult to be seen. You should use your

- full beam headlights
- rear fog lights if visibility is less than 100 metres (328 feet)
- rear fog lights if visibility is more than 100 metres (328 feet)
- dipped headlights
- sidelights only

Answers

- **rear fog lights if visibility is less than 100 metres (328 feet)**
- **dipped headlights**

You must ensure that you can be seen by others on the road. Use your lights during the day if the visibility is bad. If you use your rear fog lights, don't forget to turn them off when the visibility improves.

Question 7.27

Mark one answer

Some two-way roads are divided into three lanes. Why are these particularly dangerous?

- Traffic in both directions can use the middle lane to overtake
- Traffic can travel faster in poor weather conditions
- Traffic can overtake on the left
- Traffic uses the middle lane for emergencies only

Answer

- **Traffic in both directions can use the middle lane to overtake**

If you intend to overtake you must consider that approaching traffic could be intending the same manoeuvre. When you have considered, judged the situation and have decided it is safe, indicate your intentions early. This will show the approaching traffic that you intend to pull out.

Question 7.28

Mark two answers

Why should you be careful when riding on roads where electric trams operate?

- They cannot steer to avoid you
- They move quickly and quietly
- They are noisy and slow
- They can steer to avoid you
- They give off harmful exhaust fumes

Answers

- **They cannot steer to avoid you**
- **They move quickly and quietly**

Be aware of electric trams. They move silently and quickly and cannot steer to avoid you

Question 7.29

Mark one answer

You are driving along this road. What should you be prepared to do?

- Sound your horn and continue
- Slow down and give way
- Report the driver to the police
- Squeeze through the gap

Answer

- **Slow down and give way**

Large vehicles may need more road space at times. Be prepared to stop and wait if a vehicle needs more time and road room to turn.

Question 7.30

Mark one answer

What should you do as you approach this lorry?

- Slow down and be prepared to wait
- Make the lorry wait for you
- Flash your lights at the lorry
- Move to the right-hand side of the road

Answer

- **Slow down and be prepared to wait**

Long vehicles may need much more room on the road than other vehicles.They may take up the whole of the road space, so be prepared to give way.

SECTION 8 VEHICLE HANDLING

This section looks at the handling of your vehicle in different conditions

The questions will ask you about

- **Weather conditions**

  be aware of how wet or icy roads will affect the handling of your vehicle.

- **Road conditions**

  be aware of how the road surface may affect your vehicle.

- **Time of day**

  be aware of hazards when driving or riding at night.

- **Speed**

  be aware that it's more difficult to control your vehicle at high speeds.

- **Traffic calming**

  be aware of measures used to slow down traffic where there are pedestrians.

Question 8.1

Mark one answer

To gain basic skills in how to ride a motorcycle you should

- practise off-road with an approved training body
- ride on the road on the first dry day
- practise off-road in a public park or in a quiet cul-de-sac
- ride on the road as soon as possible

Answer

- **practise off-road with an approved training body**

All new motorcyclists must complete a course of basic training with an approved training body before going on the road. This training is given on a site which has been authorised by the Driving Standards Agency as suitable for off-road training.

Question 8.2

Mark one answer

When you are seated on a stationary motorcycle, your position should allow you to

- just touch the ground with your toes
- place both feet on the ground
- operate the centre stand
- reach the switches by stretching

Answer

- **place both feet on the ground**

When sitting astride a stationary motorcycle you should be able to place both feet on the ground for maximum control and stability.

Question 8.3

Mark two answers

As a safety measure before starting your engine, you should

- push the motorcycle forward to check the rear wheel turns freely
- engage first gear and apply the rear brake
- engage first gear and apply the front brake
- glance at the neutral light on your instrument panel

Answers

- **push the motorcycle forward to check the rear wheel turns freely**
- **glance at the neutral light on your instrument panel**

Before starting the engine you should ensure the motorcycle is in neutral. This can be done by

- moving the motorcycle to see the rear wheel turns freely
- checking the neutral lamp is lit when the ignition is turned on.

Question 8.4

Mark one answer

You should not ride with your clutch lever pulled in for longer than necessary because it

- increases wear on the gearbox
- increases petrol consumption
- reduces your control of the motorcycle
- reduces the grip of the tyres

Answer

- **reduces your control of the motorcycle**

Coasting

- gives you less steering control
- reduces the traction on the road surface
- causes the machine to pick up speed.

If you're travelling downhill your machine will gather speed quickly. The engine won't be able to assist the braking.

Question 8.5

Mark two answers

What are TWO main reasons why coasting downhill is wrong?

- Fuel consumption will be higher
- The vehicle will pick up speed
- It puts more wear and tear on the tyres
- You have less braking and steering control
- It damages the engine

Answers

- **The vehicle will pick up speed**
- **You have less braking and steering control**

It's especially important that you don't coast your vehicle

- at junctions
- approaching hazards
- on bends.

Question 8.6

Mark one answer

Why is coasting wrong?

- It will cause the car to skid
- It will make the engine stall
- The engine will run faster
- There is no engine braking

Answer

- **There is no engine braking**

Try to look ahead and read the road. Plan your approach to junctions and select the correct gear in good time. This will give you the control you need to deal with any hazards that occur.

You'll coast a little every time you change gear. This can't be avoided, but it should be kept to a minimum.

Question 8.7

Mark two answers

Hills can affect the performance of your vehicle. Which TWO apply when driving up steep hills?

- Higher gears will pull better
- You will slow down sooner
- Overtaking will be easier
- The engine will work harder
- The steering will feel heavier

Answers

- **You will slow down sooner**
- **The engine will work harder**

The engine will need more power to pull the vehicle up the hill. When approaching a steep hill you should select a lower gear to maintain your speed. You should do this without hesitation, so that you don't lose too much speed.

Question 8.8

Mark one answer

You should brake

- by using the rear brake first and then the front
- when the machine is being turned or ridden through a bend
- by pulling in the clutch before using the front brake
- when the machine is upright and moving in a straight line

Answer

- **when the machine is upright and moving in a straight line**

A motorcycle is most stable when it's upright and moving in a straight line. This is the best time to brake and normally both brakes should be used with the front brake being applied just before the rear.

Question 8.9

Mark one answer

You are following a vehicle at a safe distance on a wet road. Another driver overtakes you and pulls into the gap you have left. What should you do?

- Flash your headlights as a warning
- Try to overtake safely as soon as you can
- Drop back to regain a safe distance
- Stay close to the other vehicle until it moves on

Answer

- **Drop back to regain a safe distance**

The weather will affect the way your vehicle or machine behaves. It will increase the time it takes for you to stop and can affect your control. Drive at a speed that will allow you to stop safely and in good time.

If another vehicle pulls into the gap you've left, ease back until you've regained your stopping distance. Don't flash your lights or drive up close to it.

Question 8.10

Mark three answers

In which THREE of these situations may you overtake another vehicle on the left?

- When you are in a one-way street
- When approaching a motorway slip road where you will be turning off
- When the vehicle in front is signalling to turn right
- When a slower vehicle is travelling in the right-hand lane of a dual carriageway
- In slow-moving traffic queues when traffic in the right-hand lane is moving more slowly

Answers

- **When you are in a one-way street**
- **When the vehicle in front is signalling to turn right**
- **In slow-moving traffic queues when traffic in the right-hand lane is moving more slowly**

At certain times of the day traffic might be heavy. If traffic is moving in queues and vehicles in the right-hand lane are moving more slowly, you may overtake on the left. Don't keep changing lanes to try and beat the queue.

Question 8.11

Mark one answer

You are driving on the motorway in windy conditions. When passing high-sided vehicles you should

- increase your speed
- be wary of a sudden gust
- drive alongside very closely
- expect normal conditions

Answer

- **be wary of a sudden gust**

The draught caused by other vehicles could be strong enough to push you out of your lane. Keep both hands on the steering wheel to maintain full control.

Question 8.12

Mark one answer

When coming to a normal stop on a motorcycle, you should

- only apply the front brake
- rely just on the rear brake
- apply both brakes smoothly
- apply either of the brakes gently

Answer

- **apply both brakes smoothly**

In normal riding you should always use both brakes. Harsh or poorly-controlled use of the brakes can cause loss of control and skidding.

Question 8.13

Mark three answers

Which THREE of the following will affect your stopping distance?

- How fast you are going
- The tyres on your vehicle
- The time of day
- The weather
- The street lighting

Answers

- **How fast you are going**
- **The tyres on your vehicle**
- **The weather**

You should be aware that there are several factors that can affect the distance it takes to stop your vehicle.

Your stopping distance in wet weather will increase. You should double the separation distance from the car in front. Your tyres will have less grip on the road and therefore need more time to stop. Always drive in accordance with the conditions.

Question 8.14

Mark one answer

You are travelling in very heavy rain. Your overall stopping distance is likely to be

- doubled
- halved
- up to ten times greater
- no different

Answer

- **doubled**

Apart from the lack of visibility the road will be extremely wet. This will lesson the grip the tyres have on the road and increase the distance it takes to stop. Double your separation distance.

Question 8.15

Mark two answers

You are approaching this junction. As the motorcyclist you should

- prepare to slow down
- sound your horn
- keep near the left kerb
- speed up to clear the junction
- stop, as the car has right of way

Answers

- **prepare to slow down**
- **sound your horn**

Look out for road signs indicating side roads, even if you aren't turning off. A driver emerging might not be able to see you due to parked cars or heavy traffic. Always be prepared, and stop if it's necessary. Remember, no one has priority at unmarked crossroads.

Question 8.16

Mark one answer

What can you do to improve your safety on the road as a motorcyclist?

- Anticipate the actions of others
- Stay just above the speed limits
- Keep positioned close to the kerbs
- Remain well below speed limits

Answer

- **Anticipate the actions of others**

Always ride defensively. This means looking and planning ahead as well as anticipating the actions of other road users.

Question 8.17

Mark four answers

Which FOUR types of road surface increase the risk of skidding for motorcyclists?

- White lines
- Dry tarmac
- Tar banding
- Yellow grid lines
- Loose chippings

Answers

- **White lines**
- **Tar banding**
- **Yellow grid lines**
- **Loose chippings**

If you're riding a motorcycle you must look at the road surface ahead. The stability of your machine will depend on it. Also, look out for

- pot-holes
- drain covers (especially in the wet)
- oily surfaces
- road markings
- tram tracks
- wet mud and leaves.

Question 8.18

Mark one answer

You have to brake sharply and your machine starts to skid. You should

- continue braking and select a low gear
- apply the brakes harder for better grip
- select neutral and use the front brake only
- release the brakes and re-apply

Answer

- **release the brakes and re-apply**

If you skid as a result of too much braking you need to

- release the brakes to stop the skid
- re-apply them progressively to stop.

Question 8.19

Mark three answers

Which THREE of these can cause skidding?

- Braking too gently
- Leaning too far over when cornering
- Staying upright when cornering
- Braking too hard
- Changing direction suddenly

Answers

- **Leaning too far over when cornering**
- **Braking too hard**
- **Changing direction suddenly**

In order to keep control of your vehicle and prevent skidding you must plan well ahead to prevent harsh, late braking. Take the road and weather conditions into consideration and ride accordingly.

Question 8.20

Mark one answer

To correct a rear-wheel skid you should

- not steer at all
- steer away from it
- steer into it
- apply your handbrake

Answer

- **steer into it**

Prevention is better than cure, so it's important that you take every precaution to prevent a skid. If you do feel your vehicle beginning to skid, try to steer to recover control. Don't brake suddenly – this will only make the situation worse.

Question 8.21

Mark two answers

It is very cold and the road looks wet. You cannot hear any road noise. You should

- continue riding at the same speed
- ride slower in as high a gear as possible
- ride in as low a gear as possible
- keep revving your engine
- slow down as there may be black ice

Answers

- **ride slower in as high a gear as possible**
- **slow down as there may be black ice**

Rain freezing on roads as it falls is called black ice and isn't clearly visible. The first indication that you might have of it is when the steering becomes very light. You need to keep your speed down and ride according to the weather conditions.

Question 8.22

Mark one answer

You are approaching a road with a surface of loose chippings. What should you do?

- Ride normally
- Speed up
- Slow down
- Stop suddenly

Answer

- **Slow down**

You should

- ride at an appropriate speed
- apply both front and rear brakes evenly
- brake when travelling in a straight line and your machine is upright.

Don't make sudden changes of direction unless you are avoiding an accident.

The handling of your machine will be greatly affected by the road surface that you're riding on. Look at the road ahead and be alert if the road looks uneven or has loose chippings. Slow down in good time – braking harshly here will cause you to skid.

Question 8.23

Mark one answer

When snow is falling heavily you should

- drive as long as your headlights are used
- not drive unless you have a mobile phone
- drive only when your journey is short
- not drive unless it is essential

Answer

not drive unless it is essential

Consider if the increased risk is worth it. If the weather conditions are bad and your journey isn't essential, then stay at home.

Question 8.24

Mark one answer

You are driving on an icy road. What distance should you drive from the car in front?

- Four times the normal distance
- Six times the normal distance
- Eight times the normal distance
- Ten times the normal distance

Answer

Ten times the normal distance

Think about how far this is. It's a long way, probably further than you imagine.

Question 8.25

Mark one answer

You are driving in very wet weather. Your vehicle begins to slide. This effect is called

- hosing
- weaving
- aquaplaning
- fading

Answer

aquaplaning

Water can build up between the tyres and the road. This means that the tyres might not have contact with the road. Your vehicle could slide on the film of water, causing the steering to feel light and you to lose proper control.

Question 8.26

Mark one answer

Why should you test your brakes after this hazard?

- Because you will be on a slippery road
- Because your brakes will be soaking wet
- Because you will have gone down a long hill
- Because you will have just crossed a long bridge

Answer

- **Because your brakes will be soaking wet**

A ford is a crossing over a stream that's shallow enough to drive through. If you've driven through a ford or a deep puddle the water can affect your brakes. Be sure you check that they're working before returning to normal speed.

Question 8.27

Mark two answers

You have to make a journey in fog. What are the TWO most important things you should do before you set out?

- Top up the radiator with antifreeze
- Make sure that you have a warning triangle in the vehicle
- Check that your lights are working
- Check the battery
- Make sure that the windows are clean

Answers

- **Check that your lights are working**
- **Make sure that the windows are clean**

Don't drive in fog unless you really have to. Drive in accordance with the conditions.

Question 8.28

Mark one answer

When riding a motorcycle you should wear full protective clothing

- at all times
- only on faster, open roads
- just on long journeys
- only during bad weather

Answer

- **at all times**

Protective clothing is designed to protect you from the cold and wet and some kinds of injury.

If you allow yourself to become cold and wet you will lose concentration.

Question 8.29

Mark two answers

You have to make a journey in fog. What are the TWO most important things you should do before you set out?

- Fill up with fuel
- Make sure that you have a warm drink with you
- Check that your lights are working
- Check the battery
- Make sure that your visor is clean

Answers

- **Check that your lights are working**
- **Make sure that your visor is clean**

If you're riding a motorcycle keep your visor as clean as possible to give you a clear view of the road. It's a good idea to carry a clean, damp cloth in a polythene bag for this purpose. When the weather is foggy or misty ensure that your lights are clean and can be seen clearly by other road users.

Question 8.30

Mark one answer

You have to make a journey in foggy conditions. You should

- follow closely other vehicles' tail lights
- avoid using dipped headlights
- leave plenty of time for your journey
- keep two seconds behind other vehicles

Answer

- **leave plenty of time for your journey**

If you're planning to make a journey in foggy conditions listen to the weather reports on the radio or television. Don't drive if visibility is very low or your journey isn't necessary. If you do travel, leave plenty of time for your journey. If there's someone expecting you at the other end of your journey let them know that you'll be taking longer than normal to arrive. Take your time and don't hurry.

Question 8.31

Mark one answer

Front fog lights may be used ONLY if

- visibility is seriously reduced
- they are fitted above the bumper
- they are not as bright as the headlights
- an audible warning device is used

Answer

- **visibility is seriously reduced**

Your fog lights should have a warning light which illuminates when they are being used. You should be familiar with the layout of your dashboard so you are aware if they have been switched on in error, or you have forgotten to switch them off.

Question 8.32

Mark one answer

Front fog lights may be used ONLY if

- your headlights are not working
- they are operated with rear fog lights
- they were fitted by the vehicle manufacturer
- visibility is seriously reduced

Answer

- **visibility is seriously reduced**

It is illegal to use fog lights unless visibility is seriously reduced. Check that they have been switched off when conditions improve.

Question 8.33

Mark one answer

You may drive with front fog lights switched-on

- when visibility is less than 100 metres (328 feet)
- at any time to be noticed
- instead of headlights on high-speed roads
- when dazzled by the lights of oncoming vehicles

Answer

- **when visibility is less than 100 metres (328 feet)**

Consider if the distance you are able to see is more than 100 metre (328 feet). Turn off your fog lights as the weather improves.

Question 8.34

Mark one answer

Front fog lights should be used ONLY when

- travelling in very light rain
- visibility is seriously reduced
- daylight is fading
- driving after midnight

Answer

- **visibility is seriously reduced**

It will help others see you, but remember, they must only be used if visibility is seriously reduced to less than 100 metres (328 feet).

Question 8.35

Mark one answer

Front fog lights should be used

- when visibility is reduced to 100 metres (328 feet)
- as a warning to oncoming traffic
- when driving during the hours of darkness
- in any conditions and at any time

Answer

- **when visibility is reduced to 100 metres (328 feet)**

As visibility reduces to less than 100 metres (328 feet) switch on your fog lights if you have them fitted. It is essential, not only that you can see ahead, but that other drivers are able to see you.

Question 8.36

Mark one answer

Using front fog lights in clear daylight will

- flatten the battery
- dazzle other drivers
- improve your visibility
- increase your awareness

Answer

- **dazzle other drivers**

Fog lights can be brighter than normal dipped headlights. If the weather has improved, turn them off to prevent dazzling other road users.

Question 8.37

Mark one answer

You may use front fog lights with headlights ONLY when visibility is reduced to less than

- 100 metres (328 feet)
- 200 metres (656 feet)
- 300 metres (984 feet)
- 400 metres (1312 feet)

Answer

- **100 metres (328 feet)**

It is an offence to use them if the visibility is better than 100 metres (328 feet). Deal with patchy fog sensibly to prevent dazzling other road users in the clear patches.

Question 8.38

Mark one answer

You are following other vehicles in fog with your lights on. How else can you reduce the chances of being involved in an accident?

- Keep close to the vehicle in front
- Use your main beam instead of dipped headlights
- Keep together with the faster vehicles
- Reduce your speed and increase the gap

Answer

- **Reduce your speed and increase the gap**

Always ensure that you have your lights on and that you're seen by all other road users. Use dipped headlights. If visibility is below 100 metres (328 feet) use fog lights and high-intensity rear lights. Drive at a sensible speed and don't follow the car in front too closely. You'll need to adjust your stopping distance as the road is likely to be wet and slippery.

Question 8.39

Mark one answer

Why should you always reduce your speed when travelling in fog?

- Because the brakes do not work as well
- Because you could be dazzled by other people's fog lights
- Because the engine is colder
- Because it is more difficult to see events ahead

Answer

- **Because it is more difficult to see events ahead**

Driving in fog is hazardous. Only travel if it's really necessary. To drive or ride safely you must always look well ahead. In fog this won't be possible, and you'll have less time to react to any hazards. You must reduce your speed.

Question 8.40

Mark one answer

You are driving in fog. Why should you keep well back from the vehicle in front?

- In case it changes direction suddenly
- In case its fog lights dazzle you
- In case it stops suddenly
- In case its brake lights dazzle you

Answer

- **In case it stops suddenly**

If you're following another road user in fog, stay well back. The driver in front won't be able to see hazards until they're close, and might brake suddenly. You'll need a good separation distance as the road surface is likely to be wet and slippery.

NI

Question 8.41

Mark one answer

You should switch your rear fog lights on when visibility drops below

- your overall stopping distance
- ten car lengths
- 200 metres (656 feet)
- 100 metres (328 feet)

Answer

100 metres (328 feet)

This will help other road users to see you. Don't forget to turn off fog lights once visibility is improved. Their brightness might be mistaken for brake lights.

Question 8.42

Mark one answer

Using rear fog lights in clear daylight will

- be useful when towing a trailer
- give extra protection
- dazzle other drivers
- make following drivers keep back

Answer

dazzle other drivers

Rear fog lights shine brighter than normal rear lights so they show up in bad visibility. When the weather is clear they could dazzle the driver behind, so switch them off.

Question 8.43

Mark two answers

You are driving on a clear dry night with your rear fog lights switched on. This may

- reduce glare from the road surface
- make other drivers think you are braking
- give a better view of the road ahead
- dazzle following drivers
- help your indicators to be seen more clearly

Answers

make other drivers think you are braking

dazzle following drivers

A warning light will show on the dashboard to indicate when your rear fog lights are on. You should know the meaning of all the lights on your dashboard and check them before you move off and as you drive.

NI

Question 8.44

Mark two answers

Why is it dangerous to leave rear fog lights on when they are not needed?

- Brake lights are less clear
- Following drivers can be dazzled
- Electrical systems could be overloaded
- Direction indicators may not work properly
- The battery could fail

Answers

- **Brake lights are less clear**
- **Following drivers can be dazzled**

The drivers behind you may be confused by your rear fog lights. On a wet road surface the glare caused by bright lights makes it difficult for following drivers to know if you are braking, or if you have forgotten to turn off your rear fog lights.

This can be a real problem at speed on motorways.

Question 8.45

Mark one answer

Whilst driving, the fog clears and you can see more clearly. You must remember to

- switch off the fog lights
- reduce your speed
- switch off the demister
- close any open windows

Answer

- **switch off the fog lights**

Bright rear fog lights might be mistaken for brake lights and could be misleading for the traffic behind.

Question 8.46

Mark one answer

You have just driven out of fog. Visibility is now good. You MUST

- switch off all your fog lights
- keep your rear fog lights on
- keep your front fog lights on
- leave fog lights on in case fog returns

Answer

- **switch off all your fog lights**

Be prepared for the fact that the fog may be patchy, but you must turn off your fog lights if visibility is over 100 metres (328 feet).

NI

Question 8.47

Mark three answers

You forget to switch off your rear fog lights when the fog has cleared. This may

- dazzle other road users
- reduce battery life
- cause brake lights to be less clear
- be breaking the law
- seriously affect engine power

Answers

- **dazzle other road users**
- **cause brake lights to be less clear**
- **be breaking the law**

You could be prosecuted for driving with fog lights on in good visibility. Don't forget to switch them off as the weather improves. The high intensity of the rear fog lights can look like brakes lights, and on a high speed road this can cause following traffic to brake unnecessarily.

NI

Question 8.48

Mark one answer

You have been driving in thick fog which has now cleared. You must switch OFF your rear fog lights because

- they use a lot of power from the battery
- they make your brake lights less clear
- they will cause dazzle in your rear view mirrors
- they may not be properly adjusted

Answer

- **they make your brake lights less clear**

It is essential that the traffic behind is given a clear warning when you brake. As the rear lights could be mistaken for brake lights they will not be able to detect whether you are applying the brakes. Switch off your fog lights as the visibility improves.

Question 8.49

Mark one answer

You are driving with your front fog lights switched on. Earlier fog has now cleared. What should you do?

- Leave them on if other drivers have their lights on
- Switch them off as long as visibility remains good
- Flash them to warn oncoming traffic that it is foggy
- Drive with them on instead of your headlights

Answer

- **Switch them off as long as visibility remains good**

Switch off your fog lights if the weather improves, but be prepared to use them again if visibility reduces to less than 100 metres (328 feet).

Question 8.50

Mark one answer

While you are driving in fog, it becomes necessary to use front fog lights. You should

- only turn them on in heavy traffic conditions
- remember not to use them on motorways
- only use them with dipped headlights
- remember to switch them off as visibility improves

Answer

- **remember to switch them off as visibility improves**

It is an offence to have your fog lights on in conditions other than seriously reduced visibility i.e. less than 100 metres (328 feet).

Question 8.51

Mark one answer

You have to park on the road in fog. You should

- leave sidelights on
- leave dipped headlights and fog lights on
- leave dipped headlights on
- leave main beam headlights on

Answer

leave sidelights on

If you have to park your vehicle in foggy conditions it's important that it can be seen by other road users.

Try to find a place to park off the road. If this isn't possible, leave your vehicle facing in the same direction as the traffic. Make sure that your lights are clean and that you leave your sidelights on.

Question 8.52

Mark one answer

On a foggy day you unavoidably have to park your car on the road. You should

- leave your headlights on
- leave your fog lights on
- leave your sidelights on
- leave your hazard lights on

Answer

leave your sidelights on

Ensure that your vehicle can be seen by other road users. If possible, park your car off the road in a car park or driveway to avoid the extra risk to other road users.

Question 8.53

Mark one answer

The best place to park your motorcycle is

- on soft tarmac
- on bumpy ground
- on grass
- on firm, level ground

Answer

on firm, level ground

Parking your machine on soft ground might cause the stand to sink and the bike to fall over. The ground should also be even and level to ensure that the bike is stable. If possible, park your machine off the road.

Question 8.54

Mark one answer

You are on a motorway in fog. The left-hand edge of the motorway can be identified by reflective studs. What colour are they?

- Green

- Amber
- Red
- White

Answer

- **Red**

Be especially careful if you're driving on a motorway in fog. You must be able to stop well within the distance that you can see to be clear. Keep in the left-hand lane.

Reflective studs are used on motorways to help you in poor visibility. The studs are coloured so that you'll know which lane you're in and where slip roads join or leave the motorway.

Question 8.55

Mark one answer

When riding in windy conditions, you should

- stay close to large vehicles
- keep your speed up
- keep your speed down
- stay close to the gutter

Answer

- **keep your speed down**

Strong winds can blow motorcycles off course and even across the road. In windy conditions you need to

- slow down
- avoid riding on exposed roads
- watch for gaps in buildings and hedges where you may be affected by a sudden blast of wind.

Question 8.56

Mark one answer

In normal riding your position on the road should be

- about a foot from the kerb
- about central in your lane
- on the right of your lane
- near the centre of the road

Answer

- **about central in your lane**

If you're riding a motorcycle it's very important to ride where other road users can see you. In normal weather you should ride in the centre of your lane. This will

- help you to be seen in the mirror of the vehicle in front
- avoid uneven road surfaces in the gutter
- allow others to overtake on the right if they wish.

Question 8.57

Mark one answer

You are on a well-lit motorway at night. You must

- use only your sidelights
- always use your headlights
- always use rear fog lights
- use headlights only in bad weather

Answer

always use your headlights

If you're driving on a motorway at night you must always use your headlights, even if the road is well lit. The vehicles in front must be able to see you in their mirrors.

Question 8.58

Mark one answer

You are on a motorway at night. You MUST have your headlights switched on unless

- there are vehicles close in front of you
- you are travelling below 50 mph
- the motorway is lit
- your vehicle is broken down on the hard shoulder

Answer

your vehicle is broken down on the hard shoulder

Always use your headlights at night on a motorway unless you're stopped on the hard shoulder. If you break down and have to stop on the hard shoulder switch off the main beam. Leave the sidelights on so that other road users can see your vehicle or machine.

Question 8.59

Mark one answer

You are on a motorway at night with other vehicles just ahead of you. Which lights should you have on?

- Front fog lights
- Main beam headlights
- Sidelights only
- Dipped headlights

Answer

Dipped headlights

If you're driving or riding behind other traffic at night on the motorway

- leave a two-second time gap
- dip your headlights.

Full beam will dazzle the driver ahead. Your light beam should fall short of the vehicle in front.

Question 8.60

Mark two answers

Which TWO of the following are correct? When overtaking at night you should

- Wait until a bend so that you can see the oncoming headlights
- sound your horn twice before moving out
- be careful because you can see less
- beware of bends in the road ahead
- put headlights on full beam

Answers

- **be careful because you can see less**
- **beware of bends in the road ahead**

Only overtake the vehicle in front if it's really necessary. At night the risks are increased due to the poor visibility. Don't overtake if there's a possibility of

- road junctions
- bends ahead
- the brow of a bridge or hill, except on a dual carriageway
- pedestrian crossings
- double white lines ahead
- vehicles changing direction
- any other potential hazard.

Question 8.61

Mark one answer

You are overtaking a car at night. You must be sure that

- you flash your headlights before overtaking
- you select a higher gear
- you have switched your lights to full beam before overtaking
- you do not dazzle other road users

Answer

- **you do not dazzle other road users**

If you wish to overtake at night ensure that your lights don't reflect in the mirror of the car in front. Wait until you've overtaken before switching to full beam.

Question 8.62

Mark two answers

When riding at night you should

- wear fluorescent clothing
- ride closer to the vehicle in front
- keep your goggles or visor clean
- ride just left of centre
- use your headlights

Answers

- **keep your goggles or visor clean**
- **use your headlights**

Always make sure that you can see clearly and that other road users can see you. Make sure that your visor or goggles don't have any scratches, which might distort your view or cause dazzle. Wearing bright clothing is a good idea, but remember, only reflective clothing will adequately show up at night.

Question 8.63

Mark one answer

You are travelling at night. You are dazzled by headlights coming towards you. You should

- pull down your sun visor
- slow down or stop
- switch on your main beam headlights
- put your hand over your eyes

Answer

slow down or stop

If you're driving at night there will be extra hazards to deal with. The lights of oncoming vehicles can often distract. If you're dazzled by them don't

- close your eyes
- flash your headlights. This will only distract the other driver too.

Question 8.64

Mark one answer

You are parking on a two-way road at night. The speed limit is 40 mph. You should park on the

- left with sidelights on
- left with no lights on
- right with sidelights on
- right with dipped headlights on

Answer

left with sidelights on

On a two-way road you may only park at night without lights on

- if the road has a speed limit of 30 mph or less
- you're at least 10 metres (32 feet) away from a junction
- you're facing in the direction of the traffic flow.

Question 8.65

Mark one answer

You are on a narrow road at night. A slower-moving vehicle ahead has been signalling right for some time. What should you do?

- Overtake on the left
- Flash your headlights before overtaking
- Signal right and sound your horn
- Wait for the signal to be cancelled before overtaking

Answer

Wait for the signal to be cancelled before overtaking

If the vehicle in front has been indicating right for some time, but has made no attempt to turn, wait for the signal to be cancelled. The other driver may have misjudged the distance to the road junction or there might be a hidden hazard.

Question 8.66

Mark two answers

A rumble device is designed to

- give directions
- prevent cattle escaping
- alert you to low tyre pressure
- alert you to a hazard
- encourage you to reduce speed

Answers

- **alert you to a hazard**
- **encourage you to reduce speed**

A rumble device is usually raised markings or strips on the road's surface. These strips are in places where traffic has constantly ignored warning or restriction signs. They're there for a good reason. Slow down and be ready to deal with a hazard.

Question 8.67

Mark two answers

Which TWO are correct? The passing places on a single-track road are

- for taking a rest and break
- to pull into if an oncoming vehicle wants to proceed
- for stopping and checking your route
- to turn around in, if you are lost
- to pull into if the car behind wants to overtake

Answers

- **to pull into if an oncoming vehicle wants to proceed**
- **to pull into if the car behind wants to overtake**

If you're driving on a single-track road be prepared to pull over and let other road users pass. There are passing places to enable you to do this. These shouldn't be used for parking or turning your car around.

Question 8.68

Mark one answer

You see a vehicle coming towards you on a single-track road. You should

- go back to the main road
- do an emergency stop
- stop at a passing place
- put on your hazard warning lights

Answer

- **stop at a passing place**

You must take extra care when driving on single-track roads. You may not be able to see around bends due to high hedges or fences. Drive with caution and expect to meet oncoming vehicles around the next bend. If you do, pull over into or opposite a passing place.

Question 8.69

Mark one answer

Your motorcycle is parked on a two-way road. You should get on from the

- right and apply the rear brake
- left and leave the brakes alone
- left and apply the front brake
- right and leave the brakes alone

Answer

- **left and apply the front brake**

When you get onto a motorcycle you should

- get on from the left side to avoid putting yourself in danger from passing traffic
- apply the front brake to prevent the machine rolling either forwards or backwards.

Question 8.70

Mark one answer

When may you wait in a box junction?

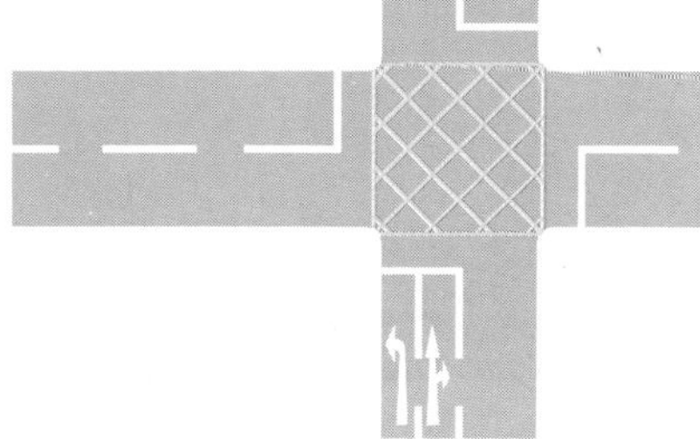

- When you are stationary in a queue of traffic
- When approaching a pelican crossing
- When approaching a zebra crossing
- When oncoming traffic prevents you turning right

Answer

- **When oncoming traffic prevents you turning right**

The purpose of this road marking is to keep the junction clear by preventing traffic from stopping in the path of crossing traffic. If there is already a vehicle waiting to turn right you're free to enter behind it and wait to turn right.

Question 8.71

Mark four answers

Which of the following may apply when dealing with this hazard?

- It could be more difficult in winter
- Use a low gear and drive slowly
- Use a high gear to prevent wheelspin
- Test your brakes afterwards
- Always switch on fog lamps
- There may be a depth gauge

Answers

- **It could be more difficult in winter**
- **Use a low gear and drive slowly**
- **Test your brakes afterwards**
- **There may be a depth gauge**

During the winter the stream is likely to flood. It is also possible that, in extreme weather it could ice over. Assess the situation carefully before you drive through. If you drive a vehicle with low suspension you will have to be extra cautious.

Question 8.72

Mark one answer

Which of these plates normally appear with this road sign?

- 

- 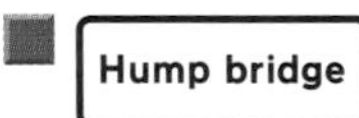

- Low bridge
- 

Answer

- Humps for ½ mile

These are in place to slow down the traffic. You should be aware that they are in places where there are often pedestrians, such as

- shopping areas
- near schools
- residential areas

Watch out for people close to the kerb or crossing the road.

Question 8.73

Mark three answers

How should a scooter be left when parking for some time in a town centre?

- On firm and level ground
- By using the sidestand leaning over the kerb
- On the centre stand if fitted
- Secure and with the fuel tap off
- On any very wide pavement

Answers

- **On firm and level ground**
- **On the centre stand if fitted**
- **Secure and with the fuel tap off**

When parking a motorcycle always try to park

- on firm level ground
- on the centre stand
- with the fuel tap turned off.

You should always secure your vehicle using any steering lock or immobiliser fitted by the manufacturer. Any additional visible motorcycle lock that helps to deter thieves is recommended.

Question 8.74

Mark one answer

You are driving along a road which has speed humps. A driver in front is travelling slower than you. You should

- sound your horn
- overtake as soon as you can
- flash your headlights
- slow down and stay behind

Answer

- **slow down and stay behind**

Normally, you should not overtake other vehicles in traffic calmed areas. Your speed may exceed that which is safe along that road, so defeating the purpose of the traffic calming measures.

Question 8.75

Mark two answers

Why should motorcyclists ride carefully where trams operate?

- They do not give way to other traffic
- They do not have mirrors and will not see you
- They do not have lights and might be difficult to see
- The rails could affect your steering and braking

Answers

- **They do not give way to other traffic**
- **The rails could affect your steering and braking**

Rails set in the road for trams can affect your steering, especially if they are above the surface of the road or if your front wheel drops into the gap between the road and the rail. They can also present a hazard if you need to brake on them, especially if the roads are wet.

Question 8.76

Mark three answers

Areas reserved for trams may have

- metal studs around them
- white line markings
- zigzag markings
- a different coloured surface
- yellow hatch markings
- a different surface texture

Answers

- **white line markings**
- **a different coloured surface**
- **a different surface texture**

Trams can run on roads used by other vehicles and pedestrians. The area of the road used by the trams is known as the 'swept area'. It should be kept clear, has a coloured surface and is usually edged with white road markings. It might also have different surface texture.

Question 8.77

Mark one answer

It rains after a long dry, hot spell. This may cause the road surface to

- be unusually slippery
- give better grip
- become covered in grit
- melt and break up

Answer

- **be unusually slippery**

Roads can become extremely slippery, especially when rain falls onto surfaces that have been subjected to a long hot dry spell. Summer showers can be as hazardous as winter frost.

Question 8.78

Mark three answers

The main causes of a motorcycle skidding are

- heavy and sharp braking
- excessive acceleration
- leaning too far when cornering
- riding in wet weather
- riding in the winter

Answers

- **heavy and sharp braking**
- **excessive acceleration**
- **leaning too far when cornering**

A good rider tries to avoid skidding. The loss of control during a skid can be lethal.

Question 8.79

Mark one answer

To stop your motorcycle quickly in an emergency you should apply

- the rear brake only
- the front brake only
- the front brake just before the rear
- the rear brake just before the front

Answer

the front brake just before the rear

You should plan ahead to avoid the need to stop suddenly. But if an emergency should arise, you must be able to stop safely. Apply the correct amount of braking effort to each wheel.

Question 8.80

Mark one answer

Chains can be fitted to your wheels to help prevent

- damage to the road surface
- wear to the tyres
- skidding in deep snow
- the brakes locking

Answer

skidding in deep snow

Snow chains can be fitted to your tyres during snowy conditions. They can help you to move off from rest or to keep moving in deep snow. This should not stop you from adjusting your driving according to the road conditions at the time.

Question 8.81

Mark one answer

Traffic calming measures are used to

- stop road rage
- help overtaking
- slow traffic down
- help parking

Answer

slow traffic down

Traffic calming measures are used to make the roads safer for vulnerable road users, such as cyclists, pedestrians and children. These can be designed as chicanes, road humps, etc., to act as obstacles forcing drivers to slow down.

This section looks at motorway rules.

The questions will ask you about

- **Speed limits**

  be aware of the speed restrictions on the motorway.

- **Lane discipline**

  keep to the left unless overtaking.

- **Stopping**

  know when and where you can stop on the motorway.

- **Lighting**

  be aware of the importance of being seen.

- **Parking**

  don't park on the motorway unless in an emergency.

Question 9.1

Mark one answer

As a provisional licence-holder you should not drive a car

- over 50 mph
- at night
- on the motorway
- with passengers in rear seats

Answer

- **on the motorway**

When you've passed your practical test ask your instructor to take you for a lesson on the motorway. You'll need to get used to the speed of traffic and how to deal with multiple lanes.

Question 9.2

Mark four answers

Which FOUR of these must NOT use motorways?

- Learner car drivers
- Motorcycles over 50 cc
- Double-deck buses
- Farm tractors
- Horse riders
- Cyclists

Answers

- **Learner car drivers**
- **Farm tractors**
- **Horse riders**
- **Cyclists**

In addition, motorways MUST NOT be used by

- pedestrians
- motorcycles under 50 cc
- certain slow-moving vehicles, without permission
- invalid carriages not weighing more than 254kg (560 lbs).

Question 9.3

Mark four answers

Which FOUR of these must NOT use motorways?

- Learner car drivers
- Motorcycles over 50 cc
- Double-deck buses
- Farm tractors
- Learner motorcyclists
- Cyclists

Answers

- **Learner car drivers**
- **Farm tractors**
- **Learner motorcyclists**
- **Cyclists**

When you've passed your practical driving test it's a good idea to have some lessons on motorways. Statistically, motorways are safer than other roads, but they have rules that you need to know before you venture out for the first time. Check with your instructor about this.

Question 9.4

Mark one answer

A motorcycle is not allowed on a motorway if it has an engine size smaller than

- 50 cc
- 125 cc
- 150 cc
- 250 cc

Answer

- **50cc**

The restricted speed of a small machine will cause a hazard to other motorway users. If you're riding a machine with a small engine, choose another route.

Question 9.5

Mark one answer

To ride on a motorway your motorcycle must be

- 50 cc or more
- 100 cc or more
- 125 cc or more
- 250 cc or more

Answer

- **50 cc or more**

Traffic on motorways travels at high speeds. Vehicles need to be capable of keeping up with the flow of traffic. For this reason low-powered vehicles are prohibited.

Question 9.6

Mark one answer

Why is it particularly important to carry out a check on your vehicle before making a long motorway journey?

- You will have to do more harsh braking on motorways
- Motorway service stations do not deal with breakdowns
- The road surface will wear down the tyres faster
- Continuous high speeds may increase the risk of your vehicle breaking down

Answer

- **Continuous high speeds may increase the risk of your vehicle breaking down**

Before you start your journey make sure that your vehicle can cope with the demands of high-speed driving. Before starting a motorway journey check your vehicle's

- oil
- water
- tyres.

Plan your rest stops if you're travelling a long way.

Question 9.7

Mark one answer

Immediately after joining a motorway you should normally

- try to overtake
- readjust your mirrors
- position your vehicle in the centre lane
- keep in the left lane

Answer

- **keep in the left lane**

Give yourself time to get used to the higher speeds of motorway traffic.

Question 9.8

Mark one answer

You are joining a motorway. Why is it important to make full use of the slip road?

- Because there is space available to turn round if you need to
- To allow you direct access to the overtaking lanes
- To build up a speed similar to traffic on the motorway
- Because you can continue on the hard shoulder

Answer

- **To build up a speed similar to traffic on the motorway**

Try to join the motorway without affecting the progress of the traffic already travelling on it. At busy times this could also mean slowing down to merge into slow-moving traffic

Question 9.9

Mark one answer

You are joining a motorway from a slip road on the left. You should

- adjust your speed to the speed of the traffic on the motorway
- accelerate as quickly as you can and ride straight out
- ride onto the hard shoulder until a gap appears
- expect drivers on the motorway to give way to you

Answer

- **adjust your speed to the speed of the traffic on the motorway**

Give way to the traffic already on the motorway and join where there's a suitable gap in the traffic. Try to avoid stopping at the end of the slip road. This might not be avoidable, however, if the motorway is exceptionally busy and there isn't a clear gap in the traffic.

Question 9.10

Mark one answer

When joining a motorway you must always

- use the hard shoulder
- stop at the end of the acceleration lane
- come to a stop before joining the motorway
- give way to traffic already on the motorway

Answer

- **give way to traffic already on the motorway**

The traffic may be travelling at high speed, so you should adjust your speed and emerge when it's safe to do so.

Question 9.11

Mark one answer

You are riding on a motorway. Unless signs show otherwise you must NOT exceed

- 50 mph
- 60 mph
- 70 mph
- 80 mph

Answer

70 mph

Ride in accordance with the conditions. Bad weather, heavy traffic or roadworks will limit your speed.

Question 9.12

Mark one answer

What is the national speed limit for cars and motorcycles in the centre lane of a three-lane motorway?

- 40 mph
- 50 mph
- 60 mph
- 70 mph

Answer

70 mph

Unless otherwise indicated the speed limit for the motorway applies to all the lanes. Be on the lookout for any indication of speed limit changes due to roadworks or traffic flow control.

Question 9.13

Mark one answer

What is the national speed limit on motorways for cars and motorcycles?

- 30 mph
- 50 mph
- 60 mph
- 70 mph

Answer

70 mph

Driving or riding at the national speed limit doesn't allow you to hog the outside lane. Always use the nearside or middle lanes whenever possible.

When leaving the motorway, always adjust your speed in good time to deal with

- bends or curves on the slip road
- traffic queuing at roundabouts.

Question 9.14

Mark one answer

You are towing a trailer on a motorway. What is your maximum speed limit?

- 40 mph
- 50 mph
- 60 mph
- 70 mph

Answer

60 mph

Don't forget that you're towing a trailer. If you're towing a small, light trailer it won't reduce your vehicle's performance by very much. Strong winds or buffeting from large vehicles might cause it to snake from side to side. Be aware of your speed and don't exceed the lower limit imposed.

Question 9.15

Mark one answer

You are driving a car on a motorway. Unless signs show otherwise you must NOT exceed

- 50 mph
- 60 mph
- 70 mph
- 80 mph

Answer

70 mph

The national speed limit for a car or motorcycle on the motorway is 70 mph.

Lower speed limits may be in force so look out for the signs. There might be a variable speed limit in operation to control a very busy motorway. The speed limit may change depending on the volume of traffic. There may be roadworks enforcing a low speed

Question 9.16

Mark one answer

On a three-lane motorway which lane should you normally use?

- Left
- Right
- Centre
- Either the right or centre

Answer

Left

On a three-lane motorway you should travel in the left-hand lane unless you're overtaking. This applies regardless of the speed you're travelling at.

Question 9.17

Mark one answer

A basic rule when on motorways is

- use the lane that has least traffic
- keep to the left lane unless overtaking
- overtake on the side that is clearest
- try to keep above 50 mph to prevent congestion

Answer

- **keep to the left lane unless overtaking**

When you've overtaken, move back into the left-hand lane as soon as it's safe to do so. Don't cut across in front of the vehicle that you're overtaking.

Question 9.18

Mark one answer

On a three-lane motorway why should you normally ride in the left lane?

- The left lane is only for lorries and motorcycles
- The left lane should only be used by smaller vehicles
- The lanes on the right are for overtaking
- Motorcycles are not allowed in the far right lane

Answer

- **The lanes on the right are for overtaking**

Change lanes only if necessary. When you do change lanes observe, signal and manoeuvre in good time. Always remember your 'lifesaver' check. This is a final,quick rearward glance before you manoeuvre.

Question 9.19

Mark one answer

You are going at 70 mph on a three-lane motorway. There is no traffic ahead. Which lane should you use?

- Any lane
- Middle lane
- Right lane
- Left lane

Answer

Left lane

Use the left-hand lane if it's free, regardless of the speed you're travelling at.

Question 9.20

Mark one answer

The left-hand lane on a three-lane motorway is for use by

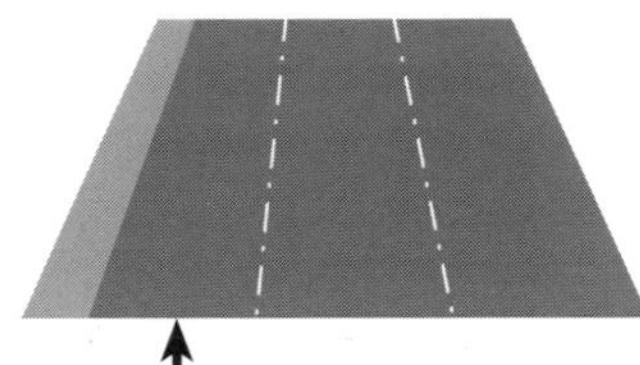

- any vehicle
- large vehicles only
- emergency vehicles only
- slow vehicles only

Answer

any vehicle

On a motorway all traffic should use the left-hand lane unless overtaking. If you need to overtake use the centre or right-hand lanes.

Make sure that you move back to the left-hand lane when you've finished overtaking. Don't stay in the middle or right-hand lanes if the left-hand lane is free.

Question 9.21

Mark one answer

The left-hand lane of a motorway should be used for

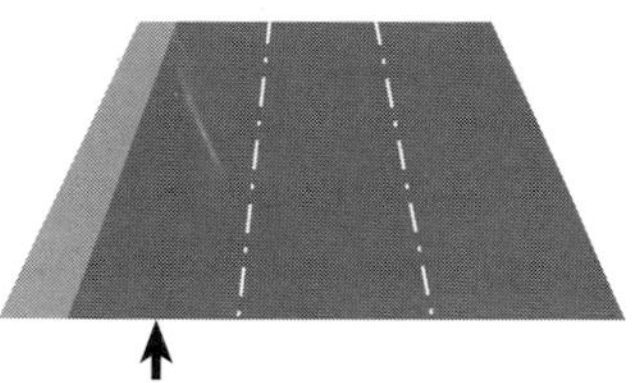

- breakdowns and emergencies only
- overtaking slower traffic in the other lanes
- slow vehicles only
- normal driving

Answer

normal driving

You should keep to the left-hand lane whenever possible for normal driving.

Question 9.22

Mark one answer

What is the right-hand lane used for on a three-lane motorway?

- Emergency vehicles only
- Overtaking
- Vehicles towing trailers
- Coaches only

Answer

Overtaking

You should keep to the left and only use the right-hand lane if you're passing slower-moving traffic.

Question 9.23

Mark one answer

Which of these IS NOT allowed to travel in the right-hand lane of a three-lane motorway?

- A small delivery van
- A motorcycle
- A vehicle towing a trailer
- A motorcycle and side-car

Answer

A vehicle towing a trailer

A vehicle with a trailer is restricted to 60 mph. For this reason it isn't allowed in the right-hand lane as it might hold up the faster-moving traffic that wishes to overtake in that lane.

Question 9.24

Mark one answer

For what reason may you use the right-hand lane of a motorway?

- For keeping out of the way of lorries
- For driving at more than 70 mph
- For turning right
- For overtaking other vehicles

Answer

For overtaking other vehicles

The right-hand lanes of the motorway are for overtaking. Sometimes you may be directed into a right-hand lane as a result of roadworks or an accident.

Be guided by the signs or police directing the traffic.

Question 9.25

Mark one answer

On motorways you should never overtake on the left UNLESS

- you can see well ahead that the hard shoulder is clear
- the traffic in the right-hand lane is signalling right
- you warn drivers behind by signalling left
- there is a queue of traffic to your right that is moving more slowly

Answer

there is a queue of traffic to your right that is moving more slowly

Only overtake on the left if traffic is moving slowly in queues and the traffic on the right is moving slower.

Question 9.26

Mark one answer

On a motorway you may ONLY stop on the hard shoulder

- in an emergency
- If you feel tired and need to rest
- if you accidentally go past the exit that you wanted to take
- to pick up a hitchhiker

Answer

- **in an emergency**

Don't stop on the hard shoulder to

- have a rest or a picnic
- pick up hitchhikers
- answer a mobile phone
- check a road map.

Never reverse along the hard shoulder if you accidentally go past the exit you wanted.

Question 9.27

Mark two answers

You are travelling on a motorway. You decide you need a rest. You should

- stop on the hard shoulder
- go to a service area
- park on the slip road
- park on the central reservation
- leave at the next exit

Answers

- **go to a service area**
- **leave at the next exit**

Stopping on the motorway in any circumstances other than an emergency or traffic queue will cause a major hazard. You should plan your journey so that you have a rest about every two hours. Stop where you are able to get out of the car for some fresh air and something to eat and drink.

Question 9.28

Mark one answer

You are driving on a motorway. The car ahead shows its hazard lights for a short time. This tells you that

- the driver wants you to overtake
- the other car is going to change lanes
- traffic ahead is slowing or stopping suddenly
- there is a police speed check ahead

Answer

- **traffic ahead is slowing or stopping suddenly**

There may be an accident or queuing traffic due to roadworks. Look well ahead, not just at the car in front, and you'll get an earlier warning of any hazard.

Question 9.29

Mark one answer

You are driving on a motorway. You have to slow down quickly due to a hazard. You should

- switch on your hazard lights
- switch on your headlights
- sound your horn
- flash your headlights

Answer

- **switch on your hazard lights**

The traffic behind you will be given an extra warning, in addition to your brake lights. Switch them off again as the queue forms behind you.

NI

Question 9.30

Mark one answer

You break down on a motorway. You need to call for help. Why may it be better to use an emergency roadside telephone rather than a mobile phone?

- It connects you to a local garage
- Using a mobile phone will distract other drivers
- It allows easy location by the emergency services
- Mobile phones do not work on motorways

Answer

- **It allows easy location by the emergency services**

On a motorway it is best to use a roadside emergency telephone so that the emergency services are able to locate you easily.

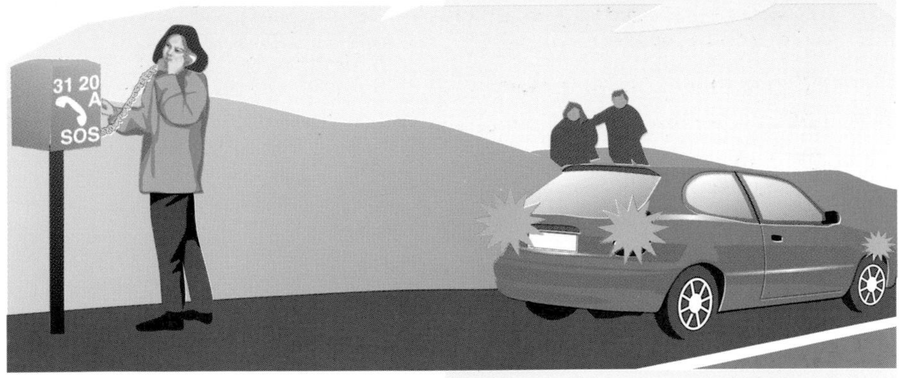

NI

Question 9.31

Mark one answer

Your vehicle breaks down on the hard shoulder of a motorway. You decide to use your mobile phone to call for help. You should

- stand at the rear of the vehicle while making the call
- try to repair the vehicle yourself
- get out of the vehicle by the right hand door
- check your location from the marker posts on the left

Answer

- **check your location from the marker posts on the left**

In the case of an emergency, time can be of the essence. The emergency services need to know your exact location. Look at the marker posts on the edge of the hard shoulder before you phone, there is a number on them, tell the services this, it will help them to locate you. Be ready to describe where you are, for example by reference to the last place or junction you passed.

Question 9.32

Mark one answer

You get a puncture on the motorway. You manage to get your vehicle onto the hard shoulder. You should

- change the wheel yourself immediately
- use the emergency telephone and call for assistance
- try to wave down another vehicle for help
- only change the wheel if you have a passenger to help you

Answer

- **use the emergency telephone and call for assistance**

Due to the danger from passing traffic you shouldn't attempt repairs on the hard shoulder, especially if you have to change an offside wheel.

Question 9.33

Mark one answer

The emergency telephones on a motorway are connected to the

- ambulance service
- police control
- fire brigade
- breakdown service

Answer

police control

The controller will ask you

- the make and colour of your vehicle
- whether you are a member of an emergency breakdown service
- the number shown on the emergency telephone casing
- whether you are travelling alone.

Question 9.34

Mark one answer

How should you use the emergency telephone on a motorway?

- Stay close to the carriageway
- Face the oncoming traffic
- Keep your back to the traffic
- Stand on the hard shoulder

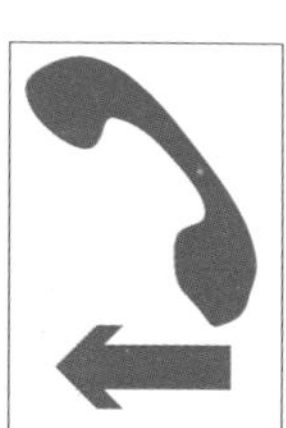

Answer

Face the oncoming traffic

Traffic is passing you at speed. The draught from a large lorry could unsteady you, so be prepared. By facing the oncoming traffic you can spot this in advance, as well as other hazards approaching.

Question 9.35

Mark one answer

What should you use the hard shoulder of a motorway for?

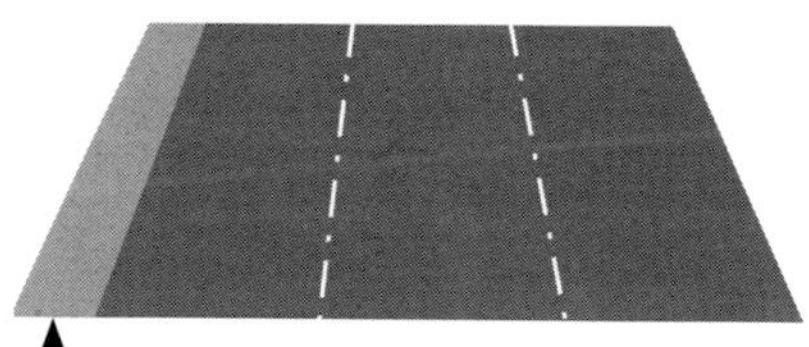

- Stopping in an emergency
- Leaving the motorway
- Stopping when you are tired
- Joining the motorway

Answer

Stopping in an emergency

Don't use the hard shoulder for stopping other than for emergencies. Drive to the next exit or service station if you're able to do so safely.

Question 9.36

Mark one answer

After a breakdown you need to rejoin the main carriageway of a motorway from the hard shoulder. You should

- move out onto the carriageway then build up your speed
- move out onto the carriageway using your hazard lights
- gain speed on the hard shoulder before moving out onto the carriageway
- wait on the hard shoulder until someone flashes their headlights at you

Answer

- **gain speed on the hard shoulder before moving out onto the carriageway**

Wait for a safe gap in the traffic before you move out. Indicate your intention but don't force your way into the traffic.

Question 9.37

Mark one answer

A crawler lane on a motorway is found

- on a steep gradient
- before a service area
- before a junction
- along the hard shoulder

Answer

- **on a steep gradient**

There are likely to be slow-moving large vehicles which might slow down the progress of other traffic. This extra lane is provided for these slow-moving vehicles helping the faster-moving traffic to flow. If the crawler lane is free then use it as you would a normal left-hand lane.

Question 9.38

Mark one answer

Your vehicle has broken down on a motorway. You are not able to stop on the hard shoulder. What should you do?

- Switch on your hazard warning lights
- Stop following traffic and ask for help
- Attempt to repair your vehicle quickly
- Stand behind your vehicle to warn others

Answer

- **Switch on your hazard warning lights**

Use your hazard warning lights to warn others. Don't try to repair the vehicle.

Question 9.39

Mark three answers

When may you stop on a motorway?

- If you have to read a map
- When you are tired and need a rest
- If red lights show above every lane
- When told to by the police
- If your mobile phone rings
- In an emergency or a breakdown

Answers

- **If red lights show above every lane**
- **When told to by the police**
- **In an emergency or a breakdown**

You may only stop on the carriageway of a motorway

- when told to do so by the police
- when flashing red lights show above every lane
- in a traffic jam
- in an emergency or breakdown.

Question 9.40

Mark one answer

You are allowed to stop on a motorway when you

- need to walk and get fresh air
- wish to pick up hitchhikers
- are told to do so by flashing red lights
- need to use a mobile telephone

Answer

- **are told to do so by flashing red lights**

If any of the other lanes show a green arrow you may move into that lane and continue if it is safe to do so. If there are red lights above every lane you must stop.

Question 9.41

Mark one answer

You are on a motorway. There are red flashing lights above every lane. You must

- pull onto the hard shoulder
- slow down and watch for further signals
- leave at the next exit
- stop and wait

Answer

- **stop and wait**

Flashing red lights above every lane mean you must not go on any further. You'll also see a red cross illuminated. Stop and wait. Don't

- change lanes
- continue
- pull onto the hard shoulder (unless in an emergency).

Question 9.42

Mark one answer

You are in the right-hand lane on a motorway. You see these overhead signs. This means

- move to the left and reduce your speed to 50 mph
- there are roadworks 50 metres (55 yards) ahead
- use the hard shoulder until you have passed the hazard
- leave the motorway at the next exit

Answer

- **move to the left and reduce your speed to 50 mph**

You must obey this sign. There might not be any visible signs of a problem ahead. However, there might be queuing traffic, fog or another hazard ahead.

Question 9.43

Mark one answer

When going through a contraflow system on a motorway you should

- ensure that you do not exceed 30 mph
- keep a good distance from the vehicle ahead
- switch lanes to keep the traffic flowing
- stay close to the vehicle ahead to reduce queues

Answer

keep a good distance from the vehicle ahead

There's likely to be a speed restriction in force. Keep to this. Don't

- switch lanes
- drive too close to other traffic.

There will be no permanent barrier between you and the traffic coming towards you. Be extra cautious.

Question 9.44

Mark one answer

You are intending to leave the motorway at the next exit. Before you reach the exit you should normally position your vehicle

- in the middle lane
- in the left-hand lane
- on the hard shoulder
- in any lane

Answer

in the left-hand lane

You'll see the first sign one mile from the exit. If you're travelling at 60 miles an hour in the right-hand lane you'll only have about 50 seconds before you reach the countdown markers. There's another sign at the half-mile point. Think about what you need to do to be in the left-hand lane in good time. Don't cut across traffic at the last moment.

Question 9.45

Mark one answer

What do these motorway signs show?

- They are countdown markers to a bridge
- They are distance markers to the next telephone
- They are countdown markers to the next exit
- They warn of a police control ahead

Answer

They are countdown markers to the next exit

The exit from a motorway is indicated by countdown markers. These are positioned 90 metres (100 yards) apart, the first being 270 metres (300 yards) from the slip road. Try to get yourself into the left lane in good time.

Question 9.46

Mark one answer

You are driving on a motorway. By mistake, you go past the exit that you wanted to take. You should

- carefully reverse on the hard shoulder
- carry on to the next exit
- carefully reverse in the left-hand lane
- make a U-turn at the next gap in the central reservation

Answer

carry on to the next exit

Don't

- reverse anywhere
- make a U-turn.

This is highly dangerous, as high-speed traffic might not be able to take evasive action.

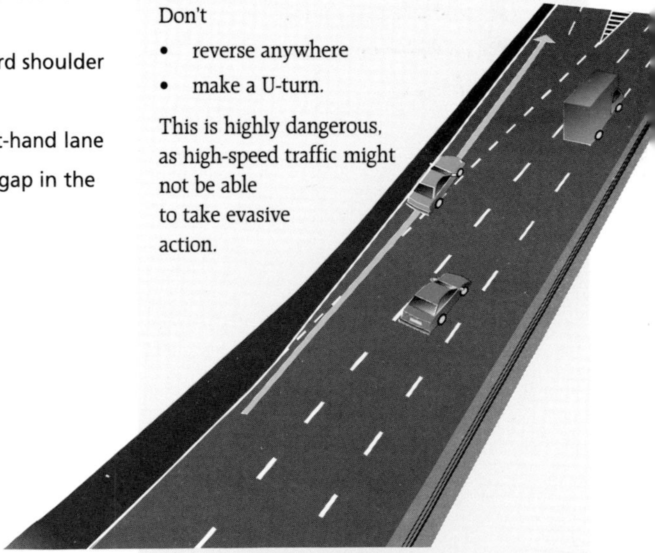

Question 9.47

Mark one answer

On a motorway the amber reflective studs can be found between

- the hard shoulder and the carriageway
- the acceleration lane and the carriageway
- the central reservation and the carriageway
- each pair of the lanes

Answer

the central reservation and the carriageway

On motorways reflective studs are fitted into the road to help you

- in the dark
- in conditions of poor visibility.

The reflective studs are coloured. These will help you to know which lane you're in and where slip roads join or leave the motorway.

Question 9.48

Mark one answer

What colour are the reflective studs between the lanes on a motorway?

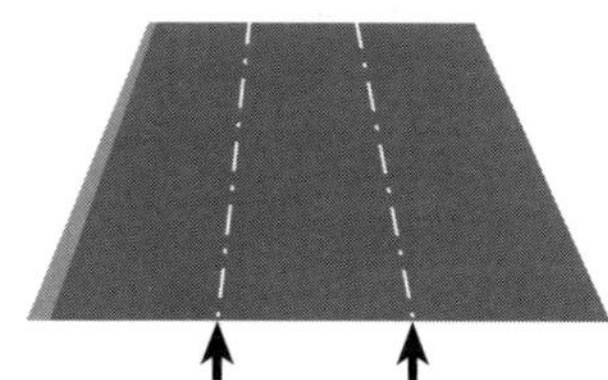

- Green
- Amber
- White
- Red

Answer

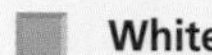

White

These are especially useful in bad weather, when visibility is restricted. The light from your headlights is reflected back highlighting the markings between the lanes.

Question 9.49

Mark one answer

You are on a three-lane motorway. There are red reflective studs on your left and white ones to your right. Where are you?

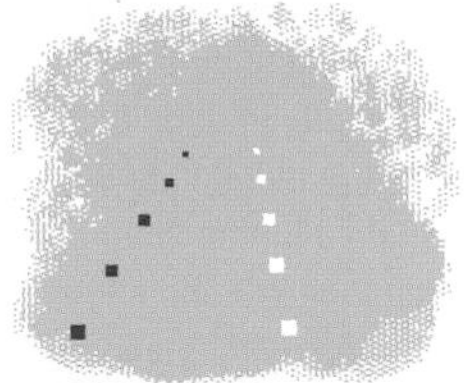

- In the right-hand lane
- In the middle lane
- On the hard shoulder
- In the left-hand lane

Answer

In the left-hand lane

The colours of the reflective studs on the motorway and their locations are

- Red – between the hard shoulder and the carriageway.
- White – lane markings.
- Amber – between the edge of the carriageway and the central reserve.
- Green – along slip road exits and entrances.
- Bright Green/Yellow – roadworks and contraflow systems.

Question 9.50

Mark one answer

What colour are the reflective studs between a motorway and its slip road?

- Amber
- White
- Green
- Red

Answer

Green

These will help you when driving in conditions of poor visibility or in the dark.

Question 9.51

Mark one answer

You are on a motorway. What colour are the reflective studs on the left of the carriageway?

- Green
- Red
- White
- Amber

Answer

- **Red**

When you have passed your practical test, ask your Instructor about lessons on the motorway. Good professional instruction will help you to become confident and safe on the motorway.

Question 9.52

Mark one answer

You have broken down on a motorway. To find the nearest emergency telephone you should always walk

- with the traffic flow
- facing oncoming traffic
- in the direction shown on the marker posts
- in the direction of the nearest exit

Answer

- **in the direction shown on the marker posts**

Along the hard shoulder there are marker posts at 100 metre intervals. These will direct you to the nearest emergency telephone.

Question 9.53

Mark one answer

You are travelling along the left lane of a three-lane motorway. Traffic is joining from a slip road. You should

- race the other vehicles
- move to another lane
- maintain a steady speed
- switch on your hazard flashers

Answer

- **move to another lane**

If it is safe to do so you should move to another lane. This can greatly assist the flow of traffic joining the motorway, especially at peak times.

NI

Question 9.54

Mark one answer

You are on a three-lane motorway towing a trailer. You may use the right hand lane when

- there are lane closures
- there is slow-moving traffic
- you can maintain a high speed
- large vehicles are in the left and centre lanes

Answer

- **there are lane closures**

You are not allowed to use the right-hand lane on a motorway with three or more lanes if you are towing a caravan or trailer.

SECTION 10 RULES OF THE ROAD

This section looks at rules of the road

The questions will ask you about

- **Speed limits**

  be aware of the speed limits for different types of vehicle.

- **Lane discipline**

  be sure you select the correct lane for the direction you wish to take.

- **Parking**

  choose a sensible place to park.

- **Lighting**

  don't let your vehicle become a hazard.

Question 10.1

Mark one answer

You are riding slowly in a town centre. Before turning left you should glance over your left shoulder to

- check for cyclists
- help keep your balance
- look for traffic signs
- check for potholes

Answer

check for cyclists

When riding slowly you must remember cyclists. They can travel quickly and fit through surprisingly narrow spaces. Before you turn left in slow moving traffic it's important to check that a cyclist isn't trying to overtake on your left.

Question 10.2

Mark one answer

You may drive over a footpath

- to overtake slow-moving traffic
- when the pavement is very wide
- if no pedestrians are near
- to get into a property

Answer

to get into a property

When you're crossing the pavement watch out for pedestrians and cyclists in both directions.

Question 10.3

Mark one answer

What is the meaning of this sign?

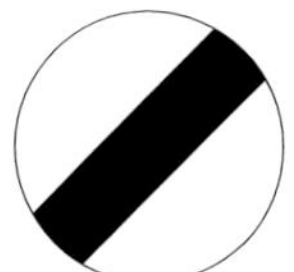

- Local speed limit applies
- No waiting on the carriageway
- National speed limit applies
- No entry to vehicular traffic

Answer

National speed limit applies

This sign doesn't tell you the speed limit in figures. You should know the speed limit for the type of road that you're on. Study your copy of *The Highway Code.*

Question 10.4

Mark one answer

What is the national speed limit on a single carriageway road for cars and motorcycles?

- 70 mph
- 60 mph
- 50 mph
- 30 mph

Answer

60 mph

Exceeding the speed limit is dangerous and can result in you receiving penalty points on your licence. It isn't worth it. Know the speed limit of the road that you're driving on by observing the road signs.

Question 10.5

Mark one answer

What is the national speed limit for cars and motorcycles on a dual carriageway?

- 30 mph
- 50 mph
- 60 mph
- 70 mph

Answer

70 mph

Ensure that you know the speed limit for the road that you're driving on.

The speed limit on a dual carriageway or motorway is 70 mph for cars and motorcycles, unless there are signs to indicate otherwise.

The speed limits for different vehicles are listed in *The Highway Code.*

Question 10.6

Mark one answer

A single carriageway road has this sign. What is the maximum permitted speed for a car towing a trailer?

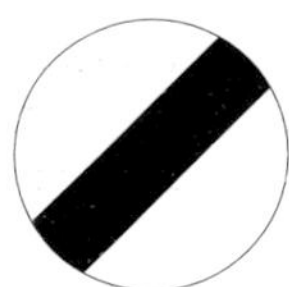

- 30 mph
- 40 mph
- 50 mph
- 60 mph

Answer

50 mph

When towing trailers, speed limits are also lower on dual carriageways and motorways. On these roads vehicles towing a trailer are restricted to 60 mph.

Question 10.7

Mark one answer

You are on a road that has no traffic signs. There are street lights. What is the speed limit?

- 20 mph
- 30 mph
- 40 mph
- 60 mph

Answer

- **30 mph**

If you aren't sure of the speed limit it can be indicated by the presence of street lights. If there is street lighting the speed limit will be 30 mph unless otherwise indicated.

Question 10.8

Mark one answer

There are no speed limit signs on the road. How is a 30 mph limit indicated?

- By hazard warning lines
- By street lighting
- By pedestrian islands
- By double or single yellow lines

Answer

- **By street lighting**

This usually indicates a 30 mph speed limit when there are no other signs to show other limits.

Question 10.9

Mark one answer

Where you see street lights but no speed limit signs the limit is usually

- 30 mph
- 40 mph
- 50 mph
- 60 mph

Answer

- **30 mph**

If you are travelling faster than the limit, slow down before you reach the sign. Check your mirror and ease off the accelerator.

Question 10.10

Mark one answer

You are towing a small caravan on a dual carriageway. You must not exceed

- 50 mph
- 40 mph
- 70 mph
- 60 mph

Answer

60 mph

Due to the increased weight and width of the combined vehicles you should plan well ahead. Be extra careful in wet or windy weather. Strong winds might cause the caravan to snake from side to side. The speed limit is reduced for vehicles towing trailers or caravans to lessen the risk of this.

Question 10.11

Mark one answer

What does this sign mean?

- Minimum speed 30 mph
- End of maximum speed
- End of minimum speed
- Maximum speed 30 mph

Answer

End of minimum speed

A red slash through this sign indicates that the restriction has ended.

Question 10.12

Mark three answers

You are going along a street with parked vehicles on the left-hand side. For which THREE reasons should you keep your speed down?

- So that oncoming traffic can see you more clearly
- You may set off car alarms
- Vehicles may be pulling out
- Drivers' doors may open
- Children may run out from between the vehicles

Answers

Vehicles may be pulling out

Drivers' doors may open

Children may run out from between the vehicles

Care must be taken where there are parked vehicles in a built-up area. Beware of

- vehicles pulling out, especially motorcycles that are small and difficult to see
- pedestrians, especially children, who may run out from between cars
- drivers opening vehicle doors.

Question 10.13

Mark one answer

You meet an obstruction on your side of the road. You should

- carry on, you have priority
- give way to oncoming traffic
- wave oncoming vehicles through
- accelerate to get past first

Answer

give way to oncoming traffic

If you have to pass a parked vehicle on your side of the road take care. Give way to oncoming traffic if there isn't enough room for you both to continue safely.

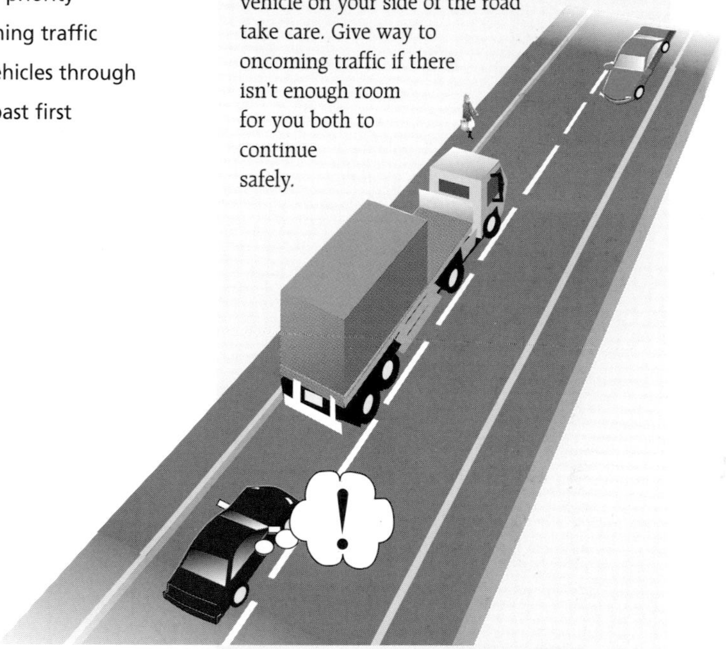

Question 10.14

Mark one answer

There is a tractor ahead of you. You wish to overtake but you are NOT sure if it is safe to do so. You should

- follow another overtaking vehicle through
- sound your horn to the slow vehicle to pull over
- speed through but flash your lights to oncoming traffic
- not overtake if you are in doubt

Answer

not overtake if you are in doubt

Always ask yourself if you really need to overtake. Can you see well down the road? If the answer is no, don't go.

Question 10.15

Mark three answers

Which three of the following are most likely to take an unusual course at roundabouts ?

- Horse riders
- Milk floats
- Delivery vans
- Long vehicles
- Estate cars
- Cyclists

Answers

- **Horse riders**
- **Long vehicles**
- **Cyclists**

Long vehicles might have to take a slightly different position when approaching the roundabout or going around it. This is to stop the rear of the vehicle cutting in and mounting the kerb. Horse riders and cyclists might also stay in the left-hand lane although they are turning right. Be aware of this and allow them room.

Question 10.16

Mark one answer

You are leaving your vehicle parked on a road. When may you leave the engine running?

- If you will be parked for less than five minutes
- If the battery is flat
- When in a 20 mph zone
- Not on any occasion

Answer

- **Not on any occasion**

When you leave your vehicle parked on a road

- switch off the engine
- make sure that there aren't any valuables visible
- shut all the windows
- lock the vehicle. Use an anti-theft device if you have one.

Question 10.17

Mark four answers

In which FOUR places must you NOT park or wait?

- On a dual carriageway
- At a bus stop
- On the slope of a hill
- Opposite a traffic island
- In front of someone else's drive
- On the brow of a hill

Answers

- **At a bus stop**
- **Opposite a traffic island**
- **In front of someone else's drive**
- **On the brow of a hill**

Care and thought should be taken when parking your own vehicle. Don't park

- on a footpath, pavement or cycle track
- near a school entrance
- on the approach to a zebra crossing (except in an authorised parking place)
- opposite another parked vehicle.

NI

Question 10.18

Mark one answer

What is the nearest you may park your vehicle to a junction?

- 10 metres (32 feet)
- 12 metres (39 feet)
- 15 metres (49 feet)
- 20 metres (66 feet)

Answer

10 metres (32 feet)

Don't park within 10 metres (32 feet) of a junction (unless in an authorised parking place) or

- where you would force other traffic to enter a tram lane
- where the kerb has been lowered to help wheelchair users
- in front of an entrance to a property
- where your vehicle might obstruct a tram.

Question 10.19

Mark one answer

You are finding it difficult to find a parking place in a busy town. You can see there is space on the zigzag lines of a zebra crossing. Can you park there?

- No, unless you stay with your car
- Yes, in order to drop off a passenger
- Yes, if you do not block people from crossing
- No, not in any circumstances

Answer

No, not in any circumstances

It's an offence to park there. You will be causing an obstruction by obscuring the view of both pedestrians and drivers.

Question 10.20

Mark two answers

In which TWO places must you NOT park?

- Near a school entrance
- Near a police station
- In a side road
- At a bus stop
- In a one-way street

Answers

Near a school entrance

At a bus stop

It may be tempting to park where you shouldn't while you run a quick errand. Careless parking is a selfish act and could endanger other road users.

NI

Question 10.21

Mark three answers

In which THREE places must you NOT park your vehicle?

- Near the brow of a hill
- At or near a bus stop
- Where there is no pavement
- Within 10 metres (32 feet) of a junction
- On a 40 mph road

Answers

- **Near the brow of a hill**
- **At or near a bus stop**
- **Within 10 metres (32 feet) of a junction**

Other traffic will have to pull out to pass you. This might mean they have to use the other side of the road where there might be oncoming traffic.

Parking near a junction could restrict the view for emerging vehicles.

Question 10.22

Mark one answer

On a clearway you must not stop

- at any time
- when it is busy
- in the rush hour
- during daylight hours

Answer

- **at any time**

Clearways are in place so that traffic can flow without the obstruction of parked vehicles. Just one parked vehicle will cause an obstruction for all other traffic. You should not even stop to pick up or set down passengers.

Question 10.23

Mark one answer

You are driving on an urban clearway. You may stop only to

- set down and pick up passengers
- use a mobile telephone
- ask for directions
- load or unload goods

Answer

- **set down and pick up passengers**

These may be provided in built up areas and times of operation will be clearly signed. You should stop only for a time that is reasonable to pick up and set down passengers. You should consider that you are not causing an obstruction for other traffic before you stop.

Question 10.24

Mark one answer

You want to park and you see this sign. On the days and times shown you should

- park in a bay and not pay
- park on yellow lines and pay
- park on yellow lines and not pay
- park in a bay and pay

Answer

- **park in a bay and pay**

Parking restrictions vary from town to town. Look at the signs carefully. Parking in the wrong place could cause an obstruction and you could be fined.

Question 10.25

Mark one answer

What is the meaning of this sign?

- No entry
- Waiting restrictions
- National speed limit
- School crossing patrol

Answer

- **Waiting restrictions**

Don't cause an obstruction by stopping or waiting where there are restrictions. You should know the meaning of road signs. Buy a copy of *Know Your Traffic Signs* (The Stationery Office) and study it.

Question 10.26

Mark one answer

What MUST you have to park in a disabled space?

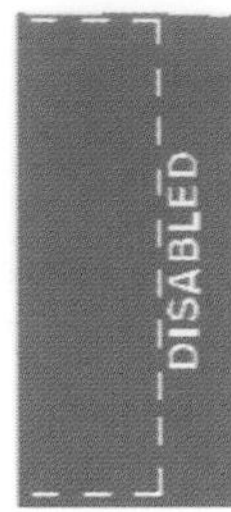

- An orange badge
- A wheelchair
- An advanced driver certificate
- A modified vehicle

Answer

An orange badge

Don't park in a space reserved for disabled people unless you or your passenger are a disabled badge-holder. The badge must be displayed on your vehicle in the bottom left-hand corner of the windscreen.

Question 10.27

Mark one answer

You are looking for somewhere to park your vehicle. The area is full EXCEPT for spaces marked 'disabled use'. You can

- use these spaces when elsewhere is full
- park if you stay with your vehicle
- use these spaces, disabled or not
- not park there unless permitted

Answer

not park there unless permitted

Don't be selfish. Find somewhere else to park even if it means that you have to walk further.

Question 10.28

Mark one answer

Your vehicle is parked on the road at night. When must you use sidelights?

- Where there are continuous white lines in the middle of the road
- Where the speed limit exceeds 30 mph
- Where you are facing oncoming traffic
- Where you are near a bus stop

Answer

Where the speed limit exceeds 30 mph

When parking at night, park in the direction of the traffic. This will enable other road users to see the reflectors on the rear of your vehicle.

Use your sidelights if the speed limit is over 30 mph or you're parking a vehicle over 1,525 kg (1.5 tons).

Question 10.29

Mark one answer

You park overnight on a road with a 40 mph speed limit. You should

- park facing the traffic
- park with sidelights on
- park with dipped headlights on
- park near a street light

Answer

park with sidelights on

Make sure that other road users can see your vehicle. Park in the direction of the traffic flow so that your vehicle isn't mistaken for a moving oncoming car.

Question 10.30

Mark one answer

You can park on the right-hand side of a road at night

- in a one-way street
- with your sidelights on
- more than 10 metres (32 feet) from a junction
- under a lamp-post

Answer

in a one-way street

Vehicles are fitted with red rear reflectors that show up when headlights shine on them. These are useful when cars are parked at night, but will only reflect if the vehicles are parked in the same direction as the traffic passing alongside. Normally you should park on the left, but if you're in a one-way street the right-hand side is OK too.

Question 10.31

Mark one answer

On a three-lane dual carriageway the right-hand lane can be used for

- overtaking only, never turning right
- overtaking or turning right
- fast-moving traffic only
- turning right only, never overtaking

Answer

overtaking or turning right

Use the left-hand lane at other times. When overtaking on a dual carriageway be on the lookout for vehicles ahead that are turning right. They're likely to be slowing or stopped. You need to see them in good time so that you can take appropriate action.

Question 10.32

Mark one answer

You are driving at night with full beam headlights on. A vehicle is overtaking you. You should dip your lights

- some time after the vehicle has passed you
- before the vehicle starts to pass you
- only if the other driver dips his headlights
- as soon as the vehicle passes you

Answer

- **as soon as the vehicle passes you**

Your lights on full beam could dazzle the driver in front. Make sure that your light beam falls short of the vehicle in front.

Question 10.33

Mark one answer

You are riding on a busy dual carriageway. When changing lanes you should

- rely totally on mirrors
- always increase your speed
- signal so others will give way
- use mirrors and shoulder checks

Answer

- **use mirrors and shoulder checks**

Before you change lanes you need to see if there's a safe gap to move across into. You have areas behind and to the side which are not covered by the mirrors. As well as using your mirrors you need to make a shoulder check to see if any vehicle is in this blind area before changing direction.

Question 10.34

Mark two answers

You are on a two-lane dual carriageway. For which TWO of the following would you use the right-hand lane?

- Turning right
- Normal progress
- Staying at the minimum allowed speed
- Constant high speed
- Overtaking slower traffic
- Mending punctures

Answers

- **Turning right**
- **Overtaking slower traffic**

If you overtake on a dual carriageway, move back into the left-hand lane as soon as it's safe. Don't cut in across the path of the vehicle you've just passed.

Question 10.35

Mark one answer

You are in the right-hand lane of a dual carriageway. You see signs showing that the right lane is closed 800 yards ahead. You should

- keep in that lane until you reach the queue
- move to the left immediately
- wait and see which lane is moving faster
- move to the left in good time

Answer

move to the left in good time

Keep a lookout for traffic signs. If you're directed to change lanes do so in good time. Don't

- push your way into traffic in another lane
- leave changing lanes until the last moment.

Question 10.36

Mark one answer

You are entering an area of roadworks. There is a temporary speed limit displayed. You must

- not exceed the speed limit
- obey the limit only during rush hour
- accept the speed limit as advisable
- obey the limit except for overnight

Answer

not exceed the speed limit

Where there are extra hazards, such as roadworks it's often necessary to slow traffic down by imposing a temporary speed limit. These speed limits aren't advisory – they must be adhered to.

Question 10.37

Mark one answer

While driving, you approach roadworks. You see a temporary maximum speed limit sign. You must

- comply with the sign during the working day
- comply with the sign at all times
- comply with the sign when the lanes are narrow
- comply with the sign during the hours of darkness

Answer

- **comply with the sign at all times**

The sign has been put there to allow traffic to deal with the hazard at a low speed. Reduce the risk and don't exceed the limit.

Question 10.38

Mark one answer

You may drive a motor car in this bus lane

- outside its operation hours
- to get to the front of a traffic queue
- at no times at all
- to overtake slow-moving traffic

Answer

- **outside its operation hours**

Make full use of bus lanes if it's permitted. This can often be at times other than rush hours. Check the sign. Times will differ from place to place.

Question 10.39

Mark three answers

As a car driver which THREE lanes are you NOT normally allowed to use?

- Crawler lane
- Bus lane
- Overtaking lane
- Acceleration lane
- Cycle lane
- Tram lane

Answers

- **Bus lane**
- **Cycle lane**
- **Tram lane**

Look out for signs or road markings that tell you which lane to use. Some lanes can only be used by certain road users. These might be to allow the traffic to flow, or to protect vulnerable road users.

Question 10.40

Mark two answers

You are driving on a road that has a cycle lane. The lane is marked by a broken white line. This means that

- you should not drive in the lane unless it is unavoidable
- you should not park in the lane unless it is unavoidable
- you can drive in the lane at any time
- the lane must be used by motorcyclists in heavy traffic

Answers

- **you should not drive in the lane unless it is unavoidable**
- **you should not park in the lane unless it is unavoidable**

Where sign or road markings show lanes are for cyclists only, leave them free. You should not drive or park in the lane unless it is unavoidable.

Question 10.41

Mark one answer

You are driving along a road that has a cycle lane. The lane is marked by a solid white line. This means that during its period of operation

- the lane may be used for parking your car
- you may drive in that lane at any time
- the lane may be used when necessary
- you must not drive in that lane

Answer

- **you must not drive in that lane**

Leave the lane free for cyclists. At other times, when the lane is not in operation you should still be aware that there still might be cyclists about. Give them room and don't pass too closely.

Question 10.42

Mark one answer

A cycle lane is marked by a solid white line. You must not drive or park in it

- at any time
- during the rush hour
- if a cyclist is using it
- during its period of operation

Answer

- **during its period of operation**

The cycle lanes are there for a reason. Keep them free and allow the cyclists to use them. Parking in the lane will force cyclists into the path of traffic on the main carriageway. This could be hazardous for both the cyclist and other road users.

Question 10.43

Mark two answers

As a motorcycle rider which TWO lanes must you NOT use?

- Crawler lane
- Overtaking lane
- Acceleration lane
- Cycle lane
- Tram lane

Answers

- **Cycle lane**
- **Tram lane**

In some towns motorcycles are permitted to use bus lanes. Check the signs carefully.

Question 10.44

Mark one answer

You are approaching a busy junction. There are several lanes with road markings. At the last moment you realise that you are in the wrong lane. You should

- continue in that lane
- force your way across
- stop until the area has cleared
- use clear arm signals to cut across

Answer

- **continue in that lane**

There are times where road markings can be obscured by queuing traffic, or you might be unsure of your correct lane. Don't cut across lanes or bully other drivers to let you in. Follow the lane you're in and find somewhere safe to turn around if you need to.

Question 10.45

Mark one answer

Where may you overtake on a one-way street?

- Only on the left-hand side
- Overtaking is not allowed
- Only on the right-hand side
- Either on the right or the left

Answer

- **Either on the right or the left**

You can overtake other traffic on either side when travelling in a one-way street. Make full use of your mirrors and ensure that it's clear all around before you attempt to overtake. Look for signs and road markings and use the most suitable lane for your destination.

Question 10.46

Mark one answer

You are going along a single-track road with passing places only on the right. The driver behind wishes to overtake. You should

- speed up to get away from the following driver
- switch on your hazard warning lights
- wait opposite a passing place on your right
- pull into a passing place on your right

Answer

- **wait opposite a passing place on your right**

Some roads are only wide enough for one vehicle. Often this type of road has special passing places where the road is widened for a short distance.

If there's a car coming toward you pull into a passing place on your left or stop opposite one on your right. Don't

- force other vehicles to reverse
- pull into the passing place on the right.

Question 10.47

Mark two answers

You are on a road that is only wide enough for one vehicle. There is a car coming towards you. Which TWO of these would be correct?

- Pull into a passing place on your right
- Force the other driver to reverse
- Pull into a passing place if your vehicle is wider
- Pull into a passing place on your left
- Wait opposite a passing place on your right
- Wait opposite a passing place on your left

Answers

- **Pull into a passing place on your left**
- **Wait opposite a passing place on your right**

If you meet another vehicle in a narrow road and the passing place is on the right, pull up opposite it. This will allow the oncoming vehicle to pull into it and pass you safely.

Question 10.48

Mark one answer

Signals are normally given by direction indicators and

- brake lights
- side lights
- fog lights
- interior lights

Answer

- **brake lights**

Your brake lights will give an indication to traffic behind that you're slowing down. Good anticipation will allow you time to check your mirrors before slowing.

If you're intending to change direction you should use your direction indicators before you brake.

Question 10.49

Mark one answer

When going straight ahead at a roundabout you should

- indicate left before leaving the roundabout
- not indicate at any time
- indicate right when approaching the roundabout
- indicate left when approaching the roundabout

Answer

- **indicate left before leaving the roundabout**

When you want to go ahead at a roundabout indicate left just after you pass the exit before the one you wish to take. Don't

- signal right on approach
- signal left on approach.

Question 10.50

Mark one answer

Which vehicle might have to use a different course to normal at roundabouts?

- Sports car
- Van
- Estate car
- Long vehicle

Answer

- **Long vehicle**

A long vehicle may have to straddle lanes either on or approaching a roundabout so that the rear wheels don't cut in over the kerb. Stay well back and give it room.

Question 10.51

Mark one answer

You are going straight ahead at a roundabout. How should you signal?

- Signal right on the approach and then left to leave the roundabout
- Signal left as you leave the roundabout
- Signal left on the approach to the roundabout and keep the signal on until you leave
- Signal left just after you pass the exit before the one you will take

Answer

- **Signal left just after you pass the exit before the one you will take**

To go straight ahead at a roundabout you should normally approach in the left-hand lane. Where there are road markings, use the lane indicated.

Ensure that you signal correctly and in good time. Other road users need to know your intentions.

Question 10.52

Mark one answer

You are turning right at a large roundabout. Just before you leave the roundabout you should

- take a 'lifesaver' glance over your left shoulder
- take a 'lifesaver' glance over your right shoulder
- put on your right indicator
- cancel the left indicator

Answer

- **take a 'lifesaver' glance over your left shoulder**

You must be aware of what's happening behind and alongside you. A final, quick rearward glance will give you the chance to react if it isn't safe to make the manoeuvre.

Question 10.53

Mark one answer

At a crossroads there are no signs or road markings. Two vehicles approach. Which has priority?

- Neither vehicle
- The vehicle travelling the fastest
- The vehicle on the widest road
- Vehicles approaching from the right

Answer

- **Neither vehicle**

At a crossroads where there are no GIVE WAY signs or road markings BE VERY CAREFUL. No vehicle has priority, even if the size of the roads are different.

Question 10.54

Mark one answer

Who has priority at an unmarked crossroads?

- The larger vehicle
- No one has priority
- The faster vehicle
- The smaller vehicle

Answer

- **No one has priority**

Practise good observation in all directions before you emerge or make a turn.

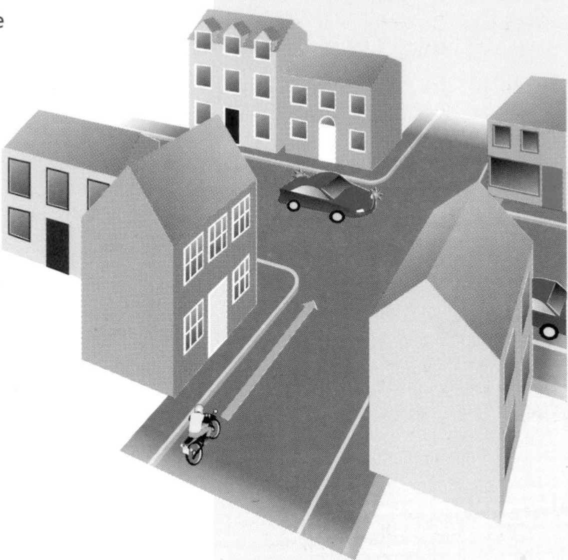

Question 10.55

Mark three answers

When filtering through slow-moving or stationary traffic you should

- watch for hidden vehicles emerging from side roads
- continually use your horn as a warning
- look for vehicles changing course suddenly
- always ride with your hazard lights on
- stand up on the footrests for a good view ahead
- look for pedestrians walking between vehicles

Answers

- **watch for hidden vehicles emerging from side roads**
- **look for vehicles changing course suddenly**
- **look for pedestrians walking between vehicles**

Other road users may not expect or look for motorcycles filtering through slow-moving or stationary traffic. The view all around will be reduced by the vehicles and you will need to watch for

- pedestrians walking between the vehicles
- vehicles suddenly changing direction
- vehicles pulling out of side roads.

Question 10.56

Mark one answer

You are intending to turn right at a crossroads. An oncoming driver is also turning right. It will normally be safer to

- keep the other vehicle to your RIGHT and turn behind it (offside to offside)
- keep the other vehicle to your LEFT and turn in front of it (nearside to nearside)
- carry on and turn at the next junction instead
- hold back and wait for the other driver to turn first

Answer

- **keep the other vehicle to your RIGHT and turn behind it (offside to offside)**

At some junctions the layout may make it difficult to turn this way. Be prepared to pass nearside to nearside, but take extra care. Your view ahead will be obscured by the vehicle turning in front of you.

Question 10.57

Mark one answer

You are both turning right at these crossroads. It is safer to keep the car to your right so you can

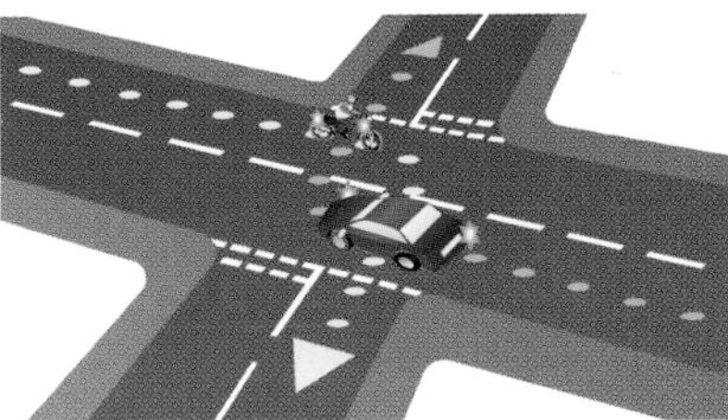

- see approaching traffic
- keep close to the kerb
- keep clear of following traffic
- make oncoming vehicles stop

Answer

- **see approaching traffic**

When turning right at this crossroads you should keep the oncoming car on your right. This will give you a clear view of the road ahead and any oncoming traffic.

Question 10.58

Mark one answer

The dual carriageway you are turning right onto has a narrow central reserve. You should

- proceed to central reserve and wait
- wait until the road is clear in both directions
- stop in first lane so that other vehicles give way
- emerge slightly to show your intentions

Answer

wait until the road is clear in both directions

If you treat this carriageway as two separate roads you could cause an obstruction to traffic in both directions.

Question 10.59

Mark one answer

While driving, you intend to turn left into a minor road. On the approach you should

- keep just left of the middle of the road
- keep in the middle of the road
- swing out wide just before turning
- keep well to the left of the road

Answer

keep well to the left of the road

Don't swing out into the centre of the road in order to make the turn. This could endanger oncoming traffic and mislead other road users of your intentions.

Question 10.60

Mark one answer

You may only enter a box junction when

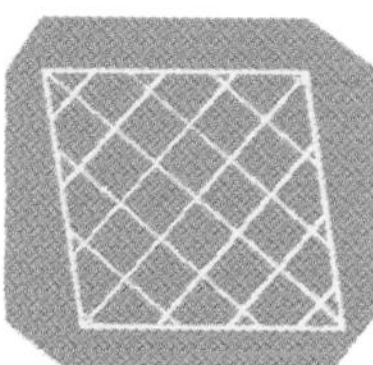

- there are less than two vehicles in front of you
- the traffic lights show green
- your exit road is clear
- you need to turn left

Answer

your exit road is clear

Box junctions are marked on the road to prevent the road becoming blocked.

Don't enter the box unless your exit road is clear. You may only wait in the box if your exit road is clear but oncoming traffic is preventing you from completing the turn.

Question 10.61

Mark one answer

You may wait in a yellow box junction when

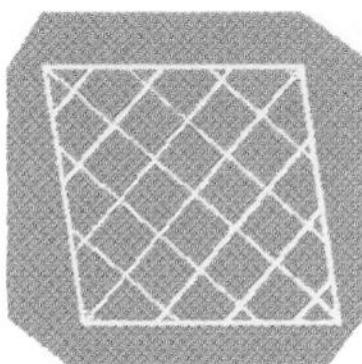

- oncoming traffic is preventing you from turning right
- you are in a queue of traffic turning left
- you are in a queue of traffic to go ahead
- you are on a roundabout

Answer

oncoming traffic is preventing you from turning right

The purpose of this road marking is to keep the centre of the junction clear of queuing traffic when the lights change priority. Don't stop in it if you aren't turning right.

Question 10.62

Mark one answer

You want to turn right at a box junction. There is oncoming traffic. You should

- wait in the box junction if your exit is clear
- wait before the junction until it is clear of all traffic
- drive on: you cannot turn right at a box junction
- drive slowly into the box junction when signalled by oncoming traffic

Answer

wait in the box junction if your exit is clear

As the lights change priority the oncoming traffic will stop, allowing you to proceed.

Question 10.63

Mark three answers

On which THREE occasions MUST you stop your vehicle?

- When involved in an accident
- At a red traffic light
- When signalled to do so by a police officer
- At a junction with double broken white lines
- At a pelican crossing when the amber light is flashing and no pedestrians are crossing

Answers

- **When involved in an accident**
- **At a red traffic light**
- **When signalled to do so by a police officer**

Don't stop or hold up traffic unnecessarily. However you MUST stop when signalled to do so by

- a police officer
- a school crossing patrol
- a red traffic light

or when you have had an accident.

Question 10.64

Mark three answers

You MUST stop when signalled to do so by which THREE of these?

- A police officer
- A pedestrian
- A school crossing patrol
- A bus driver
- A red traffic light

Answers

- **A police officer**
- **A school crossing patrol**
- **A red traffic light**

Looking well ahead and 'reading' the road will help you to anticipate hazards. This will allow you to stop safely if asked to do so by a person or a road sign.

Question 10.65

Mark three answers

At roadworks which of the following can control traffic flow?

- A STOP–GO board
- Flashing amber lights
- A policeman
- Flashing red lights
- Temporary traffic lights

Answers

- **A STOP–GO board**
- **A policeman**
- **Temporary traffic lights**

As you approach the warning signs you should be considering what actions you need to take. You might have to slow right down or stop. Obey any instructions you are given and don't try to beat any lights by driving up to them quickly.

Question 10.66

Mark one answer

You are waiting at a level crossing. The red warning lights continue to flash after a train has passed by. What should you do?

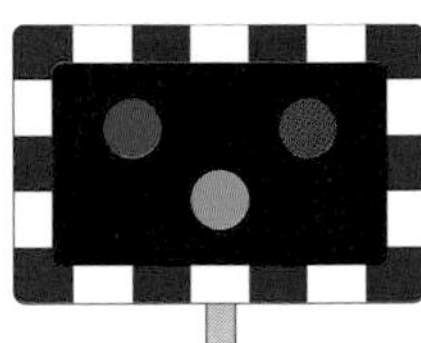

- Get out and investigate
- Telephone the signal operator
- Continue to wait
- Drive across carefully

Answer

Continue to wait

At a level crossing flashing red lights mean you should stop. If the train passes but the lights keep flashing, wait. There may be another train coming.

Question 10.67

Mark one answer

You are driving over a level crossing. The warning lights come on and a bell rings. What should you do?

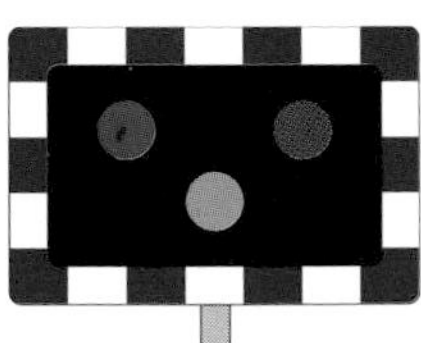

- Get everyone out of the vehicle immediately
- Stop and reverse back to clear the crossing
- Keep going and clear the crossing
- Stop immediately and use your hazard warning lights

Answer

Keep going and clear the crossing

Keep going – don't stop on the crossing. If the warning lights come on as you're approaching the crossing, stop. Don't try to dart across before the train comes.

Question 10.68

Mark one answer

You are waiting at a level crossing. A train has passed but the lights keep flashing. You must

- carry on waiting
- phone the signal operator
- edge over the stop line and look for trains
- park your vehicle and investigate

Answer

carry on waiting

If the lights at a level crossing continue to flash after a train has passed WAIT – there might be another train coming. Time seems to pass slowly when you're held up in a queue. Be patient and wait until the lights stop flashing.

Question 10.69

Mark one answer

You will see these markers when approaching

- the end of a motorway
- a concealed level crossing
- a concealed speed limit sign
- the end of a dual carriageway

Answer

a concealed level crossing

There may be a bend before a level crossing, in which case you won't be able to see barriers or waiting traffic ahead. These signs give you an early warning that you may find these hazards just around the bend.

Question 10.70

Mark one answer

Someone is waiting to cross at a zebra crossing. They are standing on the pavement. You should normally

- go on quickly before they step onto the crossing
- stop before you reach the zigzag lines and let them cross
- stop, let them cross, wait patiently
- ignore them as they are still on the pavement

Answer

 **stop, let them cross, wait patiently**

The pedestrian is showing an intention to cross. If you are looking well down the road you will give yourself enough time to slow down and stop correctly. Don't forget to check your mirrors before slowing down.

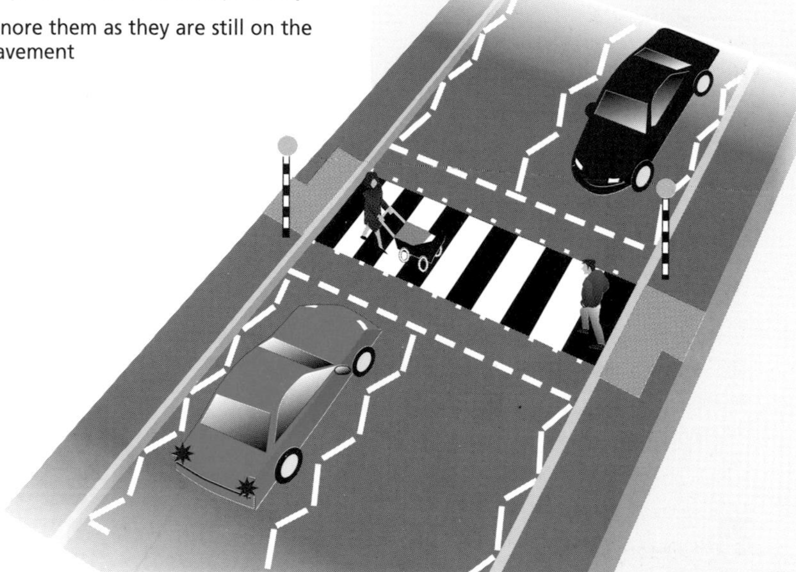

Question 10.71

Mark one answer

At toucan crossings, apart from pedestrians you should be aware of

- emergency vehicles emerging
- buses pulling out
- trams crossing in front
- cyclists riding across

Answer

cyclists riding across

The use of cycles is being encouraged and more toucan crossings are being installed. These crossings enable pedestrians and cyclists to cross the path of other traffic. Watch out as cyclists will approach the crossing faster than a pedestrian.

Question 10.72

Mark two answers

Who can use a toucan crossing?

- Trains
- Cyclists
- Buses
- Pedestrians
- Trams

Answers

- **Cyclists**
- **Pedestrians**

Toucan crossings are similar to pelican crossings. Cyclists share the crossing with pedestrians without the need to dismount. They're shown a green cycle when it's safe to cross.

Question 10.73

Mark one answer

At a pelican crossing, what does a flashing amber light mean?

- You must not move off until the lights stop flashing
- You must give way to pedestrians still on the crossing
- You can move off, even if pedestrians are still on the crossing
- You must stop because the lights are about to change to red

Answer

- **You must give way to pedestrians still on the crossing**

If the road is clear then proceed. The green light will show after the flashing amber.

Question 10.74

Mark one answer

You are waiting at a pelican crossing. The red light changes to flashing amber. This means you must

- wait for pedestrians on the crossing to clear
- move off immediately without any hesitation
- wait for the green light before moving off
- get ready and go when the continuous amber light shows

Answer

- **wait for pedestrians on the crossing to clear**

This light allows time for the pedestrians already on the crossing to get to the other side in their own time, without undue hurry. Don't rev your engine or start to move off while they are still crossing.

Question 10.75

Mark one answer

You are on a busy main road and find that you are travelling in the wrong direction. What should you do?

- Turn into a side road on the right and reverse into the main road
- Make a U-turn in the main road
- Make a 'three-point' turn in the main road
- Turn round in a side road

Answer

Turn round in a side road

Don't

- turn in a busy street
- reverse into a main road.

Find a quiet side road. Choose a place where you won't obstruct an entrance or exit, and look out for pedestrians and cyclists as well as other traffic.

Question 10.76

Mark one answer

You may remove your seat belt when carrying out a manoeuvre that involves

- reversing
- a hill start
- an emergency stop
- driving slowly

Answer

reversing

Don't forget to click your seat belt back on when you've finished reversing.

Question 10.77

Mark one answer

You must not reverse

- for longer than necessary
- for more than a car's length
- into a side road
- in a built-up area

Answer

for longer than necessary

You may decide to turn your vehicle around by reversing into an opening or side road. When you reverse, always look behind and watch for pedestrians. Don't

- reverse for longer than is necessary
- reverse from a side road into a main road.

Question 10.78

Mark one answer

You are parked in a busy high street. What is the safest way to turn your vehicle around to go the opposite way?

- Find a quiet side road to turn round in
- Drive into a side road and reverse into the main road
- Get someone to stop the traffic
- Do a U-turn

Answer

- **Find a quiet side road to turn round in**

You should carry out the manoeuvre without causing a hazard to other vehicles.

Question 10.79

Mark one answer

When you are NOT sure that it is safe to reverse your vehicle you should

- use your horn
- rev your engine
- get out and check
- reverse slowly

Answer

- **get out and check**

If you can't see all around your vehicle, get out and have a look. You could also ask someone outside the vehicle to guide you. A small child could easily be hidden directly behind you. Don't take risks.

Question 10.80

Mark one answer

When may you reverse from a side road into a main road?

- Only if both roads are clear of traffic
- Not at any time
- At any time
- Only if the main road is clear of traffic

Answer

- **Not at any time**

Don't reverse into a main road from a side road. The main road is likely to be busy and the traffic on it moving quickly. Cut down the risks by using a quiet side road to reverse into.

Question 10.81

Mark one answer

You are reversing your vehicle into a side road. When would the greatest hazard to passing traffic occur?

- After you've completed the manoeuvre
- Just before you actually begin to manoeuvre
- After you've entered the side road
- When the front of your vehicle swings out

Answer

- **When the front of your vehicle swings out**

Always check road and traffic conditions in all directions. Act on what you see and wait if you need to.

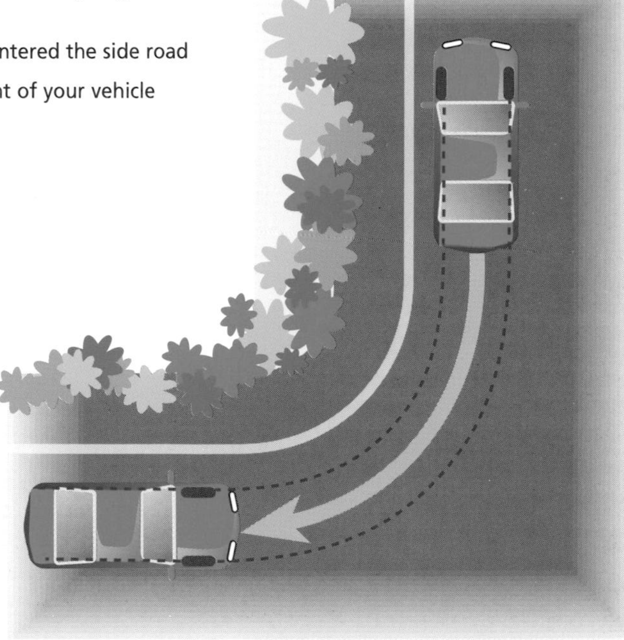

Question 10.82

Mark one answer

You want to tow a trailer with your motorcycle. Your engine must be more than

- 50 cc
- 125 cc
- 525 cc
- 1000 cc

Answer

- **125 cc**

You must remember that towing a trailer requires special care. You must obey the speed limit restrictions which apply to all vehicles towing trailers.

DO NOT FORGET IT IS THERE.

Question 10.83

Mark one answer

What is the national speed limit on a single carriageway?

- 40mph
- 50mph
- 60mph
- 70mph

Answer

 **60mph**

You don't have to ride up to the speed limit. Use your own judgement and, if appropriate, ride at a slower speed that suits the prevailing road and traffic conditions.

Question 10.84

Mark one answer

What does this sign mean?

- No parking for solo motorcycles
- Parking for solo motorcycles
- Passing place for motorcycles
- Police motorcycles only

Answer

Parking for solo motorcycles

In some towns and cities there are special areas reserved for the parking of motorcycles. Look out for these signs.

Question 10.85

Mark three answers

Your motorcycle will be parked for a long time. You should

- use the centre stand if fitted
- park on a wide pavement
- lean it against a wall
- switch off the fuel tap
- park where the ground is firm and level
- park with your lights on in daytime

Answers

- **use the centre stand if fitted**
- **switch off the fuel tap**
- **park where the ground is firm and level**

Park on firm and level ground. Your centre stand, if fitted, will give greater stability. Don't forget to switch off your fuel tap and take the ignition key with you.

Question 10.86

Mark one answer

You are riding towards road works. The temporary traffic lights are at red. The road ahead is clear. What should you do?

- Ride on with extreme caution
- Ride on at normal speed
- Carry on if approaching cars have stopped
- Wait for the green light

Answer

Wait for the green light

You must obey all traffic signs. Just because the lights are temporary it does not mean that you can disregard them.

Question 10.87

Mark one answer

You are travelling on a well lit road at night in a built-up area. By using dipped headlights you will be able to

- see further along the road
- go at a much faster speed
- switch to main beam quickly
- be easily seen by others

Answer

be easily seen by others

Travelling on a well-lit road you may still be difficult to see. Dipped headlights will make you more conspicuous than if you use only sidelights.

Question 10.88

Mark one answer

When can you park on the left opposite these road markings?

- If the line nearest to you is broken
- When there are no yellow lines
- To pick up or set down passengers
- During daylight hours only

Answer

To pick up or set down passengers

You must not park or stop on a road marked with double white lines, except to pick up or set down passengers.

SECTION 11 ROAD AND TRAFFIC SIGNS

This section looks at road and traffic signs.

The questions will ask you about

- **Road signs**

  these tell you about the road ahead.

- **Speed limits**

  recognise signs showing speed limits.

- **Road markings**

  be aware that directions might be painted on the road surface.

- **Regulations**

  these can be shown to you by means of a road sign.

Question 11.1

Mark one answer

You MUST obey signs giving orders. These signs are mostly in

- green rectangles
- red triangles
- blue rectangles
- red circles

Answer

- **red circles**

Traffic signs can be divided into three classes – those giving orders, those warning and those informing. On the road each class of sign has a different shape.

Question 11.2

Mark one answer

Traffic signs giving orders are generally which shape?

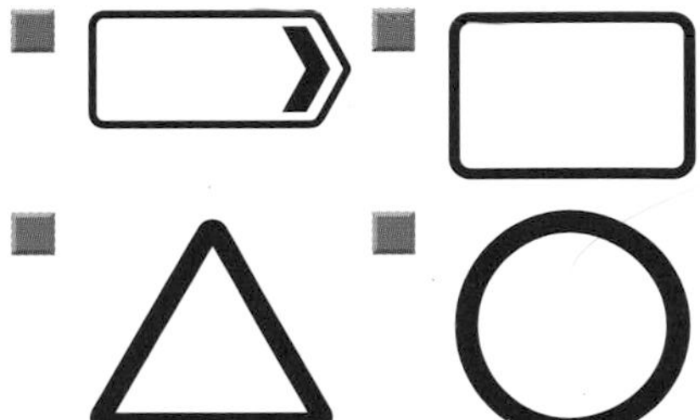

Answer

Road signs in the shape of a circle give orders. Those with a red circle are mostly prohibitive. The stop sign is octagonal to give it greater prominence. These signs must always be obeyed.

Question 11.3

Mark one answer

Which type of sign tells you NOT to do something?

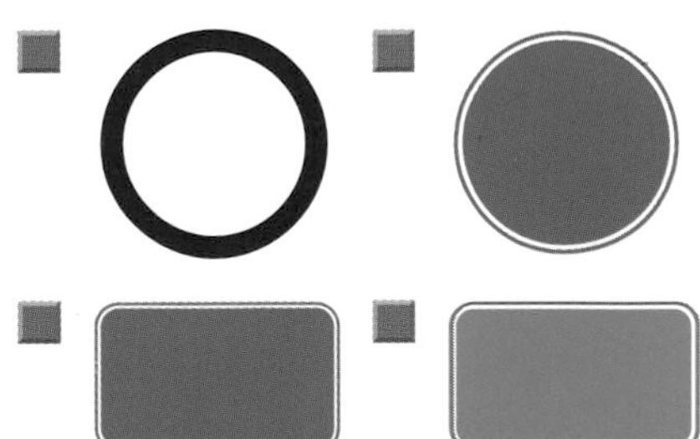

Answer

Signs in the shape of a circle mean that you aren't allowed to do something. Study Know Your Traffic Signs to ensure that you understand the order you're shown.

Question 11.4

Mark one answer

What does this sign mean?

- Maximum speed limit with traffic calming
- Minimum speed limit with traffic calming
- '20 cars only' parking zone
- Only 20 cars allowed at any one time

Answer

Maximum speed limit with traffic calming

If you're driving in areas where there are likely to be pedestrians such as

- outside schools
- near parks
- residential areas
- shopping areas

be extra cautious and keep your speed down. Many local authorities have taken measures to slow traffic down by creating traffic calming measures such as speed humps. They're there for a reason: slow down.

Question 11.5

Mark one answer

Which sign means no motor vehicles are allowed?

Answer

Certain areas are set aside for pedestrians to walk free of traffic.

Question 11.6

Mark one answer

Which of these signs means no motor vehicles?

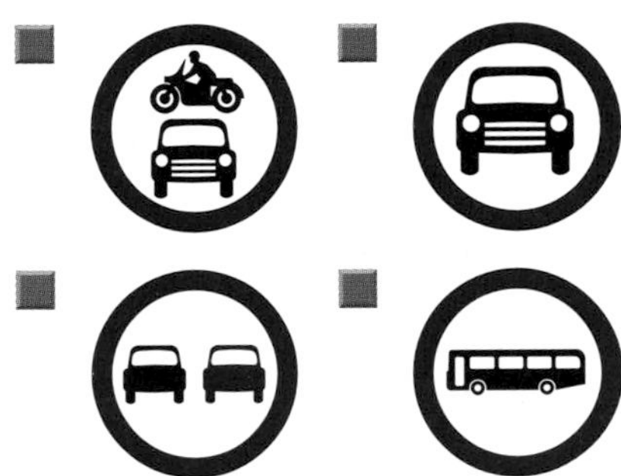

Answer

If you are driving a motor vehicle or riding a motorcycle you must not enter. This area has been especially designated for pedestrians.

Question 11.7

Mark one answer

What does this sign mean?

- New speed limit 20 mph
- No vehicles over 30 tonnes
- Minimum speed limit 30 mph
- End of 20 mph zone

Answer

End of 20 mph zone

Where you see this sign the 20 mph restriction ends. Only increase your speed if it's safe to do so. Check all around and well down the road before increasing your speed.

Question 11.8

Mark one answer

This traffic sign means there is

- a compulsory maximum speed limit
- an advisory maximum speed limit
- a compulsory minimum speed limit
- an advised separation distance

Answer

a compulsory maximum speed limit

In this picture the traffic is slow moving; this could be due to road works or another temporary obstruction. The sign gives you an early warning of a speed restriction. If you are travelling at a higher speed, slow down in good time.

Question 11.9

Mark one answer

What does this sign mean?

- No overtaking
- No motor vehicles
- Clearway (no stopping)
- Cars and motorcycles only

Answer

No motor vehicles

Traffic may be prohibited from certain roads. A sign will indicate which types of vehicles aren't allowed to use it. Make sure that you know which signs apply to the vehicle you're using.

Question 11.10

Mark one answer

What does this sign mean?

- No parking
- No road markings
- No through road
- No entry

Answer

No entry

Not knowing the meaning of a road sign could lead you into a dangerous situation.

Question 11.11

Mark one answer

What does this sign mean?

- Bend to the right
- Road on the right closed
- No traffic from the right
- No right turn

Answer

- **No right turn**

The road on the right might be a no entry or the sign could be there to allow the traffic on the main road to flow by stopping cars queuing to turn right.

Question 11.12

Mark one answer

Which sign means 'no entry'?

Answer

Look out for traffic signs as you drive. Disobeying or not seeing a sign could not only be dangerous, but also an offence; you could be fined.

Question 11.13

Mark one answer

What does this sign mean?

- Route for trams only
- Route for buses only
- Parking for buses only
- Parking for trams only

Answer

- **Route for trams only**

Avoid blocking tram routes. Trams are fixed on their route and can't dodge around other vehicles or pedestrians. Modern trams travel quickly and are quiet, so you might not hear them approaching.

Question 11.14

Mark one answer

Which type of vehicle does this sign apply to?

- Wide vehicles
- Long vehicles
- High vehicles
- Heavy vehicles

Answer

- **High vehicles**

The triangular shapes at the top and bottom of the sign mean that the sign is showing you the restricted height.

Question 11.15

Mark one answer

Which sign means NO motor vehicles allowed?

Answer

This sign is used to enable pedestrians to walk free from traffic. It's often found in shopping areas.

Question 11.16

Mark one answer

What does this sign mean?

- You have priority
- No motor vehicles
- Two-way traffic
- No overtaking

Answer

No overtaking

Road signs that show no overtaking will be placed in locations where passing the vehicle in front is dangerous. If you see this sign don't attempt to overtake. The sign is there for a reason and you must obey it.

Question 11.17

Mark one answer

What does this sign mean?

- Keep in one lane
- Give way to oncoming traffic
- Do not overtake
- Form two lanes

Answer

Do not overtake

If you're behind a slow-moving vehicle be patient. Wait until the restriction no longer applies and you can overtake safely.

Question 11.18

Mark one answer

Which sign means no overtaking?

Answer

This sign indicates that overtaking here would be dangerous. Don't take risks.

Question 11.19

Mark one answer

What does this sign mean?

- Waiting restrictions apply
- Waiting permitted
- National speed limit applies
- Clearway (no stopping)

Answer

Waiting restrictions apply

There will be a plate or additional sign to tell you when the restrictions apply.

Question 11.20

Mark one answer

What does this sign mean?

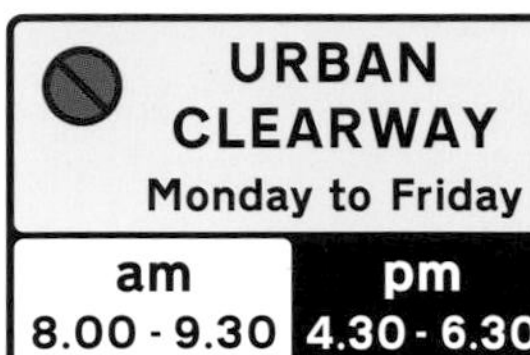

- You can park on the days and times shown
- No parking on the days and times shown
- No parking at all from Monday to Friday
- You can park at any time; the urban clearway ends

Answer

- **No parking on the days and times shown**

Before you leave your vehicle parked at the side of the road, check that the space isn't restricted. Parking times vary from place to place, so always check the sign before securing and leaving your car.

Question 11.21

Mark one answer

What does this sign mean?

- End of restricted speed area
- End of restricted parking area
- End of clearway
- End of cycle route

Answer

- **End of restricted parking area**

Even though there are no restrictions make sure that you park where you won't cause an obstruction or endanger other road users.

Question 11.22

Mark one answer

Which sign means 'no stopping'?

Answer

Stopping where you see this sign is likely to cause congestion. Allow the traffic to flow by obeying the signs.

Question 11.23

Mark one answer

What does this sign mean?

- Roundabout
- Crossroads
- No stopping
- No entry

Answer

No stopping

This sign is in place to ensure a clear route for traffic. Don't stop except in an emergency.

Question 11.24

Mark one answer

You see this sign ahead. It means

- national speed limit applies
- waiting restrictions apply
- no stopping
- no entry

Answer

no stopping

There are stretches of road where you aren't allowed to stop (unless in an emergency). These are called 'clearways'. You'll see this sign. Stopping where these restrictions apply may be dangerous and could cause an obstruction. Restrictions might apply for several miles and this may be indicated on the sign.

Question 11.25

Mark one answer

What does this sign mean?

- Distance to parking place ahead
- Distance to public telephone ahead
- Distance to public house ahead
- Distance to passing place ahead

Answer

Distance to parking place ahead

If you intend to stop and rest, note this early indication. This sign allows you time to ask any passengers if they need to stop for any reason.

Question 11.26

Mark one answer

What does this sign mean?

- Vehicles may not park on the verge or footway
- Vehicles may park on the left-hand side of the road only
- Vehicles may park fully on the verge or footway
- Vehicles may park on the right-hand side of the road only

Answer

Vehicles may park fully on the verge or footway

In order to keep roads free from parked cars there are some areas where you're allowed to park on the verge. Only do this where you see the sign. Parking on verges or kerbs in other areas could lead to a fine.

Question 11.27

Mark one answer

What does this traffic sign mean?

- No overtaking allowed
- Give priority to oncoming traffic
- Two way traffic
- One-way traffic only

Answer

Give priority to oncoming traffic

Priority signs are normally shown where the road is narrow and there isn't enough room for two vehicles to pass, such as

- a narrow bridge
- at roadworks
- a width restriction.

Make sure that you know who has priority. Comply with the sign and don't force your way through. Show courtesy and consideration to other road users.

Question 11.28

Mark one answer

What is the meaning of this traffic sign?

- End of two-way road
- Give priority to vehicles coming towards you
- You have priority over vehicles coming towards you
- Bus lane ahead

Answer

You have priority over vehicles coming towards you

Don't force your way through. Show courtesy and consideration to other road users. Although you have priority make sure oncoming traffic is going to give way.

Question 11.29

Mark one answer

Which sign means 'traffic has priority over oncoming vehicles'?

Answer

Even though you may have priority, give way if proceeding is likely to cause an accident, congestion or confrontation.

Question 11.30

Mark one answer

What MUST you do when you see this sign?

- Stop, ONLY if traffic is approaching
- Stop, even if the road is clear
- Stop, ONLY if children are waiting to cross
- Stop, ONLY if a red light is showing

Answer

- **Stop, even if the road is clear**

A stop sign is shown on an octagonal-shaped background. The sign will be at a junction where visibility is restricted or there's heavy traffic.

IT MUST BE OBEYED. YOU MUST STOP.

Practice good all-round observation before moving off.

Question 11.31

Mark one answer

What does this sign mean?

- No overtaking
- You are entering a one-way street
- Two-way traffic ahead
- You have priority over vehicles from the opposite direction

Answer

- **You have priority over vehicles from the opposite direction**

Don't force the issue. Slow down and give way to avoid confrontation or an accident.

Question 11.32

Mark one answer

What shape is a STOP sign at a junction?

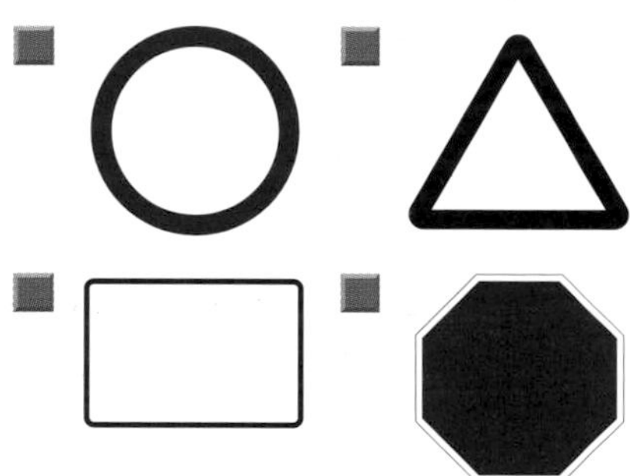

Answer

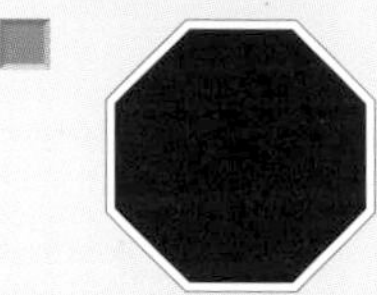

The STOP sign is distinctive and the only sign of this shape. You must stop and take effective observation before proceeding.

Question 11.33

Mark one answer

At a junction you see this sign partly covered by snow. What does it mean?

- Cross roads
- Give way
- Stop
- Turn right

Answer

- **Stop**

The STOP sign is the only sign this shape. This is to give it greater prominence. Although the snow has covered the wording you must still be able to recognise and obey this sign.

Question 11.34

Mark one answer

Which shape is used for a GIVE WAY sign?

Answer

Other warning signs are the same shape and colour, but the GIVE WAY sign points downwards. You must give way to traffic already on the major road.

Question 11.35

Mark one answer

What does this sign mean?

- Service area 30 miles ahead
- Maximum speed 30 mph
- Minimum speed 30 mph
- Lay-by 30 miles ahead

Answer

Minimum speed 30 mph

This sign is shown where slow-moving vehicles would impede the flow of traffic. However, if you need to slow down to avoid a potential accident you should do so.

Question 11.36

Mark one answer

Which of these signs means turn left ahead?

Answer

This sign gives a clear instruction. You should be looking out for signs as you drive. Prepare to negotiate a left-hand turn.

Question 11.37

Mark one answer

At a mini-roundabout you should

- give way to traffic from the right
- give way to traffic from the left
- give way to traffic from the other way
- stop even when clear

Answer

give way to traffic from the right

Look out for other traffic as you approach. Vehicles entering the mini-roundabout from your left or ahead might prevent traffic on your right from proceeding. Watch for their signals and continue if it's safe to do so.

Question 11.38

Mark one answer

What does this sign mean?

- Buses turning
- Ring road
- Mini roundabout
- Keep right

Answer

Mini roundabout

Look out for any direction signs and judge whether you need to signal your intentions. Do this in good time so that other road users approaching the roundabout can assess the situation.

Question 11.39

Mark one answer

What does this sign mean?

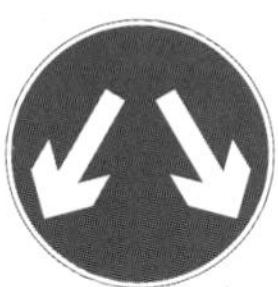

- Give way to oncoming vehicles
- Approaching traffic passes you on both sides
- Turn off at the next available junction
- Pass either side to get to the same destination

Answer

Pass either side to get to the same destination

These signs are often seen in one-way streets that have more than one lane. Use the route that's the most convenient and doesn't require a late change of direction.

Question 11.40

Mark one answer

What does this sign mean?

- Route for trams
- Give way to trams
- Route for buses
- Give way to buses

Answer

Route for trams

Take extra care when you first encounter trams. Look out for road markings and signs that alert you to them. Modern trams are very quiet and you may not hear them approaching.

Question 11.41

Mark one answer

What does a circular traffic sign with a blue background do?

- Give warning of a motorway ahead
- Give directions to a car park
- Give motorway information
- Give an instruction

Answer

Give an instruction

Signs with blue circles give a positive instruction. They will often be seen in towns or urban areas. For example mini-roundabout or pass either side.

Question 11.42

Mark one answer

Which of these signs means that you are entering a one-way street?

Answer

If the road has two lanes you can use either lane and overtake on either side. Use the lane that's more convenient for your destination.

Question 11.43

Mark one answer

Where would you see a contraflow bus and cycle lane?

- On a dual carriageway
- On a roundabout
- On an urban motorway
- On a one-way street

Answer

On a one-way street

Contraflow' means that the bus or cycle lane is going in the opposite direction to the other lanes in the road. Don't drive in or straddle these lanes.

Question 11.44

Mark one answer

What does this sign mean?

- Bus station on the right
- Contraflow bus lane
- With-flow bus lane
- Give way to buses

Answer

Contraflow bus lane

There will also be markings on the road surface to indicate the bus lane. Don't use this lane for parking or overtaking.

Question 11.45

Mark one answer

What does this sign mean?

- With-flow bus and cycle lane
- Contraflow bus and cycle lane
- No buses and cycles allowed
- No waiting for buses and cycles

Answer

With-flow bus and cycle lane

In this case buses and cycles may travel in this lane in the same direction as other traffic. There may be times shown on the sign to indicate when the lane is in use.

Question 11.46

Mark one answer

What does a sign with a brown background show?

- Tourist directions
- Primary roads
- Motorway routes
- Minor routes

Answer

Tourist directions

Signs with a brown background give directions to places of interest. They will often be seen on the motorway directing you along the easiest route.

Question 11.47

Mark one answer

This sign means

- tourist attraction
- beware of trains
- level crossing
- beware of trams

Answer

tourist attraction

These signs indicate places of interest and are designed to guide you by the easiest route. If you are a tourist you're likely to be unfamiliar with the area, so these signs are particularly useful.

Question 11.48

Mark one answer

What are triangular signs for?

- To give warnings
- To give information
- To give orders
- To give directions

Answer

To give warnings

This type of sign will tell you about the road ahead and what to expect. Get into the habit of checking each sign that you pass. They will warn you of the hazards ahead.

Question 11.49

Mark one answer

What does this sign mean?

- Turn left ahead
- T-junction
- No through road
- Give way

Answer

T-junction

Look well down the road and check the road signs as you drive. You'll then be able to anticipate any junction hazards.

Question 11.50

Mark one answer

What does this sign mean?

- Multi-exit roundabout
- Risk of ice
- Six roads converge
- Place of historical interest

Answer

Risk of ice

It will take up to ten times longer to stop when it's icy. Consider this and drive carefully. Don't brake or steer harshly as your tyres could lose their grip on the road.

Question 11.51

Mark one answer

What does this sign mean?

- Crossroads
- Level crossing with gate
- Level crossing without gate
- Ahead only

Answer

- **Crossroads**

The priority through the junction is shown by the broader line. However, be aware of the danger when other traffic is crossing a major road.

Question 11.52

Mark one answer

What does this sign mean?

- Ring road
- Mini-roundabout
- No vehicles
- Roundabout

Answer

- **Roundabout**

Prepare yourself for approaching hazards by checking signs as you drive.

Decide which exit you wish to take. Prepare to position your vehicle correctly as you approach the roundabout.

Question 11.53

Mark four answers

Which FOUR of these would be indicated by a triangular road sign?

- Road narrows
- Ahead only
- Low bridge
- Minimum speed
- Children crossing
- T-junction

Answers

- **Road narrows**
- **Low bridge**
- **Children crossing**
- **T-junction**

Make use of the warning sign and be prepared for the hazard ahead.

Question 11.54

Mark one answer

What does this sign mean?

- Cyclists must dismount
- Cycles are not allowed
- Cycle route ahead
- Cycle in single file

Answer

Cycle route ahead

Where there's a cycle route ahead, a sign will show a bicycle in a red warning triangle. Watch out for children on bicycles and cyclists rejoining the main road.

Question 11.55

Mark one answer

Which sign means that pedestrians may be walking along the road?

Answer

Be extra cautious, especially if there is a bend in the road and you're unable to see well ahead. When you pass, leave plenty of room. Consider that you might have to use the right hand side of the road, so look well ahead down the road, as well as in your mirrors, before you pull out.

Question 11.56

Mark one answer

Which of these signs warn you of a pedestrian crossing?

Answer

Look well ahead and check the pavements and surrounding areas for pedestrians. Keep an eye on those who are walking towards the crossing. Check your mirrors for traffic behind, in case you have to slow down or stop.

Question 11.57

Mark one answer

What does this sign mean?

- No footpath ahead
- Pedestrians only ahead
- Pedestrian crossing ahead
- School crossing ahead

Answer

Pedestrian crossing ahead

There are many signs relating to pedestrians. Study The Highway Code and Know Your Traffic Signs. Some of the signs look similar but give different warnings. Make a mental note as you drive so that you're prepared for any potential hazard.

Question 11.58

Mark one answer

What does this sign mean?

- School crossing patrol
- No pedestrians allowed
- Pedestrian zone – no vehicles
- Pedestrian crossing ahead

Answer

Pedestrian crossing ahead

Look well ahead and be ready to stop for any pedestrians crossing the road. Also check the pavements for anyone who looks like they might step off into the road.

Question 11.59

Mark one answer

Which of these signs means there is a double bend ahead?

Answer

Triangular signs give you a warning of hazards ahead. They're there to give you time to adjust your speed and drive accordingly.

Question 11.60

Mark one answer

What does this sign mean?

- Wait at the barriers
- Wait at the crossroads
- Give way to trams
- Give way to farm vehicles

Answer

Give way to trams

Obey the 'GIVE WAY' signs. Trams are unable to steer around you or change their specific route.

Question 11.61

Mark one answer

What does this sign mean?

- Humpback bridge
- Humps in the road
- Entrance to tunnel
- Soft verges

Answer

- **Humps in the road**

These have been put in place to slow the traffic down. They're usually found in residential areas. Slow down and drive at an appropriate speed.

Question 11.62

Mark one answer

What does this sign mean?

- Low bridge ahead
- Tunnel ahead
- Ancient monument ahead
- Accident black spot ahead

Answer

- **Tunnel ahead**

Be prepared to switch on your headlights, if required. Reduce your speed. Your eyes might need to adjust to the sudden darkness.

Question 11.63

Mark one answer

What does this sign mean?

- Two-way traffic straight ahead
- Two-way traffic crossing a one-way street
- Two-way traffic over a bridge
- Two-way traffic crosses a two-way road

Answer

- **Two-way traffic crossing a one-way street**

Be prepared for traffic approaching from junctions on either side of you.

Try to avoid unnecessary changing of lanes just before the junction.

Question 11.64

Mark one answer

Which sign means 'two-way traffic crosses a one-way road'?

Answer

Traffic could be joining the road you're in from either direction. Unless you need to turn, don't change lanes as you approach the junction.

Question 11.65

Mark one answer

Which of these signs means the end of a dual carriageway?

Answer

If you're travelling in the right-hand lane, prepare and move over into the left-hand lane as soon as it's safe to do so.

Question 11.66

Mark one answer

What does this sign mean?

- End of dual carriageway
- Tall bridge
- Road narrows
- End of narrow bridge

Answer

End of dual carriageway

Don't leave moving into the left-hand lane until the last moment. Early planning will prevent you having to rely on other traffic letting you in.

Question 11.67

Mark one answer

What does this sign mean?

- Two-way traffic ahead across a one-way street
- Traffic approaching you has priority
- Two-way traffic straight ahead
- Motorway contraflow system ahead

Answer

Two-way traffic straight ahead

This sign may be at the end of a dual carriageway or a one-way street. The sign is there to warn you of oncoming traffic.

Question 11.68

Mark one answer

What does this sign mean?

- Crosswinds
- Road noise
- Airport
- Adverse camber

Answer

Crosswinds

Where weather conditions are often bad, signs will give you a warning. A sign with a picture of a windsock will indicate there may be strong crosswinds. This sign is often found on exposed roads.

Question 11.69

Mark one answer

What does this traffic sign mean?

- Slippery road ahead
- Tyres liable to punctures ahead
- Danger ahead
- Service area ahead

Answer

- **Danger ahead**

A sign showing an exclamation mark (!) will alert you to the likelihood of danger ahead. Be ready for any situation that requires you to reduce your speed.

Question 11.70

Mark one answer

You are about to overtake when you see this sign. You should

- overtake the other driver as quickly as possible
- move to the right to get a better view
- switch your headlights on before overtaking
- hold back until you can see clearly ahead

Answer

- **hold back until you can see clearly ahead**

You won't be able to see any hazards that might be out of sight in the dip.

Imagine there might be

- cyclists
- horse riders
- parked vehicles
- pedestrians.

There might also be oncoming traffic to deal with.

Question 11.71

Mark one answer

What does this sign mean?

- Level crossing with gate or barrier
- Gated road ahead
- Level crossing without gate or barrier
- Cattle grid ahead

Answer

Level crossing with gate or barrier

Some crossings have gates but no attendant or signals. You should

- stop
- look both ways
- listen and make sure that there is no train approaching.

If there is a telephone contact the signal operator to make sure that it's safe to cross.

Question 11.72

Mark one answer

What does this sign mean?

- No trams ahead
- Oncoming trams
- Trams crossing ahead
- Trams only

Answer

Trams crossing ahead

This is a warning sign. Watch out for trams. If you are not used to driving in a town where there are trams, be especially careful at junctions. Watch out for road signs.

Question 11.73

Mark one answer

What does this sign mean?

- Adverse camber
- Steep hill downwards
- Uneven road
- Steep hill upwards

Answer

Steep hill downwards

This warning sign will give you an early indication. Prepare to alter your speed and gear. Looking at the sign from left to right, will show you whether it's up or downhill.

Question 11.74

Mark one answer

What does this sign mean?

- Quayside or river bank
- Steep hill downwards
- Slippery road
- Road liable to flooding

Answer

Quayside or river bank

Be aware that the road surface in this location is likely to be wet and slippery.

Question 11.75

Mark one answer

What does this sign mean?

- Uneven road surface
- Bridge over the road
- Road ahead ends
- Water across the road

Answer

Water across the road

This sign is found where a shallow stream crosses the road. Heavy rainfall could increase the flow of water. If the water looks too deep or the stream has swelled over a large distance, stop and find another route.

Question 11.76

Mark one answer

What does this sign mean?

- Humpback bridge
- Traffic calming hump
- Low bridge
- Uneven road

Answer

Humpback bridge

Slow right down. Driving over a humpback bridge too fast could cause your wheels to leave the road surface and result in a loss of control.

Question 11.77

Mark one answer

What does this sign mean?

- Turn left for parking area
- No through road on the left
- No entry for traffic turning left
- Turn left for ferry terminal

Answer

No through road on the left

Signs are there to help you to drive and to help you to avoid making late decisions. If you intend to take a left turn this sign shows you that you can't get through to another route.

Question 11.78

Mark one answer

What does this sign mean?

- T-junction
- No through road
- Telephone box ahead
- Toilet ahead

Answer

No through road

You will not be able to find a through route to another road. Only use this road for access.

Question 11.79

Mark one answer

Which sign means 'no through road'?

Answer

This sign is found at the entrance to the road.

Question 11.80

Mark one answer

Which of the following signs informs you that you are coming to a No Through Road?

Answer

This sign is found at the entrance to the road.

Question 11.81

Mark one answer

What does this sign mean?

- Direction to park and ride car park
- No parking for buses or coaches
- Directions to bus and coach park
- Parking area for cars and coaches

Answer

Direction to park and ride car park

To ease the congestion in centres, some cities and towns provide a park and ride scheme. This allows you to park in a designated area and ride by bus into the centre. This is usually cheaper and easier than car parking in the centre.

Question 11.82

Mark one answer

You are going through a tunnel and you see this sign. What does it mean?

- Direction to emergency pedestrian exit
- Beware of pedestrians, no footpath ahead
- No access for pedestrians
- Beware of pedestrians crossing ahead

Answer

- **Direction to emergency pedestrian exit**

If you find yourself having to evacuate a tunnel, do so as quickly as you can. Follow the signs, these will direct you to the nearest exit point. If there are several people, don't panic but try to leave in a calm and orderly manner.

Question 11.83

Mark one answer

Which is the sign for a ring road?

Answer

Ring roads are designed to relieve congestion in towns and cities.

Question 11.84

Mark one answer

What does this sign mean?

- Route for lorries
- Ring road
- Rest area
- Roundabout

Answer

- **Ring road**

Signs are also designed to give you advice. Ring road signs direct traffic around major towns and cities. Ring roads help the traffic to flow and ease congestion in town centres.

Question 11.85

Mark one answer
What does this sign mean?

- Hilly road
- Humps in road
- Holiday route
- Hospital route

Answer

Holiday route

In some areas where the volume of traffic increases during the summer months signs show a route that diverts traffic away from town centres. This helps the traffic to flow, decreasing queues.

Question 11.86

Mark one answer
What does this sign mean?

- The right-hand lane ahead is narrow
- Right-hand lane for buses only
- Right-hand lane for turning right
- The right-hand lane is closed

Answer

The right-hand lane is closed

Temporary signs may tell you about roadworks or lane restrictions. Look well ahead. If you have to change lanes, do so in good time.

Question 11.87

Mark one answer

What does this sign mean?

- Change to the left lane
- Leave at the next exit
- Contraflow system
- One-way street

Answer

- **Contraflow system**

If you use the right-hand lane, you'll be travelling with no permanent barrier between your vehicle and the traffic coming towards you. Observe speed limits and keep a good distance from the car ahead.

Question 11.88

Mark three answers

To avoid an accident when entering a contraflow system, you should

- reduce speed in good time
- switch lanes anytime to make progress
- choose an appropriate lane early
- keep the correct separation distance
- increase speed to pass through quickly
- follow other motorists closely to avoid long queues

Answers

- **reduce speed in good time**
- **choose an appropriate lane early**
- **keep the correct separation distance**

In a contraflow system you will be travelling close to oncoming traffic and sometimes in narrow lanes. You should

- obey the temporary signs governing speed limits
- get into the correct lane in good time
- keep a safe separation distance from the vehicle ahead.

Question 11.89

Mark one answer

What does this sign mean?

- Leave motorway at next exit
- Lane for heavy and slow vehicles
- All lorries use the hard shoulder
- Rest area for lorries

Answer

Lane for heavy and slow vehicles

Where there's a long, steep, uphill gradient on a motorway there may be a crawler lane. This type of lane helps the traffic to flow by diverting the slower heavy vehicles into an extra lane on the left.

Question 11.90

Mark one answer

You see this traffic light ahead. Which light(s) will come on next?

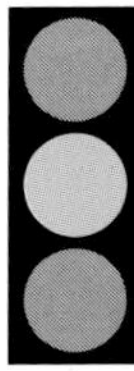

- Red alone
- Red and amber together
- Green and amber together
- Green alone

Answer

Red alone

At junctions controlled by traffic lights you must stop behind the white line until the lights change to green. Don't

- move forward when the red and amber lights are showing together
- proceed when the light is green if your exit road is blocked.

If you're approaching traffic lights that are visible from a distance and the light has been green for some time it's likely to change. Try to anticipate this. Be ready to slow down and stop.

Question 11.91

Mark one answer

You are approaching a red traffic light. The signal will change from red to

- red and amber, then green
- green, then amber
- amber, then green
- green and amber, then green

Answer

red and amber, then green

If you know which light is going to show next you can plan your approach accordingly. This will prevent excessive braking or hesitation at the junction.

Question 11.92

Mark one answer

A red traffic light means

- you should stop unless turning left
- stop, if you are able to brake safely
- you must stop and wait behind the stop line
- proceed with caution

Answer

you must stop and wait behind the stop line

Learn the sequence of traffic lights.

- RED means stop and wait behind the stop line.
- RED-AND-AMBER also means stop. Don't go until the green light shows.
- GREEN means you may go if your way is clear. Don't proceed if your exit road is blocked, and don't block the junction. Look out for pedestrians.
- AMBER means stop at the stop line. You may go if the amber light appears after you've crossed the stop line or you're so close to it that to pull up might cause an accident.

Question 11.93

Mark one answer

At traffic lights, amber on its own means

- prepare to go
- go if the way is clear
- go if no pedestrians are crossing
- stop at the stop line

Answer

stop at the stop line

If the lights have been on green for a while they're likely to change to red as you approach. Anticipate this so that you're able to stop in time.

Question 11.94

Mark one answer

A red traffic light means

- you must stop behind the white stop line
- you may drive straight on if there is no other traffic
- you may turn left if it is safe to do so
- you must slow down and prepare to stop if traffic has started to cross

Answer

you must stop behind the white stop line

The white line is positioned so that pedestrians have room to cross in front of waiting vehicles. If pedestrians are crossing make sure your handbrake is on.

Question 11.95

Mark one answer

You are approaching traffic lights. Red and amber are showing. This means

- pass the lights if the road is clear
- there is a fault with the lights – take care
- wait for the green light before you pass the lights
- the lights are about to change to red

Answer

- **wait for the green light before you pass the lights**

Other traffic might still be clearing the junction. Don't take risks.

Question 11.96

Mark one answer

You are at a junction controlled by traffic lights. When should you NOT proceed at green?

- When pedestrians are waiting to cross
- When your exit from the junction is blocked
- When you think the lights may be about to change
- When you intend to turn right

Answer

- **When your exit from the junction is blocked**

As you approach the lights look into the road you wish to take. Only proceed if your exit road is clear. If the road is blocked hold back, even if you have to wait for the next green signal.

Question 11.97

Mark one answer

You are in the left-hand lane at traffic lights. You are waiting to turn left. At which of these traffic lights must you NOT move on?

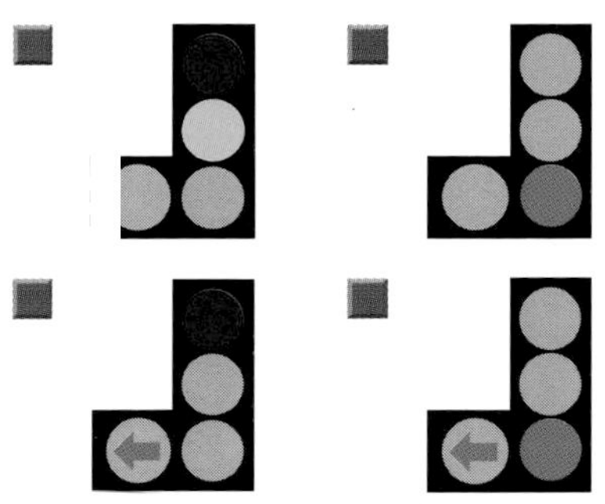

Answer

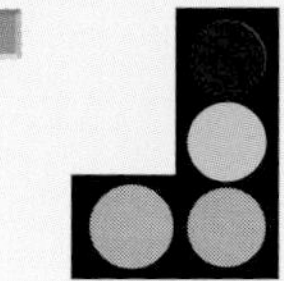

At some junctions there may be a separate signal for each lane. These are called 'filter' lights. They're designed to help traffic flow at major junctions. Make sure that you're in the correct lane and proceed if the green light shows.

Question 11.98

Mark one answer

What does this sign mean?

- Traffic lights out of order
- Amber signal out of order
- Temporary traffic lights ahead
- New traffic lights ahead

Answer

Traffic lights out of order

Where traffic lights are out of order you might see this sign. Proceed with caution as nobody has priority at the junction.

Question 11.99

Mark one answer

You see this sign at a crossroads. You should

- maintain the same speed
- carry on with great care
- find another route
- telephone the police

Answer

- **carry on with great care**

Only do so if the road is clear. Treat the road as if it is an unmarked junction, that is, no one has priority.

Question 11.100

Mark one answer

When traffic lights are out of order, who has priority?

- Traffic going straight on
- Traffic turning right
- Nobody
- Traffic turning left

Answer

- **Nobody**

Treat the junction as an unmarked crossroads. Deal with the situation with caution.

Question 11.101

Mark three answers

These flashing red lights mean STOP. In which THREE of the following places could you find them?

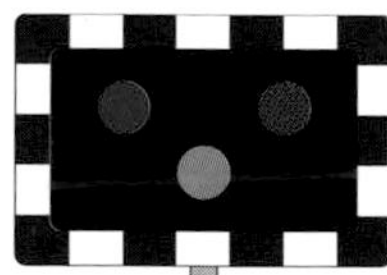

- Pelican crossings
- Lifting bridges
- Zebra crossings
- Level crossings
- Motorway exits
- Fire stations

Answers

- **Lifting bridges**
- **Level crossings**
- **Fire stations**

Don't take risks by trying to beat the lights, even if it's clear. You must stop.

Question 11.102

Mark one answer

What do these zigzag lines at pedestrian crossings mean?

- No parking at any time
- Parking allowed only for a short time
- Slow down to 20 mph
- Sounding horns is not allowed

Answer

No parking at any time

The approach to hazards may be marked with signs on the road surface. The approach to a pedestrian crossing is marked with zigzag lines.

Don't

- park on them
- overtake the leading vehicle when approaching the crossing.

Parking here will block the view for pedestrians and the approaching traffic.

Question 11.103

Mark one answer

You are approaching a zebra crossing where pedestrians are waiting. Which arm signal might you give?

Answer

A 'slowing down' signal will indicate your intentions to oncoming and following vehicles. Be aware that pedestrians might start to cross as soon as they see this signal.

Question 11.104

Mark one answer

The white line along the side of the road

- shows the edge of the carriageway
- shows the approach to a hazard
- means no parking
- means no overtaking

Answer

shows the edge of the carriageway

This is found at the edge of the road other than at junctions. It can be especially useful when visibility is restricted.

Question 11.105

Mark one answer

The white line painted in the centre of the road means

- the area is hazardous and you must not overtake
- you should give priority to oncoming vehicles
- do not cross the line unless the road ahead is clear
- the area is a national speed limit zone

Answer

do not cross the line unless the road ahead is clear

A long white line with short gaps is a warning line, so if you wish to overtake or need to turn, consider the risks.

Question 11.106

Mark one answer

When may you cross a double solid white line in the middle of the road?

- To pass traffic that is queuing back at a junction
- To pass a car signalling to turn left ahead
- To pass a road maintenance vehicle travelling at 10 mph or less
- To pass a vehicle that is towing a trailer

Answer

- **To pass a road maintenance vehicle travelling at 10 mph or less**

Only overtake such a vehicle if you're sure that you can complete the manoeuvre safely. Keep well back before you overtake so that you have a clear view of the road. Double solid white lines indicate that there are hazards, such as bends in the road or junctions, so be extra cautious.

Question 11.107

Mark one answer

A white line like this along the centre of the road is a

- bus lane marking
- hazard warning
- 'give way' marking
- lane marking

Answer

- **hazard warning**

Make a note of hazard lines as you drive. Look well ahead and around so that you're prepared for any potential dangers.

Question 11.108

Mark one answer

You see this white arrow on the road ahead. It means

- entrance on the left
- all vehicles turn left
- keep left of the hatched markings
- road bending to the left

Answer

keep left of the hatched markings

Don't attempt to overtake here; there might be unseen hazards over the brow of the hill. Keep to the left.

Question 11.109

Mark one answer

What does this road marking mean?

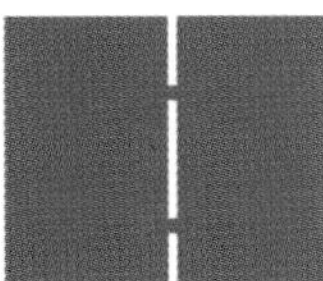

- Do not cross the line
- No stopping allowed
- You are approaching a hazard
- No overtaking allowed

Answer

You are approaching a hazard

Road markings will warn you of a hazard ahead. A single broken line, with long markings and short gaps, along the centre of the road is a hazard warning line. Don't cross it unless you can see that the road is clear WELL ahead.

Question 11.110

Mark one answer

This marking appears on the road just before a

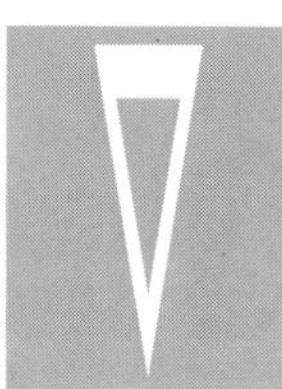

- no entry sign
- give way sign
- stop sign
- no through road sign

Answer

give way sign

You must give way to the traffic on the main road. This road marking might not be used at junctions where there is relatively little traffic. The give way rules still apply.

Question 11.111

Mark one answer

Where would you see this road marking?

- At traffic lights
- On road humps
- Near a level crossing
- At a box junction

Answer

On road humps

Due to the dark colour of the road, changes in surface aren't easily seen. White triangles painted on the road surface give you an indication of where there are road humps.

Question 11.112

Mark one answer

Which is a hazard warning line?

- 
- 
- 
- 

Answer

Look out for places where the single broken line on the road surface gets longer. This will mean there's a hazard ahead.

Question 11.113

Mark one answer

At this junction there is a stop sign with a solid white line on the road surface. Why is there a stop sign here?

- Speed on the major road is de-restricted
- It is a busy junction
- Visibility along the major road is restricted
- There are hazard warning lines in the centre of the road

Answer

Visibility along the major road is restricted

If your view is restricted at a road junction you must stop. There may also be a stop sign. Don't emerge until you're sure there's no traffic approaching.

IF YOU DON'T KNOW, DON'T GO.

Question 11.114

Mark one answer

You see this line across the road at the entrance to a roundabout. What does it mean?

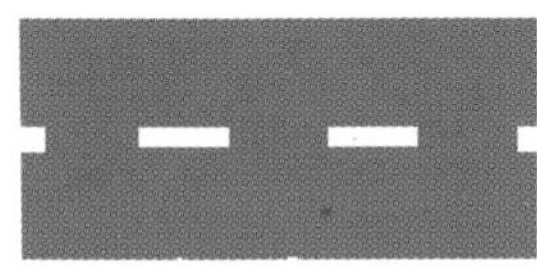

- Give way to traffic from the right
- Traffic from the left has right of way
- You have right of way
- Stop at the line

Answer

- **Give way to traffic from the right**

Slow down as you approach, checking the traffic as you do so. If you need to stop and give way, stay behind the broken line until it is safe to emerge onto the roundabout.

Question 11.115

Mark one answer

Where would you find this road marking?

- At a railway crossing
- At a junction
- On a motorway
- On a pedestrian crossing

Answer

- **At a junction**

This marking indicates the direction in which the traffic should flow.

Question 11.116

Mark one answer

How will a police officer in a patrol vehicle normally get you to stop?

- Flash the headlights, indicate left and point to the left
- Wait until you stop, then approach you
- Use the siren, overtake, cut in front and stop
- Pull alongside you, use the siren and wave you to stop

Answer

- **Flash the headlights, indicate left and point to the left**

You must obey signals given by the police. If a police officer in a patrol vehicle wants you to stop he or she will indicate this without causing danger to you or other traffic.

Question 11.117

Mark one answer

There is a police car following you. The police officer flashes the headlights and points to the left. What should you do?

- Turn at the next left
- Pull up on the left
- Stop immediately
- Move over to the left

Answer

- **Pull up on the left**

You must pull up on the left, as soon as it's safe to do so, and switch off your engine.

Question 11.118

Mark one answer

You approach a junction. The traffic lights are not working. A police officer gives this signal. You should

- turn left only
- turn right only
- stop level with the officer's arm
- stop at the stop line

Answer

- **stop at the stop line**

If a police officer or traffic wardens are directing traffic you must obey them. They will use the arm signals shown in *The Highway Code.* Learn what these mean and act accordingly.

Question 11.119

Mark one answer

The driver of the car in front is giving this arm signal. What does it mean?

- The driver is slowing down
- The driver intends to turn right
- The driver wishes to overtake
- The driver intends to turn left

Answer

- **The driver intends to turn left**

There might be an occasion where another driver uses an arm signal. This may be because the vehicle's indicators are obscured by other traffic. In order for such signals to be effective all drivers should know the meaning of them.

Be aware that the 'left turn' signal might look similar to the 'slowing down' signal.

Question 11.120

Mark one answer

The driver of this car is giving an arm signal. What is he about to do?

- Turn to the right
- Turn to the left
- Go straight ahead
- Let pedestrians cross

Answer

- **Turn to the left**

This could be used where there is a complicated junction and you wish to make your intentions clear.

For arm signals to be effective all road users should know their meaning.

Question 11.121

Mark one answer

Which arm signal tells a following vehicle that you intend to turn left?

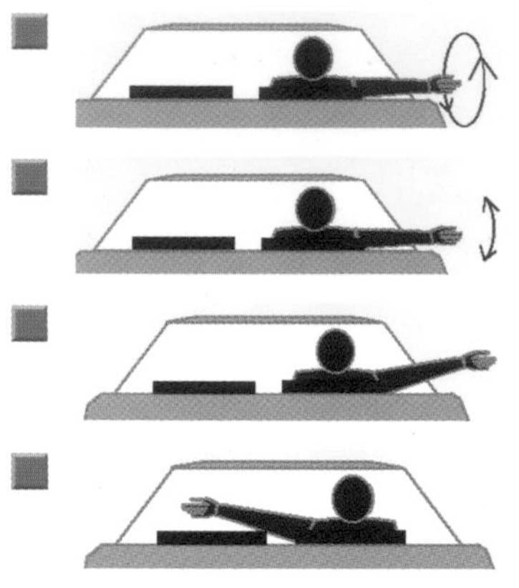

Answer

There may be occasions when you need to give an arm signal. For example

- where other road users can't see your indicators
- in bright sunshine, when your indicator may be difficult to see
- to reinforce a signal at a complex road layout.

Make sure that they're clear, correct and decisive.

Question 11.122

Mark one answer

How should you give an arm signal to turn left?

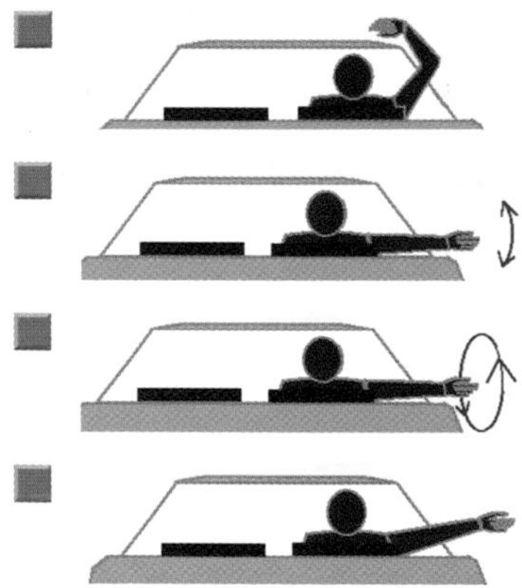

Answer

There may be occasions where other road users are unable to see your indicator, such as in bright sunlight, or at a busy, complicated junction. In these cases a hand signal will help others to understand your intentions.

Question 11.123

Mark one answer

You are signalling to turn right in busy traffic. How would you confirm your intention safely?

- Sound the horn
- Give an arm signal
- Flash your headlights
- Position over the centre line

Answer

Give an arm signal

In some situations you may feel your indicators cannot be seen by other road users. If you feel you need to make your intention more clearly seen give the arm signal shown in *The Highway Code.*

Question 11.124

Mark one answer

How should you give an arm signal to turn left?

Answer

Arm signals are very effective during daylight, especially when you're wearing bright clothing.

Practise giving arm signals when you're learning. You need to be able to keep full control of your machine with one hand off the handlebars.

Question 11.125

Mark one answer

Your indicators are difficult to see due to bright sunshine. When using them you should

- also give an arm signal
- sound your horn
- flash your headlamp
- keep both hands on the handlebars

Answer

also give an arm signal

Arm signals are effective when you aren't sure that your indicators can be seen by other road users. Make sure that your signal is decisive, and return your hand to the handlebars before you turn.

Question 11.126

Mark one answer

You are giving an arm signal ready to turn left. Why should you NOT continue with the arm signal while you turn?

- Because you might hit a pedestrian on the corner
- Because you will have less steering control
- Because you will need to keep the clutch applied
- Because other motorists will think that you are stopping on the corner

Answer

- **Because you will have less steering control**

Don't maintain an arm signal when turning. You should have full control of your machine at all times.

Question 11.127

Mark one answer

You want to turn right at a junction but you think that your indicators cannot be seen clearly. What should you do?

- Get out and check if your indicators can be seen
- Stay in the left-hand lane
- Keep well over to the right
- Give an arm signal as well as an indicator signal

Answer

- **Give an arm signal as well as an indicator signal**

If you think that your indicators can't be seen clearly due to other vehicles obscuring them, make sure that your signal is seen by using an arm signal too.

Question 11.128

Mark one answer

When may you sound the horn on your vehicle?

- To give you right of way
- To attract a friend's attention
- To warn others of your presence
- To make slower drivers move over

Answer

- **To warn others of your presence**

Don't use the horn aggressively. You must not sound it

- between 11.30 pm and 7 am
- when your vehicle's stationary unless a moving vehicle poses a danger.

Question 11.129

Mark one answer

You must not use your horn when your vehicle is stationary

- unless a moving vehicle may cause you danger
- at any time whatsoever
- unless it is used only briefly
- except for signalling that you have just arrived

Answer

- **unless a moving vehicle may cause you danger**

Do this only if you think that there is a risk of an accident. Don't use it to attract the attention of others for social reasons.

Question 11.130

Mark one answer

When motorists flash their headlights at you it means

- that there is a radar speed trap ahead
- that they are giving way to you
- that they are warning you of their presence
- that there is something wrong with your vehicle

Answer

- **that they are warning you of their presence**

If other drivers flash their headlights this isn't a signal to show priority. The flashing of headlights has the same meaning as sounding the horn – it's a warning of their presence.

Question 11.131

Mark one answer

Why should you make sure that you have cancelled your indicators after turning?

- To avoid flattening the battery
- To avoid misleading other road users
- To avoid dazzling other road users
- To avoid damage to the indicator relay

Answer

- **To avoid misleading other road users**

If you haven't taken a sharp turn your indicators might not turn off automatically. Be aware of this if you've used them for slight deviations, such as passing parked vehicles.

Question 11.132

Mark one answer

You are waiting at a T-junction. A vehicle is coming from the right with the left signal flashing. What should you do?

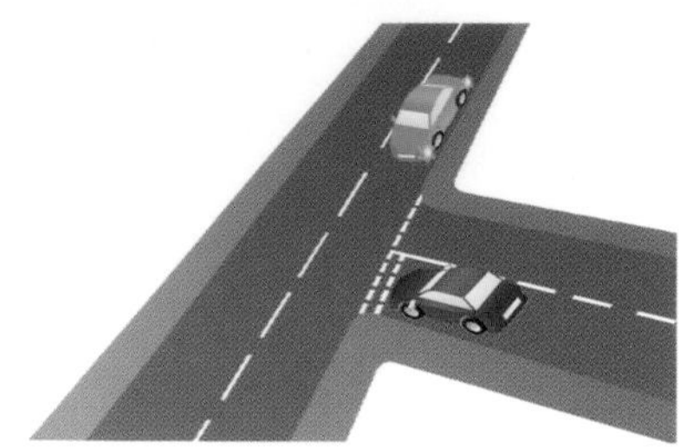

- Move out and accelerate hard
- Wait until the vehicle starts to turn in
- Pull out before the vehicle reaches the junction
- Move out slowly

Answer

Wait until the vehicle starts to turn in

Other road users may give misleading signals. When you're waiting at a junction don't emerge until you're sure of their intentions.

Pulling out safely calls for accurate judgement.

Question 11.133

Mark one answer

When may you use hazard warning lights when driving?

- Instead of sounding the horn in a built-up area between 11.30 pm and 7 am
- On a motorway or unrestricted dual carriageway, to warn of a hazard ahead
- On rural routes, after a warning sign of animals
- On the approach to toucan crossings where cyclists are waiting to cross

Answer

On a motorway or unrestricted dual carriageway, to warn of a hazard ahead

Where there's queuing traffic ahead and you have to slow down and maybe stop, showing your hazard warning lights will alert the traffic behind to the situation. Don't forget to switch them off as the queue forms behind you.

Question 11.134

Mark one answer

Where would you see these road markings?

- At a level crossing
- On a motorway slip road
- At a pedestrian crossing
- On a single-track road

Answer

On a motorway slip road

You must not enter into the area marked except in an emergency.

Question 11.135

Mark one answer

When may you NOT overtake on the left?

- On a free-flowing motorway or dual carriageway
- When the traffic is moving slowly in queues
- On a one-way street
- When the car in front is signalling to turn right

Answer

On a free-flowing motorway or dual carriageway

You may only overtake on the left

- when traffic is moving slowly in queues
- when a vehicle ahead is positioned to turn right and there's room to pass on the left
- in a one-way street.

Don't overtake on the left if the traffic on a dual carriageway is flowing freely. Other road users won't anticipate your action.

Question 11.136

Mark one answer

You are driving on a motorway. There is a slow-moving vehicle ahead. On the back you see this sign. You should

- pass on the right
- pass on the left
- leave at the next exit
- drive no further

Answer

pass on the left

You'll have to change lanes in order to pass the vehicle. Use your mirror and signal. If it's safe to do so move over into the lane on your left. Look well down the road so that you can spot such hazards early, leaving you time to complete the manoeuvre safely.

Question 11.137

Mark one answer

What does this motorway sign mean?

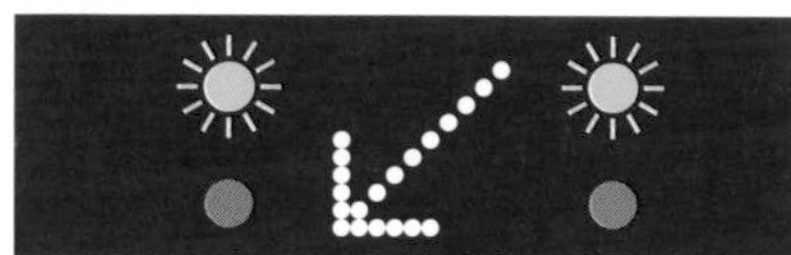

- Change to the lane on your left
- Leave the motorway at the next exit
- Change to the opposite carriageway
- Pull up on the hard shoulder

Answer

Change to the lane on your left

On the motorway, signs might show temporary warnings. This allows for different traffic or weather conditions and might indicate

- lane closures
- speed limits
- weather warnings.

Question 11.138

Mark one answer

What does this motorway sign mean?

- Temporary minimum speed 50 mph
- No services for 50 miles
- Obstruction 50 metres (164 feet) ahead
- Temporary maximum speed 50 mph

Answer

- **Temporary maximum speed 50 mph**

Look out for signs above your lane or on the central reserve. These will give you important information or warnings about the road ahead.

Due to the high speeds of motorway traffic these signs may light up some distance from any hazard. Don't ignore the signs just because the road looks clear to you.

Question 11.139

Mark one answer

What does this sign mean?

- Through traffic to use left lane
- Right-hand lane T-junction only
- Right-hand lane closed ahead
- 11 tonne weight limit

Answer

- **Right-hand lane closed ahead**

Move over as soon as you see the sign and it's safe to do so. Don't stay in the lane, which is closed ahead, until the last moment to beat a queue of traffic.

Question 11.140

Mark one answer

On a motorway this sign means

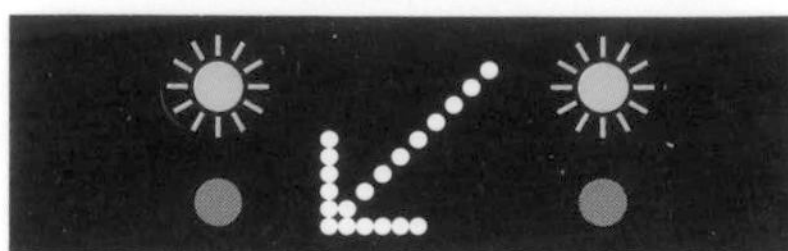

- move over onto the hard shoulder
- overtaking on the left only
- leave the motorway at the next exit
- move to the lane on your left

Answer

move to the lane on your left

On the motorway, signs might show temporary warnings. This allows for different traffic or weather conditions and might indicate

- lane closures
- speed limits
- weather warnings.

Question 11.141

Mark one answer

What does '25' mean on this motorway sign?

- The distance to the nearest town
- The route number of the road
- The number of the next junction
- The speed limit on the slip road

Answer

The number of the next junction

Before you set out on your journey use a road map to plan your route. You should give yourself enough time to get into the correct lane for the exit that you wish to take. Uncertainty at road junctions can lead to danger.

Question 11.142

Mark one answer

You are on a motorway. Red flashing lights appear above your lane only. What should you do?

- Continue in that lane and await further information
- Go no further in that lane
- Pull onto the hard shoulder
- Stop and wait for an instruction to proceed

Answer

Go no further in that lane

Flashing red lights above your lane show that your lane is closed. You should move into a clear lane in plenty of time.

Question 11.143

Mark one answer
The right-hand lane of a three-lane motorway is

- for lorries only
- an overtaking lane
- the right-turn lane
- an acceleration lane

Answer

an overtaking lane

Motorways today can become very busy. If a vehicle in the right-hand lane is preventing traffic to the rear from overtaking, or is travelling at a slower speed than those on the nearside, bunching can occur. This means that drivers will begin to travel too close to the vehicle in front of them. If you aren't overtaking, use the left-hand lane.

Question 11.144

Mark one answer
Where can you find reflective amber studs on a motorway?

- Separating the slip road from the motorway
- On the left-hand edge of the road
- On the right-hand edge of the road
- Separating the lanes

Answer

On the right-hand edge of the road

At night or in poor visibility reflective studs on the road will help you to judge your position on the carriageway.

Question 11.145

Mark one answer
Where on a motorway would you find green reflective studs?

- Separating driving lanes
- Between the hard shoulder and the carriageway
- At slip road entrances and exits
- Between the carriageway and the central reservation

Answer

At slip road entrances and exits

Knowing the colours of the reflective studs on the road will help you in foggy conditions or when visibility is poor.

Question 11.146

Mark one answer

You are travelling along a motorway. You see this sign. You should

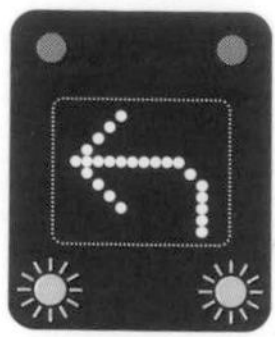

- leave the motorway at the next exit
- turn left immediately
- change lane
- move onto the hard shoulder

Answer

leave the motorway at the next exit

You'll see this sign if the motorway is closed ahead. When you see it prepare to get into the nearside lane so that you can take the exit safely. Don't leave it to the last moment.

Question 11.147

Mark one answer

You see these signs overhead on the motorway. They mean

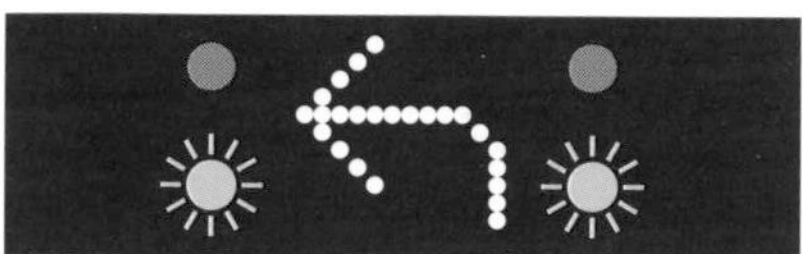

- leave the motorway at the next exit
- all vehicles use the hard shoulder
- sharp bend to the left ahead
- stop, all lanes ahead closed

Answer

leave the motorway at the next exit

There has been an incident ahead and the motorway is closed. You must obey the sign. Make sure that you prepare to leave as soon as you see the warning sign. Don't leave it until the last moment by cutting across other traffic.

Question 11.148

Mark one answer

What does this sign mean?

- No motor vehicles
- End of motorway
- No through road
- End of bus lane

Answer

End of motorway

When you leave the motorway make sure that you check your speedometer. You may be going faster than you realise. Slow down using the slip road. Look out for speed limit signs.

Question 11.149

Mark one answer

Which of these signs means that the national speed limit applies?

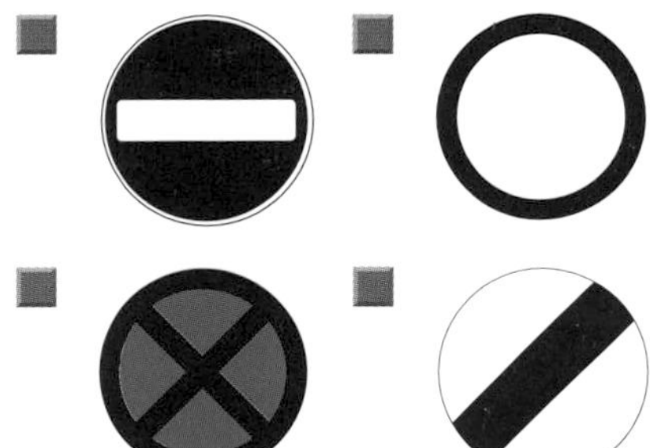

Answer

You should know the speed limit for the road that you're travelling on and the vehicle that you're driving. Study your copy of *The Highway Code*, where the limits are clearly shown.

Question 11.150

Mark one answer

What is the maximum speed on a single carriageway road?

- 50 mph
- 60 mph
- 40 mph
- 70 mph

Answer

60 mph

If you're travelling on a dual carriageway that becomes a single carriageway road, cut your speed gradually so that you aren't exceeding the limit as you enter. There might not be a sign to remind you of the limit, so learn the speed limits.

Question 11.151

Mark one answer

What does this sign mean?

- Motorcycles only
- No cars
- Cars only
- No motorcycles

Answer

No motorcycles

You must comply with all traffic signs and be especially aware of those signs which apply specifically to the type of vehicle you are using.

Question 11.152

Mark one answer

You are on a motorway. You see this sign on a lorry that has stopped in the right-hand lane. You should

- move into the right-hand lane
- stop behind the flashing lights
- pass the lorry on the left
- leave the motorway at the next exit

Answer

pass the lorry on the left

Sometimes it is possible to carry out work on the motorway without closing the lanes. In such cases, signs are mounted on the back of lorries to warn other road users of road works ahead.

Question 11.153

Mark one answer

This sign is of particular importance to motorcyclists. It means

- side winds
- airport
- slippery road
- service area

Answer

side winds

Strong crosswinds can suddenly blow you off course. Keep your speed down when it is very windy, especially on exposed roads.

Question 11.154

Mark one answer

What does this sign mean?

- End of motorway
- End of restriction
- Lane ends ahead
- Free recovery ends

Answer

End of restriction

At the end of the restriction you will see this sign without any flashing lights.

Question 11.155

Mark one answer

This sign is advising you to

- follow the route diversion
- follow the signs to the picnic area
- give way to pedestrians
- give way to cyclists

Answer

follow the route diversion

These symbols guide drivers on diversion routes that may have been imposed by a road closure or an accident on a motorway or other main road.

Question 11.156

Mark one answer

Why would this temporary speed limit sign be shown?

- To warn of the end of the motorway
- To warn you of a low bridge
- To warn you of a junction ahead
- To warn of road works ahead

Answer

To warn of road works ahead

To lessen the chance of accidents happening, most major roadworks have reduced speed limits imposed. You should always comply with them.

Question 11.157

Mark one answer

Which one of these signs are you allowed to ride past on a solo motorcycle?

Answer

Most regulatory signs are circular; a red circle gives a prohibitory instruction.

Question 11.158

Mark one answer

Which of these signals should you give when slowing or stopping your motorcycle?

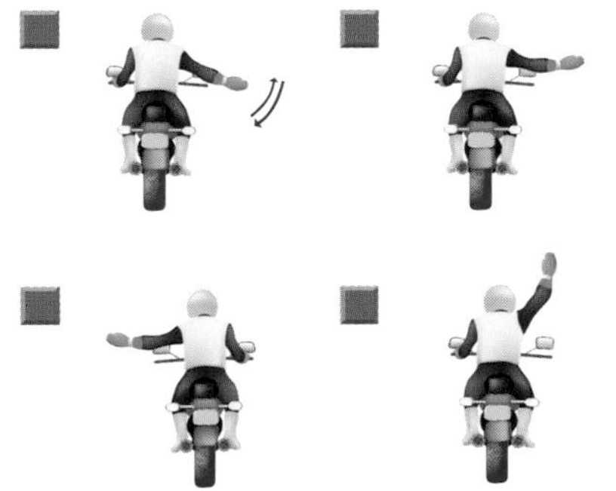

Answer

Arm signals can be given to reinforce your flashing indicators, especially if the indicator signal could cause confusion, e.g., if you intend to pull up close to a side road.

SECTION 12 DOCUMENTS

This section looks at the documents needed for drivers and their vehicles.

The questions will ask you about

- **Licences**

  you must know what the law requires.

- **Insurance**

  you must have the cover you need to drive or ride.

- **MOT test certificate**

  you should be aware of the safety checks your vehicle must undergo to gain an MOT certificate.

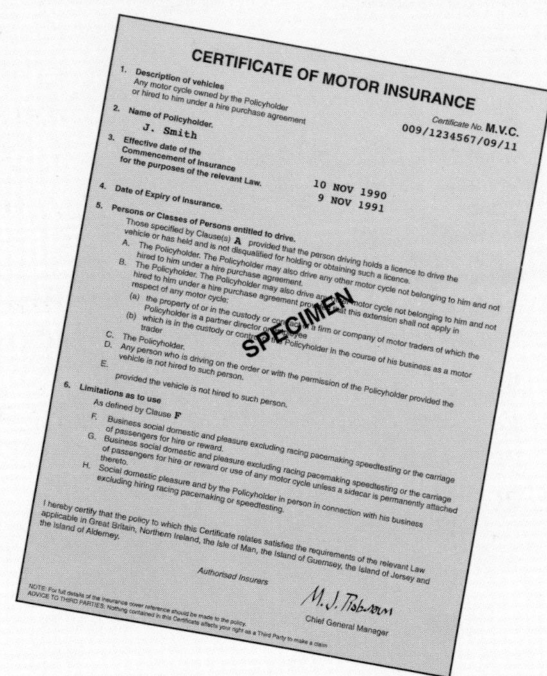

CERTIFICATE OF MOTOR INSURANCE

Certificate No. **M.V.C.** 009/1234567/09/11

1. **Description of vehicles**
   Any motor cycle owned by the Policyholder or hired to him under a hire purchase agreement
2. **Name of Policyholder.**
   J. Smith
3. **Effective date of the Commencement of Insurance for the purposes of the relevant Law.** 10 NOV 1990
4. **Date of Expiry of Insurance.** 9 NOV 1991
5. **Persons or Classes of Persons entitled to drive.**
   Those specified by Clause(s) **A** provided that the person driving holds a licence to drive the vehicle or has held and is not disqualified for holding or obtaining such a licence.
   A. The Policyholder. The Policyholder may also drive any other motor cycle not belonging to him and not hired to him under a hire purchase agreement.
   B. The Policyholder. The Policyholder may also drive an[illegible] motor cycle not belonging to him and not hired to him under a hire purchase agreement pro[illegible] this extension shall not apply in respect of any motor cycle:
   (a) the property of or in the custody or con[illegible] a firm or company of motor traders of which the Policyholder is a partner director or [illegible]
   (b) which is in the custody or contr[illegible] Policyholder in the course of his business as a motor trader
   C. The Policyholder.
   D. Any person who is driving on the order or with the permission of the Policyholder provided the vehicle is not hired to such person.
   E.
   provided the vehicle is not hired to such person.
6. **Limitations as to use**
   As defined by Clause **F**
   F. Business social domestic and pleasure excluding racing pacemaking speedtesting or the carriage of passengers for hire or reward.
   G. Business social domestic and pleasure excluding racing pacemaking speedtesting or the carriage of passengers for hire or reward or use of any motor cycle unless a sidecar is permanently attached thereto.
   H. Social domestic pleasure and by the Policyholder in person in connection with his business excluding hiring racing pacemaking or speedtesting.

I hereby certify that the policy to which this Certificate relates satisfies the requirements of the relevant Law applicable in Great Britain, Northern Ireland, the Isle of Man, the Island of Guernsey, the Island of Jersey and the Island of Alderney.

Authorised Insurers

M. J. Robson
Chief General Manager

NOTE: For full details of the insurance cover reference should be made to the policy.
ADVICE TO THIRD PARTIES: Nothing contained in this Certificate affects your right as a Third Party to make a claim

SPECIMEN

Question 12.1

Mark one answer

To drive on the road learners MUST

- have NO penalty points on their licence
- have taken professional instruction
- have a signed, valid provisional licence
- apply for a driving test within 12 months

Answer

- **have a signed, valid provisional licence**

Before you drive on the road you must have a signed provisional licence in the category of vehicle that you're driving. As soon as you've received your licence, sign it. It isn't valid until you've done so.

Question 12.2

Mark two answers

To supervise a learner driver you must

- have held a full licence for at least 3 years
- be at least 21
- be an approved driving instructor
- hold an advanced driving certificate

Answers

- **have held a full licence for at least 3 years**
- **be at least 21**

Don't just take someone's word that they are qualified to supervise you. The person who sits alongside you while you are learning should be a responsible adult.

Question 12.3

Mark one answer

Your driving licence must be signed by

- a police officer
- a driving instructor
- your next of kin
- yourself

Answer

- **yourself**

Do this as soon as you receive it through the post. Don't drive until you've signed it.

NI

Question 12.4

Mark four answers

You have passed CBT (Compulsory Basic Training). You want a Direct Access test. You must

- be aged 21 or over
- not exceed 60 mph
- have an approved instructor with you
- remain in radio contact while learning
- only learn in daylight hours
- wear fluorescent or reflective clothing

Answers

- **be aged 21 or over**
- **have an approved instructor with you**
- **remain in radio contact while learning**
- **wear fluorescent or reflective clothing**

If you wish to learn to ride a motorcycle via the direct access route you must be at least 21 years old. When practising on the road you must

- have L plates fitted (or D plates in Wales)
- be accompanied by an approved instructor in radio contact
- wear fluorescent or reflective safety clothing.

NI

Question 12.5

Mark one answer

You want a licence to ride a large motorcycle via direct access. You will

- not require L plates if you have passed a car test
- require L plates only when learning on your own machine
- require L plates while learning with a qualified instructor
- not require L plates if you have passed a moped test

Answer

- **require L plates while learning with a qualified instructor**

While training through the direct access scheme you must be accompanied by an instructor on another motorcycle and in radio contact. You will have to display L plates on your motorcycle and follow all normal learner restrictions.

Question 12.6

Mark one answer

You are a learner motorcyclist. The law states that you can carry a passenger when

- your motorcycle is no larger than 125 cc
- your pillion passenger is a full licence-holder
- you have passed your test for a full licence
- you have had three years' experience of riding

Answer

- **you have passed your test for a full licence**

When you're a learner motorcyclist you must comply with certain legal restrictions. The law states that you must

- display L plates (or D plates in Wales) to the front and rear on your machine
- not carry pillion passengers
- not use the motorway.

Question 12.7

NI

Mark three answers

What should you bring with you when taking your motorcycle test?

- A service record book
- An insurance certificate
- A signed driving licence
- An MOT certificate
- A CBT (Compulsory Basic Training) certificate
- Signed photo identity

Answers

- **A signed driving licence**
- **A CBT (Compulsory Basic Training) certificate**
- **Signed photo identity**

When you attend a motorcycle test your examiner will ask to see

- your driving licence
- your CBT certificate (except in Northern Ireland).
- signed photo ID

Question 12.8

NI

Mark one answer

Before taking a motorcycle test you need

- a full moped licence
- a full car licence
- a CBT (Compulsory Basic Training) certificate
- 12 months riding experience

Answer

- **a CBT (Compulsory Basic Training) certificate**

You can find out about a CBT course by asking your motorcycle dealer or by telephoning 0115 901 2595.

In Northern Ireland the CBT scheme doesn't operate, so all reference to CBT isn't applicable.

Question 12.9

NI

Mark one answer

Compulsory Basic Training (CBT) can only be carried out by

- any ADI (Approved Driving Instructor)
- any road safety officer
- any DSA (Driving Standards Agency) approved training body
- any motorcycle main dealer

Answer

- **any DSA (Driving Standards Agency) approved training body**

DSA approves bodies to provide training in a safe environment. Frequent checks are made to ensure a high standard of instruction. Taking a CBT course will provide you with the right start to your motorcycling life.

NI

Question 12.10

Mark one answer

After passing your motorcycle test you must exchange the pass certificate for a full motorcycle licence within

- six months
- one year
- two years
- five years

Answer

two years

When you pass your practical motorcycle test you'll be issued with a pass certificate (form D.10 – DL8 in Northern Ireland). You must exchange the certificate for a full licence within two years of passing your test. If you don't

- the certificate will lapse
- you'll have to retake your test if you wish to resume full motorcycle licence entitlement.

Question 12.11

Mark two answers

For which TWO of these must you show your motor insurance certificate?

- When you are taking your driving test
- When buying or selling a vehicle
- When a police officer asks you for it
- When you are taxing your vehicle
- When having an MOT inspection

Answers

When a police officer asks you for it

When you are taxing your vehicle

When you take out motor insurance you'll be issued with a Certificate of Insurance. This contains details explaining who and what is insured. You'll have to produce your Certificate of Insurance when you're paying your vehicle excise duty (road tax).

If a police officer asks for your Certificate of Insurance and you don't have it with you, you may produce it at a police station within seven days (five days in Northern Ireland).

Question 12.12

Mark one answer

Vehicle excise duty is often called 'Road Tax' or 'The Tax Disc'. You must

- keep it with your registration document
- display it clearly on your vehicle
- keep it concealed safely in your vehicle
- carry it on you at all times

Answer

display it clearly on your vehicle

It should be displayed on the left hand bottom of the windscreen. This allows it to be easily seen from the kerbside. It must be current, and you can't transfer the disc from vehicle to vehicle.

Question 12.13

Mark two answers

For which TWO of these must you show your motorcycle insurance certificate?

- When you are taking your motorcycle test
- When buying or selling a machine
- When a police officer asks you for it
- When you are taxing your machine
- When having an MOT inspection

Answers

- **When a police officer asks you for it**
- **When you are taxing your machine**

You don't have to carry it with you at all times. However, it must be valid and available to present at a police station (within seven days) if requested.

NI

Question 12.14

Mark one answer

A police officer asks to see your documents. You do not have them with you. You may produce them at a police station within

- five days
- seven days
- 14 days
- 21 days

Answer

- **seven days**

You don't have to carry your documents with you. If a police officer asks to see them and you don't have them with you, you may produce them at a police station within seven days (five days in Northern Ireland).

Question 12.15

Mark one answer

Before riding anyone else's motorcycle you should make sure that

- the machine owner has third party insurance cover
- your own machine has insurance cover
- the machine is insured for your use
- the owner has the insurance documents with them

Answer

- **the machine is insured for your use**

If you borrow a motorcycle you must make sure that you're insured. Find out yourself. Don't take anyone else's word for it.

Question 12.16

Mark one answer

Before driving anyone else's motor vehicle you should make sure that

- the vehicle owner has third party insurance cover
- your own vehicle has insurance cover
- the vehicle is insured for your use
- the owner has left the insurance documents in the vehicle

Answer

- **the vehicle is insured for your use**

Don't take someone else's word on the matter. New drivers are considered a high risk and this is reflected in high insurance costs. If you're careful and don't have an accident, the cost of your insurance will come down, although other factors, such as your occupation and where you live, are taken into account.

Question 12.17

Mark one answer

What is the legal minimum insurance cover you must have to drive or ride on public roads?

- Third party, fire and theft
- Fully comprehensive
- Third party only
- Personal injury cover

Answer

- **Third party only**

The minimum insurance requirement by law is third party cover. This covers others involved in an accident but not damage to your vehicle. Basic third party insurance won't cover theft or fire damage. Check with your insurance company for advice on the best cover for you. Make sure that you read the policy carefully.

Question 12.18

Mark three answers

You have third party insurance. What does this cover?

- Damage to your own vehicle
- Damage to your vehicle by fire
- Injury to another person
- Damage to someone's property
- Damage to other vehicles
- Injury to yourself

Answers

- **Injury to another person**
- **Damage to someone's property**
- **Damage to other vehicles**

Third party insurance doesn't cover damage to your own vehicle or injury to yourself. If you have an accident and you damage your vehicle you might have to carry out the repairs at your own expense.

NI

Question 12.19

Mark one answer

The cost of your insurance may be reduced if

- your car is large and powerful
- you are using the car for work purposes
- you have penalty points on your licence
- you are over 25 years old

Answer

- **you are over 25 years old**

Provided you haven't had previous accidents or committed any driving offences, your insurance should be less costly as you get beyond the age of 25. This is because statistics show that most accidents are caused by or involve young and/or inexperienced drivers.

Question 12.20

Mark one answer

Motor cars and motorcycles must FIRST have an MOT test certificate when they are

- one year old
- three years old
- five years old
- seven years old

Answer

- **three years old**

The vehicle you drive must be in good condition and roadworthy. If it's over three years old it must have a valid MOT test certificate.

In Northern Ireland a vehicle first needs an MOT test certificate when it's four years old.

Question 12.21

Mark one answer

An MOT certificate is normally valid for

- three years after the date it was issued
- 10,000 miles
- one year after the date it was issued
- 30,000 miles

Answer

- **one year after the date it was issued**

Make a note of the date that your vehicle is due for an MOT. Some garages remind you, but not all of them.

Question 12.22

Mark one answer

Your car needs an MOT certificate. If you drive without one this could invalidate your

- vehicle service record
- insurance
- road tax disc
- vehicle registration document

Answer

- **insurance**

You are driving a vehicle which is illegal and could be unsafe. As there is a higher risk of an accident your insurance company would not cover you for any damage incurred.

NI

Question 12.23

Mark one answer

When is it legal to drive a car over three years old without an MOT certificate?

- Up to seven days after the old certificate has run out
- When driving to an MOT centre to arrange an appointment
- Just after buying a secondhand car with no MOT
- When driving to an appointment at an MOT centre

Answer

- **When driving to an appointment at an MOT centre**

If a car is over three years old it must have a valid MOT certificate if you want to use it on the road. The only time a car is exempt is when it's being driven to an appointment at an MOT testing station.

In Northern Ireland the time limit before an MOT test is first needed is four years.

Question 12.24

Mark one answer

Your vehicle needs a current MOT certificate. You do not have one. Until you do have one you will not be able to renew your

- driving licence
- vehicle insurance
- road tax disc
- vehicle registration document

Answer

- **road tax disc**

You'll have to produce your MOT certificate when you renew your road tax disc (road fund licence).

Question 12.25

Mark two answers

Which TWO of these are NOT required to have an MOT certificate?

- Motor cycle
- Small trailer
- Ambulance
- Caravan

Answers

- **Small trailer**
- **Caravan**

Despite not needing an MOT certificate, you should ensure that your trailer is in good order and properly serviced. Tyres, wheel nuts, lights and indicators should be checked regularly.

Question 12.26

Mark three answers

Which THREE of the following do you need before you can drive or ride legally?

- A valid signed driving licence
- A valid tax disc displayed on your vehicle
- Proof of your identity
- Proper insurance cover
- Breakdown cover
- A vehicle handbook

Answers

- **A valid signed driving licence**
- **A valid tax disc displayed on your vehicle**
- **Proper insurance cover**

Make sure that your vehicle's not only safe but legal.

Question 12.27

NI

Mark one answer

CBT (Compulsory Basic Training) completion certificates (DL196) issued on or after 01 July 1996 are valid for

- two years
- three years
- five years
- indefinitely

Answer

- **three years**

In order to complete the CBT course you'll have to demonstrate that you can ride confidently and safely in a variety of road and traffic conditions. Your certificate will enable you to apply for your tests. If you don't pass your tests within its three-year life you'll have to complete the CBT course again.

Question 12.28

Mark one answer

When you buy a motorcycle you will need a vehicle registration document from

- any MOT testing station
- the person selling the motorcycle
- your local council offices
- your local trading standards officer

Answer

- **the person selling the motorcycle**

You must fill in your details and send it to the Driver and Vehicle Licensing Agency (DVLA) at the address given on the document.

Question 12.29

Mark three answers

Which THREE pieces of information are found on a vehicle registration document?

- Registered keeper
- Make of the vehicle
- Service history details
- Date of the MOT
- Type of insurance cover
- Engine size

Answers

- **Registered keeper**
- **Make of the vehicle**
- **Engine size**

Every vehicle used on the road has a registration document. This is issued by the Driver Vehicle Licensing Agency (DVLA) or the Driver and Vehicle Licensing Northern Ireland (DVLNI), and it keeps a record of the change of ownership. The document states

- date of first registration
- registration number
- previous keeper
- registered keeper
- make of vehicle
- engine size and chassis number
- year of manufacture
- colour.

Question 12.30

Mark three answers

You have a duty to contact the licensing authority when

- you go abroad on holiday
- you change your vehicle
- you change your name
- your job status is changed
- your permanent address changes
- your job involves travelling abroad

Answers

- **you change your vehicle**
- **you change your name**
- **your permanent address changes**

The licensing authority need to keep their records up to date. You will receive a reminder when your road tax is due and they will need your current address for this purpose. Every vehicle in the country is registered, so it's possible to trace it's history.

Question 12.31

Mark three answers

You must notify the licensing authority when

- your health affects your driving
- your eyesight does not meet a set standard
- you intend lending your vehicle
- your vehicle requires an MOT certificate
- you change your vehicle

Answers

- **your health affects your driving**
- **your eyesight does not meet a set standard**
- **you change your vehicle**

The Driver and Vehicle Licensing Agency (DVLA) hold the records of all vehicles and drivers in Great Britain. They need to know of any change in circumstances so that they can keep their records up to date. Your health might affect your ability to drive safely. This should not be underestimated as you and others on the road could be at risk.

Question 12.32

Mark one answer

You have just bought a secondhand vehicle. When should you tell the licensing authority of change of ownership?

- Immediately
- After 28 days
- When an MOT is due
- Only when you insure it

Answer

- **Immediately**

As soon as you can, fill out the registration document of the vehicle and send it off. The requirements will be written on the document. It is an offence not to notify the licensing agency.

Question 12.33

Mark two answers

Your vehicle is insured third party only. This covers

- damage to your vehicle
- damage to other vehicles
- injury to yourself
- injury to others
- all damage and injury

Answers

- **damage to other vehicles**
- **injury to others**

This type of insurance cover is usually cheaper than fully comprehensive. However, it does not cover any damage to your own vehicle or property. It is solely to cover damage and/or injury to others.

Question 12.34

Mark three answers

You hold a provisional motorcycle licence. This means you must NOT

- exceed 30 mph
- ride on a motorway
- ride after dark
- carry a pillion passenger
- ride without 'L' plates displayed

Answers

- **ride on a motorway**
- **carry a pillion passenger**
- **ride without 'L' plates displayed**

Provisional entitlement means that many restrictions apply to your use of motorcycles.

Most of the requirements are there to protect you and other road users. Make sure you are well aware of the requirements before you ride your machine on the road.

Question 12.35

Mark three answers

Which of the following information is found on your motorcycle registration document?

- Make and model
- Service history record
- Ignition key security number
- Engine size and number
- Purchase price
- Year of first registration

Answers

- **Make and model**
- **Engine size and number**
- **Year of first registration**

The vehicle registration document contains details of your motorcycle's make and model.

- when it was first registered
- engine size and number

If you buy a new machine the dealer will register your motorcycle with the licensing authority who will send the registration document to you.

Question 12.36

Mark one answer

A theory test pass certificate will not be valid after

- 6 months
- 1 year
- 18 months
- 2 years

Answer

- **2 years**

A theory test pass certificate is valid for two years. If after two years you have not passed your practical test you will have to retake your theory test again.

Question 12.37

Mark one answer

A theory test pass certificate is valid for

- two years
- three years
- four years
- five years

Answer

- **two years**

Your pass certificate is valid for only two years. If you don't pass your practical test for that category of vehicle within two years you will have to retake your theory test.

Question 12.38

Mark one answer

Your motor insurance policy has an excess of £100. What does this mean?

- The insurance company will pay the first £100 of any claim
- You will be paid £100 if you do not have an accident
- Your vehicle is insured for a value of £100 if it is stolen
- You will have to pay the first £100 of any claim

Answer

- **You will have to pay the first £100 of any claim**

You will have to pay the first £100 of any claim. It is a method that insurance companies use to keep annual premiums down. It is usually the case where the higher the excess you choose to pay, then the lower the annual premium you will be charged.

Question 12.39

Mark two answers

You have just passed your driving test. Within two years you get six penalty points on your licence. You will have to

- retake only your theory test
- retake your theory and practical tests
- retake only your practical test
- re-apply for your full licence immediately
- re-apply for your provisional licence

Answers

- **retake your theory and practical tests**
- **re-apply for your provisional licence**

Your licence will be revoked if the number of penalty points on your licence reaches six or more, as a result of offences you commit before the two years are over. This includes offences you committed before you passed your test.

You may only drive as a learner until you pass both the theory and practical tests again.

Question 12.40

Mark one answer

A cover note is a document issued before you receive your

- driving licence
- insurance certificate
- registration document
- MOT certificate

Answer

insurance certificate

Sometimes an insurance company will issue a temporary insurance certificate called a cover note. It gives you the same insurance cover as your certificate, but will only last for a limited period, usually one month.

Question 12.41

Mark one answer

When you apply to renew your vehicle excise licence (tax disc) you must produce

- a valid insurance certificate
- the old tax disc
- the vehicle handbook
- a valid driving licence

Answer

a valid insurance certificate

Tax discs can be renewed at most post offices, your nearest vehicle registration office or by post to the licensing authority. Make sure you take all the relevant documents with your application.

Question 12.42

Mark one answer

What is the legal minimum insurance cover you must have to drive on public roads?

- Fire and theft
- Theft only
- Third party
- Fire only

Answer

Third party

Third party insurance is the minimum cover you must have to be able to drive or ride on the public roads. This means it only covers damage and/or injury that you may cause to other persons or property. It does not cover any damage to your vehicle or property.

Question 12.43

Mark one answer

A full category A1 licence will allow you to ride a motorcycle up to

- 125 cc
- 250 cc
- 350 cc
- 425 cc

Answer

125 cc

When you pass your test on a motorcycle between 75 cc and 125 cc you will be issued with a full light motorcycle licence of category A1. You will then be allowed to ride any motorcycle up to 125 cc, and with a power output of 11 Kw (14.6 bhp).

NI

Question 12.44

Mark two answers

The cost of your insurance may be reduced if you

- are over 25 years old
- are under 25 years old
- do not wear glasses
- pass the driving test first time
- complete the Pass Plus scheme

Answers

- **are over 25 years old**
- **complete the Pass Plus scheme**

The cost of insurance varies with your age. Usually, the younger you are the more expensive it is especially if you are under 25 years of age. The Pass Plus scheme is recognised by many insurance companies now and if you complete this form of extra training you could benefit with a reduced first premium.

Question 12.45

Mark one answer

How old must you be to supervise a learner driver?

- 18 years old
- 19 years old
- 20 years old
- 21 years old

Answer

- **21 years old**

As well as least 21 years old, to accompany a learner driver you must have held a full EC/EEA driving licence for at least three years and still hold one for the category of vehicle being driven.

Question 12.46

Mark one answer

A newly qualified driver must

- display green 'L' plates
- not exceed 40 mph for 12 months
- be accompanied on a motorway
- have valid motor insurance

Answer

- **have valid motor insurance**

It is your responsibility to make sure you are properly insured for the vehicle you are driving.

SECTION 13 ACCIDENTS

This section looks at what to do in the event of an accident.

The questions will ask you about

- **First Aid**

  if you have the knowledge, your fast, effective action might save a life.

- **Warning devices**

  know how to warn other road users of an accident.

- **Reporting procedures**

  know where and when to report an accident.

- **Safety regulations**

  know what to do if a vehicle carrying hazardous loads is involved in an accident.

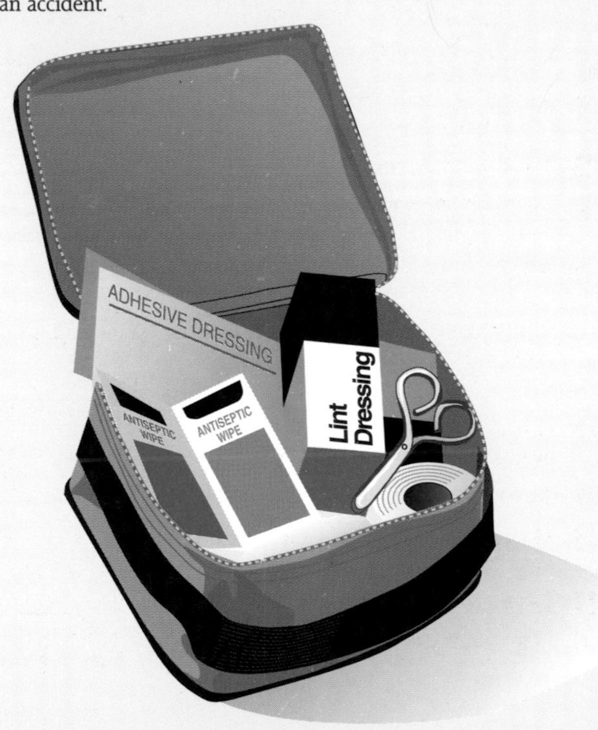

Question 13.1

Mark three answers

Which of these items should you carry in your vehicle for use in the event of an accident?

- Road map
- Can of petrol
- Jump leads
- Fire extinguisher
- First Aid kit
- Warning triangle

Answers

- **Fire extinguisher**
- **First Aid kit**
- **Warning triangle**

This equipment could be invaluable and a small price to pay if it helps prevent or lessen injury.

Question 13.2

Mark one answer

At the scene of an accident you should

- not put yourself at risk
- go to those casualties who are screaming
- pull everybody out of their vehicles
- leave vehicle engines switched on

Answer

- **not put yourself at risk**

It's important that those at the scene of an accident do not create a further risk to themselves or other road users. If the accident has occurred on a motorway, traffic will be approaching at speed. Consider this when trying to help casualties or warn other drivers.

Question 13.3

Mark four answers

You are the first to arrive at the scene of an accident. Which FOUR of these should you do?

- Leave as soon as another motorist arrives
- Switch off the vehicle engine(s)
- Move uninjured people away from the vehicle(s)
- Call the emergency services
- Warn other traffic

Answers

- **Switch off the vehicle engine(s)**
- **Move uninjured people away from the vehicle(s)**
- **Call the emergency services**
- **Warn other traffic**

If you're involved in, or arrive at, the scene of an accident, there are certain actions you should take. It's important to know what to do and also what NOT to do. You could save someone's life, or endanger it.

Question 13.4

Mark one answer

An accident has just happened. An injured person is lying in the busy road. What is the FIRST thing you should do to help?

- Treat the person for shock
- Warn other traffic
- Place them in the recovery position
- Make sure the injured person is kept warm

Answer

- **Warn other traffic**

You could do this by

- displaying an advance warning signal, if you have one
- switching on hazard warning lights or other lights
- any other means that does not put you at risk.

Question 13.5

Mark three answers

You are the first person to arrive at an accident where people are badly injured. Which THREE should you do?

- Switch on your own hazard warning lights
- Make sure that someone telephones for an ambulance
- Try and get people who are injured to drink something
- Move the people who are injured clear of their vehicles
- Get people who are not injured clear of the scene

Answers

- **Switch on your own hazard warning lights**
- **Make sure that someone telephones for an ambulance**
- **Get people who are not injured clear of the scene**

If you're the first person to arrive at the scene of an accident, further collision and fire are the first concerns. Switching off vehicle engines will reduce the risk of fire. Your hazard warning lights will let approaching traffic know that there's a need for caution.

Don't assume someone else has called the emergency services.

Question 13.6

Mark one answer

You arrive at the scene of a motorcycle accident. The rider is injured. When should the helmet be removed?

- Only when it is essential
- Always straight away
- Only when the motorcyclist asks
- Always, unless they are in shock

Answer

- **Only when it is essential**

If a motorcyclist has been injured in an accident it's important not to remove their helmet unless it is necessary to keep them alive.

Question 13.7

Mark three answers

You arrive at a serious motorcycle accident. The motorcyclist is unconscious and bleeding. Your main priorities should be to

- try to stop the bleeding
- make a list of witnesses
- check the casualty's breathing
- take the numbers of the vehicles involved
- sweep up any loose debris
- check the casualty's airways

Answers

- **try to stop the bleeding**
- **check the casualty's breathing**
- **check the casualty's airways**

At a road accident the danger of further collisions and fire need to be dealt with first. Injuries should be dealt with in the order

- Airway
- Breathing
- Circulation and bleeding.

Question 13.8

Mark one answer

You arrive at an accident. A motorcyclist is unconscious. Your FIRST priority is the casualty's

- breathing
- bleeding
- broken bones
- bruising

Answer

- **breathing**

At the scene of an accident you must first make sure there is no danger from further collisions or fire before dealing with any casualties.

The first priority when dealing with an unconscious person is to make sure they can breathe. This may involve clearing their airway if they're having difficulty or some obstruction is obvious.

Question 13.9

Mark three answers

At an accident a casualty is unconscious. Which THREE of the following should you check urgently?

- Circulation
- Airway
- Shock
- Breathing
- Broken bones

Answers

- **Circulation**
- **Airway**
- **Breathing**

An unconscious casualty may have difficulty breathing. Check that their tongue has not fallen back, blocking their airway. Do this by tilting the head back slightly.

Question 13.10

Mark three answers

You arrive at the scene of an accident. It has just happened and someone is unconscious. Which of the following should be given urgent priority to help them?

- Clear the airway and keep it open
- Try to get them to drink water
- Check that they are breathing
- Look for any witnesses
- Stop any heavy bleeding
- Take the numbers of vehicles involved

Answers

- **Clear the airway and keep it open**
- **Check that they are breathing**
- **Stop any heavy bleeding**

Stay with the casualty and send someone to ring for an ambulance.

Question 13.11

Mark three answers

At an accident someone is unconscious. Your main priorities should be to

- sweep up the broken glass
- take the names of witnesses
- count the number of vehicles involved
- check the airway is clear
- make sure they are breathing
- stop any heavy bleeding

Answers

- **check the airway is clear**
- **make sure they are breathing**
- **stop any heavy bleeding**

Remember this procedure by saying ABC. Airway – Breathing – Circulation

Question 13.12

Mark three answers

You have stopped at the scene of an accident to give help. Which THREE things should you do?

- Keep injured people warm and comfortable
- Keep injured people calm by talking to them reassuringly
- Keep injured people on the move by walking them around
- Give injured people a warm drink
- Make sure that injured people are not left alone

Answers

- **Keep injured people warm and comfortable**
- **Keep injured people calm by talking to them reassuringly**
- **Make sure that injured people are not left alone**

If you stop at the scene of an accident to give help and there are casualties don't

- move injured people, unless further danger is threatened
- give the injured anything to drink.

Question 13.13

Mark three answers

You arrive at the scene of an accident. It has just happened and someone is injured. Which THREE of the following should be given urgent priority?

- Stop any severe bleeding
- Get them a warm drink
- Check that their breathing is OK
- Take numbers of vehicles involved
- Look for witnesses
- Clear their airway and keep it open

Answers

- **Stop any severe bleeding**
- **Check that their breathing is OK**
- **Clear their airway and keep it open**

When you have done this, call the emergency services, they are the experts.
If you feel you are not capable of carrying out first aid, then consider doing some training. It could save a life.

Question 13.14

Mark two answers

At an accident a casualty has stopped breathing. You should

- remove anything that is blocking the mouth
- keep the head tilted forwards as far as possible
- raise the legs to help with circulation
- try to give the casualty something to drink
- keep the head tilted back as far as possible

Answers

- **remove anything that is blocking the mouth**
- **keep the head tilted back as far as possible**

These actions will ensure that the casualty has clear airways and is in the correct position if mouth to mouth ventilation is required.

Question 13.15

Mark four answers

You are at the scene of an accident. Someone is suffering from shock. You should

- reassure them constantly
- offer them a cigarette
- keep them warm
- avoid moving them if possible
- loosen any tight clothing
- give them a warm drink

Answers

- **reassure them constantly**
- **keep them warm**
- **avoid moving them if possible**
- **loosen any tight clothing**

The effects of trauma may not be immediately obvious. Prompt treatment can help to minimise the effects of shock.

- lay the casualty down
- loosen tight clothing
- call an ambulance
- check their breathing and pulse.

Question 13.16

Mark one answer

Which of the following should you NOT do at the scene of an accident?

- Warn other traffic by switching on your hazard warning lights
- Call the emergency services immediately
- Offer someone a cigarette to calm them down
- Ask drivers to switch off their engines

Answer

- **Offer someone a cigarette to calm them down**

Keeping casualties or witnesses calm is important, but never offer a cigarette because of the risk of fire. Check for any signs of shock, such as,

- sweating
- clammy skin
- giddiness
- rapid or shallow breathing
- a weak pulse.

Question 13.17

Mark two answers

There has been an accident. The driver is suffering from shock. You should

- give them a drink
- reassure them
- not leave them alone
- offer them a cigarette
- ask who caused the accident

Answers

- **reassure them**
- **not leave them alone**

They could have an injury that is not immediately obvious. Loosen any tight clothing and check that their breathing is not rapid or slow.

Question 13.18

Mark three answers

You are at the scene of an accident. Someone is suffering from shock. You should

- offer them a cigarette
- offer them a warm drink
- keep them warm
- loosen any tight clothing
- reassure them constantly

Answers

- **keep them warm**
- **loosen any tight clothing**
- **reassure them constantly**

People who seem to be unhurt may be suffering from shock. So try to reassure everyone involved at the scene and keep everybody calm.

Question 13.19

Mark one answer

You have to treat someone for shock at the scene of an accident. You should

- reassure them constantly
- walk them around to calm them down
- give them something cold to drink
- cool them down as soon as possible

Answer

- **reassure them constantly**

You should lay the casualty down, loosen any tight clothing, whilst reassuring them. If possible, get someone else to call an ambulance to avoid leaving the casualty alone.

Question 13.20

Mark one answer

You arrive at the scene of a motorcycle accident. No other vehicle is involved. The rider is unconscious, lying in the middle of the road. The first thing you should do is

- move the rider out of the road
- warn other traffic
- clear the road of debris
- give the rider reassurance

Answer

- **warn other traffic**

The motorcyclist is in an extremely vulnerable position, exposed to further danger from traffic. The traffic needs to slow right down and be aware of the hazard in good time.

Question 13.21

Mark one answer

At an accident a small child is not breathing. When giving mouth to mouth you should breathe

- sharply
- gently
- heavily
- rapidly

Answer

- **gently**

With a small child breathe gently into the nose and mouth until you see the chest rise.

Question 13.22

Mark three answers

To start mouth to mouth on a casualty you should

- tilt their head forward
- clear the airway
- turn them on their side
- tilt their head back
- pinch the nostrils together
- put their arms across their chest

Answers

- **clear the airway**
- **tilt their head back**
- **pinch the nostrils together**

Use your finger to check for and move any obvious obstruction in the mouth. It's important to ensure that the air ways are clear

Question 13.23

Mark one answer

When you are giving mouth to mouth you should only stop when

- you think the casualty is dead
- the casualty can breathe without help
- the casualty has turned blue
- you think the ambulance is coming

Answer

- **the casualty can breathe without help**

Don't give up. Look for signs of recovery and check the casualty's pulse. When the casualty starts to breathe, place them in the recovery position.

Question 13.24

Mark one answer

You arrive at the scene of an accident. There has been an engine fire and someone's hands and arms have been burnt. You should NOT

- douse the burn thoroughly with cool liquid
- lay the casualty down
- remove anything sticking to the burn
- reassure them constantly

Answer

- **remove anything sticking to the burn**

This could cause further damage and infection to the wound. Your first priorities are to cool the burn and check the patient for shock.

Question 13.25

Mark one answer

You arrive at an accident where someone is suffering from severe burns. You should

- apply lotions to the injury
- burst any blisters
- remove anything stuck to the burns
- douse the burns with cool liquid

Answer

- **douse the burns with cool liquid**

Try to find fluid that is clean, cold and non-toxic. Its coolness will stop the burn and relieve the pain. Keep the wound doused for at least ten minutes. If blisters appear don't attempt to burst them as this could lead to infection.

Question 13.26

Mark one answer

You arrive at an accident where someone is suffering from severe burns. You should

- burst any blisters
- douse the burns thoroughly with cool liquid
- apply lotions to the injury
- remove anything sticking to the burns

Answer

- **douse the burns thoroughly with cool liquid**

Do this for about ten minutes making sure that the casualty is comfortable. If any clothing is stuck to the wound, don't try to remove it

Question 13.27

Mark two answers

You arrive at the scene of an accident. A pedestrian has a severe bleeding wound on their leg, although it is not broken. What should you do?

- Dab the wound to stop bleeding
- Keep both legs flat on the ground
- Apply firm pressure to the wound
- Raise the leg to lessen bleeding
- Fetch them a warm drink

Answers

- **Apply firm pressure to the wound**
- **Raise the leg to lessen bleeding**

As soon as you can, apply a pad to the wound with a bandage or a clean length of cloth. Raising the leg will lessen the flow of blood. Be aware that any restriction of blood circulation for more than a short period of time may result in long-term injury.

Question 13.28

Mark one answer

You arrive at the scene of an accident. A passenger is bleeding badly from an arm wound. What should you do?

- Apply pressure over the wound and keep the arm down
- Dab the wound
- Get them a drink
- Apply pressure over the wound and raise the arm

Answer

- **Apply pressure over the wound and raise the arm**

If possible, lay the casualty down. Raising the arm above the level of the heart will stem the flow of blood.

Question 13.29

Mark one answer

You arrive at the scene of an accident. A pedestrian is bleeding heavily from a leg wound, but the leg is not broken. What should you do?

- Dab the wound to stop the bleeding
- Keep both legs flat on the ground
- Apply firm pressure to the wound
- Fetch them a warm drink

Answer

- **Apply firm pressure to the wound**

Lift the casualty's leg so that the wound is higher than their heart. This should reduce the flow of blood.

Question 13.30

Mark one answer

At an accident a casualty is unconscious but still breathing. You should only move them if

- an ambulance is on its way
- bystanders advise you to
- there is further danger
- bystanders will help you to

Answer

- **there is further danger**

Moving them could cause further injury. So it's important that this is only done if there is obvious danger to the casualty.

Question 13.31

Mark one answer

At an accident you suspect a casualty has back injuries. The area is safe. You should

- offer them a drink
- not move them
- raise their legs
- offer them a cigarette

Answer

- **not move them**

Talk to the casualty and keep them calm. If you attempt to move them it could cause further injury. Call an ambulance at the first opportunity.

Question 13.32

Mark one answer

At an accident it is important to look after the casualty. When the area is safe, you should

- get them out of the vehicle
- give them a drink
- give them something to eat
- keep them in the vehicle

Answer

- **keep them in the vehicle**

Don't move casualties who are trapped in vehicles unless they are in danger.

Question 13.33

Mark one answer

A tanker is involved in an accident. Which sign would show that the tanker is carrying dangerous goods?

- 

- 

- 
- 

Answer

- 

There will be an orange label on the side and rear of the lorry. Look at this carefully and report what it says when you phone the emergency services.

Question 13.34

Mark one answer

While driving, a warning light on your vehicle's instrument panel comes on. You should

- continue if the engine sounds alright
- hope that it is just a temporary electrical fault
- deal with the problem when there is more time
- check out the problem quickly and safely

Answer

- **check out the problem quickly and safely**

An illuminated warning light could mean that your car is unsafe to drive. Don't take risks. If you aren't sure about the problem get a qualified mechanic to check it.

Question 13.35

Mark two answers

For which TWO should you use hazard warning lights?

- When you slow down quickly on a motorway because of a hazard ahead
- When you have broken down
- When you wish to stop on double yellow lines
- When you need to park on the pavement

Answers

- **When you slow down quickly on a motorway because of a hazard ahead**
- **When you have broken down**

Hazard warning lights are fitted to all modern cars and some motorcycles. They should be used to warn other road users of a hazard ahead.

Question 13.36

Mark three answers

For which THREE should you use your hazard warning lights?

- When you are parking in a restricted area
- When you are temporarily obstructing traffic
- To warn following traffic of a hazard ahead
- When you have broken down
- When only stopping for a short time

Answers

- **When you are temporarily obstructing traffic**
- **To warn following traffic of a hazard ahead**
- **When you have broken down**

Use them on the motorway when you have to slow down suddenly because of a queue of traffic ahead. This is to warn following traffic that you're slowing suddenly and rapidly.

Question 13.37

Mark one answer

When are you allowed to use hazard warning lights?

- When stopped and temporarily obstructing traffic
- When travelling during darkness without headlights
- When parked for shopping on double yellow lines
- When travelling slowly because you are lost

Answer

- **When stopped and temporarily obstructing traffic**

Don't use hazard lights

- to excuse yourself for illegal, dangerous or inconsiderate parking
- when you're moving slowly because you're lost
- when you're moving slowly due to bad weather.

Question 13.38

Mark one answer

You have broken down on a two-way road. You have a warning triangle. You should place the warning triangle at least how far from your vehicle?

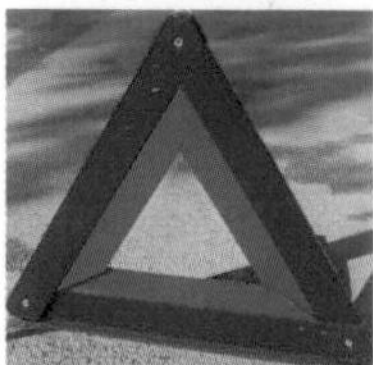

- 5 metres (16 feet)
- 25 metres (82 feet)
- 45 metres (147 feet)
- 100 metres (328 feet)

Answer

45 metres (147 feet)

Carry an advance warning triangle in your vehicle. They fold flat and don't take up much room. Use it to warn other road users if your vehicle has broken down or there's been an accident. Place your warning triangle at least 45 metres (147 feet) from your vehicle on a straight, level road

Question 13.39

Mark one answer

You are in an accident on a two-way road. You have a warning triangle with you. At what distance before the obstruction should you place the warning triangle?

- 25 metres (82 feet)
- 45 metres (147 feet)
- 100 metres (328 feet)
- 150 metres (492 feet)

Answer

45 metres (147 feet)

If there's a bend or hump in the road place the triangle so that approaching traffic slows down before the bend. You must give traffic enough time to react to the warning.

Use your hazard warning lights as well as a warning triangle, especially in the dark.

Question 13.40

Mark one answer

Your motorcycle has broken down on a motorway. How will you know the direction of the nearest emergency telephone?

- By walking with the flow of traffic
- By following an arrow on a marker post
- By walking against the flow of traffic
- By remembering where the last phone was

Answer

By following an arrow on a marker post

If you break down on a motorway you should

- pull onto the hard shoulder and stop as far over to the left as you can
- switch on hazard lights (if they are fitted)
- make your way to the nearest emergency telephone.

Marker posts spaced every 100 metres will direct you to the nearest telephone.

Question 13.41

Mark one answer

You have broken down on a two-way road. You have a warning triangle. It should be displayed

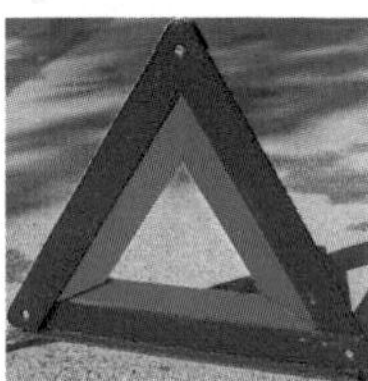

- on the roof of your vehicle
- at least 150 metres (492 feet) behind your vehicle
- at least 45 metres (147 feet) behind your vehicle
- just behind your vehicle

Answer

- **at least 45 metres (147 feet) behind your vehicle**

If you need to display a warning triangle make sure that it can be seen clearly by other road users. Place it on the same side of the road and clear of any obstruction.

Question 13.42

Mark three answers

The police may ask you to produce which THREE of these documents following an accident?

- Vehicle registration document
- Driving licence
- Theory test certificate
- Insurance certificate
- MOT test certificate
- Road tax disc

Answers

- **Driving licence**
- **Insurance certificate**
- **MOT test certificate**

The first thing you must do is stop. It is an offence not to do so.

Question 13.43

Mark four answers

You are involved in an accident with another driver. Someone is injured. Your vehicle is damaged. Which FOUR of the following should you find out?

- Whether the driver owns the other vehicle involved
- The other driver's name, address and telephone number
- The car make and registration number of the other vehicle
- The occupation of the other driver
- The details of the other driver's vehicle insurance
- Whether the other driver is licensed to drive

Answers

- **Whether the driver owns the other vehicle involved**
- **The other driver's name, address and telephone number**
- **The car make and registration number of the other vehicle**
- **The details of the other driver's vehicle insurance**

Try to keep calm and don't rush the proceedings. Take your time. You might be a little shaken by the incident, but try to ensure that you have all the details before you leave the scene.

Question 13.44

Mark one answer

At a railway level crossing the red light signal continues to flash after a train has gone by. What should you do?

- Phone the signal operator
- Alert drivers behind you
- Wait
- Proceed with caution

Answer

- **Wait**

Don't

- proceed
- phone the signal operator immediately
- zigzag between the gates.

There may be another train coming.

Question 13.45

Mark three answers

You break down on a level crossing. The lights have not yet begun to flash. Which THREE things should you do?

- Telephone the signal operator
- Leave your vehicle and get everyone clear
- Walk down the track and signal the next train
- Move the vehicle if a signal operator tells you to
- Tell drivers behind what has happened

Answers

- **Telephone the signal operator**
- **Leave your vehicle and get everyone clear**
- **Move the vehicle if a signal operator tells you to**

Keep calm. Don't

- walk up the track to warn approaching trains
- try to restart the engine
- try to move the vehicle unless told to do so by the signal operator.

Question 13.46

Mark one answer

You have stalled in the middle of a level crossing and cannot restart the engine. The warning bell starts to ring. You should

- get out and clear of the crossing
- run down the track to warn the signal operator
- carry on trying to restart the engine
- push the vehicle clear of the crossing

Answer

- **get out and clear of the crossing**

Try not to panic, and stay calm, especially if you have passengers on board. If you can't restart your engine before the warning bells ring, then leave the vehicle.

Question 13.47

Mark one answer

Your vehicle has broken down on an automatic railway level crossing. What should you do FIRST?

- Get everyone out of the vehicle and clear of the crossing
- Phone the signal operator so that trains can be stopped
- Walk along the track to give warning to any approaching trains
- Try to push the vehicle clear of the crossing as soon as possible

Answer

- **Get everyone out of the vehicle and clear of the crossing**

Ensure that everyone is WELL clear of the crossing. In the event of an accident debris could be scattered in several directions.

Question 13.48

Mark two answers

Your tyre bursts while you are driving. Which TWO things should you do?

- Pull on the handbrake
- Brake as quickly as possible
- Pull up slowly at the side of the road
- Hold the steering wheel firmly to keep control
- Continue on at a normal speed

Answers

- **Pull up slowly at the side of the road**
- **Hold the steering wheel firmly to keep control**

A tyre bursting can lead to a loss of control, especially if you're travelling at high speed. The correct procedure can help to stop the vehicle safely.

Question 13.49

Mark two answers

Which TWO things should you do when a front tyre bursts?

- Apply the handbrake to stop the vehicle
- Brake firmly and quickly
- Let the vehicle roll to a stop
- Hold the steering wheel lightly
- Grip the steering wheel firmly

Answers

- **Let the vehicle roll to a stop**
- **Grip the steering wheel firmly**

Try not to react by applying the brakes harshly. This could lead to further loss of steering control. Indicate your intention to pull up at the side of the road and roll to a stop.

Question 13.50

Mark one answer

Your vehicle has a puncture on a motorway. What should you do?

- Drive slowly to the next service area to get assistance
- Pull up on the hard shoulder. Change the wheel as quickly as possible
- Pull up on the hard shoulder. Use the emergency phone to get assistance
- Switch on your hazard lights. Stop in your lane

Answer

- **Pull up on the hard shoulder. Use the emergency phone to get assistance**

Pull up on the hard shoulder and make your way to the nearest emergency telephone and request assistance. It is dangerous to try and change an offside wheel, due to fast traffic passing very close to your vehicle.

Question 13.51

Mark one answer

You should use the engine cut-out switch to

- stop the engine in an emergency
- stop the engine on short journeys
- save wear on the ignition switch
- start the engine if you lose the key

Answer

- **stop the engine in an emergency**

Most motorcycles are fitted with an engine cut-out switch. This is designed to stop the engine in an emergency and so reduce the risk of fire.

Question 13.52

Mark one answer

You see a car on the hard shoulder of a motorway with a HELP pennant displayed. This means the driver is most likely to be

- a disabled person
- first aid trained
- a foreign visitor
- a rescue patrol person

Answer

a disabled person

The driver might not be able to walk the distance to the emergency telephone. Disabled persons can show this sign to alert police controls.

Question 13.53

Mark one answer

On the motorway the hard shoulder should be used

- to answer a mobile phone
- when an emergency arises
- for a short rest when tired
- to check a road atlas

Answer

when an emergency arises

Pull onto the hard shoulder and use the emergency telephone to report your problem. The telephone connects you to police control, who will put you through to an emergency breakdown service. Never cross the carriageway to use the telephone on the other side.

Question 13.54

Mark two answers

What TWO safeguards could you take against fire risk to your vehicle?

- Keep water levels above maximum
- Carry a fire extinguisher
- Avoid driving with a full tank of petrol
- Use unleaded petrol
- Check out any strong smell of petrol
- Use low octane fuel

Answers

Carry a fire extinguisher

Check out any strong smell of petrol

The fuel in your vehicle can be a dangerous fire hazard. Don't

- use a naked flame near the vehicle if you can smell fuel
- smoke when refuelling your vehicle.

Question 13.55

Mark three answers

You have broken down on a motorway. When you use the emergency telephone you will be asked

- for the number on the telephone that you are using
- for your driving licence details
- for the name of your vehicle insurance company
- for details of yourself and your vehicle
- whether you belong to a motoring organisation

Answers

- **for the number on the telephone that you are using**
- **for details of yourself and your vehicle**
- **whether you belong to a motoring organisation**

Have these details ready before you phone to save time. Be sure to give the correct information. It is safer to always face the traffic when you speak on the telephone.

Question 13.56

Mark one answer

You are on the motorway. Luggage falls from your vehicle. What should you do?

- Stop at the next emergency telephone and contact the police
- Stop on the motorway and put on hazard lights whilst you pick it up
- Walk back up the motorway to pick it up
- Pull up on the hard shoulder and wave traffic down

Answer

- **Stop at the next emergency telephone and contact the police**

Pull over onto the hard shoulder near an emergency telephone and phone for assistance. Don't

- stop on the carriageway
- attempt to retrieve anything.

Question 13.57

Mark one answer

You are travelling on a motorway. A bag falls from your motorcycle. There are valuables in the bag. What should you do?

- Go back carefully and collect the bag as quickly as possible
- Stop wherever you are and pick up the bag, but only when there is a safe gap
- Stop on the hard shoulder and use the emergency telephone to inform the police
- Stop on the hard shoulder and then retrieve the bag yourself

Answer

- **Stop on the hard shoulder and use the emergency telephone to inform the police**

However important you think retrieving your property may be, DON'T walk onto the motorway. Your bag might be creating a hazard, but not as great a hazard as you would be.

Question 13.58

Mark one answer

You are on a motorway. A large box falls onto the road from a lorry. The lorry does not stop. You should

- go to the next emergency telephone and inform the police
- catch up with the lorry and try to get the driver's attention
- stop close to the box until the police arrive
- pull over to the hard shoulder, then remove the box

Answer

- **go to the next emergency telephone and inform the police**

Lorry drivers are sometimes unaware of objects falling from their vehicles. If you see something fall off a lorry onto the motorway, watch to see if the driver pulls over. If the lorry doesn't stop you should

- pull over onto the hard shoulder near an emergency telephone
- report the hazard to the police.

Question 13.59

Mark two answers

You are on a motorway. When can you use hazard warning lights?

- When a vehicle is following too closely
- When you slow down quickly because of danger ahead
- When you are towing another vehicle
- When driving on the hard shoulder
- When you have broken down on the hard shoulder

Answers

- **When you slow down quickly because of danger ahead**
- **When you have broken down on the hard shoulder**

Hazard lights will warn the traffic travelling behind you that your vehicle is a potential hazard. Don't forget to turn them off again when you return to the carriageway or normal speed.

Question 13.60

Mark one answer

You are on a motorway. The car in front switches on its hazard warning lights whilst moving. This means

- they are going to take the next exit
- there is a danger ahead
- there is a police car in the left lane
- they are trying to change lanes

Answer

- **there is a danger ahead**

Hazard lights should only be used when driving if you're on a

- motorway
- dual carriageway subject to the national speed limit

and you need to warn following traffic of a danger ahead.

SECTION 14 VEHICLE LOADING

This section looks at the safety of loads.

The questions will ask you about

- **Stability**

  make sure that your load doesn't affect the stability of your vehicle.

- **Towing regulations**

  be aware of the effects of towing a trailer and the rules that apply.

Question 14.1

Mark two answers

Overloading your vehicle can seriously affect the

- gearbox
- steering
- handling
- battery life
- journey time

Answers

- **steering**
- **handling**

Any load will have an affect on the handling of your vehicle, and this becomes worse if you overload it. Any change in the centre of gravity or the weight the vehicle is carrying will affect it's handling on bends.

Question 14.2

Mark one answer

Who is responsible for making sure that a vehicle is not overloaded?

- The driver or rider of the vehicle
- The owner of the items being carried
- The person who loaded the vehicle
- The owner of the vehicle

Answer

- **The driver or rider of the vehicle**

Your vehicle must not be overloaded. This will affect control and handling characteristics. If your vehicle is overloaded and it causes an accident, you'll be responsible.

Question 14.3

Mark two answers

On which TWO occasions might you inflate your tyres to more than the recommended normal pressure?

- When the roads are slippery
- When driving fast for a long distance
- When the tyre tread is worn below 2 mm
- When carrying a heavy load
- When the weather is cold
- When the vehicle is fitted with anti-lock brakes

Answers

- **When driving fast for a long distance**
- **When carrying a heavy load**

Check the vehicle hand book, which should give you guidance on the correct tyre pressure in these circumstances.

Travelling at speed for long distances can cause the tyres to become hot, which could damage the side walls.

Question 14.4

Mark one answer

Any load that is carried on a luggage rack MUST be

- securely fastened when riding
- carried only when strictly necessary
- visible when you are riding
- covered with plastic sheeting

Answer

- **securely fastened when riding**

Don't risk losing any luggage off your machine. It could fall into the path of following vehicles and cause danger. It's an offence to travel with an insecure load.

Question 14.5

Mark one answer

Any load that is carried on a roof rack MUST be

- securely fastened when driving
- carried only when strictly necessary
- as light as possible
- covered with plastic sheeting

Answer

- **securely fastened when driving**

If you wish to carry items on the roof there are roof boxes available from automotive supply stores. These will help to keep your luggage secure and dry.

Question 14.6

Mark one answer

A heavy load on your roof rack will

- improve the road holding
- reduce the stopping distance
- make the steering lighter
- reduce stability

Answer

- **reduce stability**

Be aware of this when you negotiate bends and corners. Your vehicle and/or load could become unstable. You could lose control.

Question 14.7

Mark three answers

Which THREE are suitable restraints for a child under three years?

- A child seat
- An adult holding a child
- An adult seat belt
- A lap belt
- A harness
- A baby carrier

Answers

- **A child seat**
- **A harness**
- **A baby carrier**

The driver is responsible for ensuring that children under three wear suitable child restraints. If the child is in the front seat, a restraint must be used. If the child is in the rear seat, restraints must be used if available.

A harness or booster seat should be appropriate to the child's weight.

Question 14.8

Mark one answer

What do child locks in a vehicle do?

- Lock the seat belt buckles in place
- Lock the rear windows in the up position
- Stop children from opening rear doors
- Stop the rear seats from tipping forward

Answer

- **Stop children from opening rear doors**

Child locks are fitted to most modern cars. They prevent the door being opened from the inside.

Question 14.9

Mark one answer

Your vehicle is fitted with child safety door locks. You should use these so that children inside the car cannot open

- the right-hand doors
- the left-hand doors
- the rear doors
- any of the doors

Answer

- **the rear doors**

If you're travelling with children in the rear seats, fitting child safety locks is a sensible safety precaution. There will be times when children are eager to get out of the car as it comes to a stop, and child safety locks will prevent them until you're sure it's safe for them to do so.

Question 14.10

Mark one answer

You want to tow a trailer with your motorcycle. Which one applies?

- The motorcycle should be attached to a sidecar
- The trailer should weigh more than the motorcycle
- The trailer should be fitted with brakes
- The trailer should not be more than 1 metre (3 feet 3 inches) wide

Answer

- **The trailer should not be more than 1 metre (3 feet 3 inches) wide**

To tow a trailer behind a motorcycle you must

- have a full motorcycle licence
- have a motorcycle with an engine larger than 125 cc.

Motorcycle trailers must not exceed 1 metre (3 feet 3 inches) wide.

Question 14.11

Mark one answer

You are planning to tow a caravan. Which of these will mostly help to aid the vehicle handling?

- A jockey-wheel fitted to the towbar
- Power steering fitted to the towing vehicle
- Anti-lock brakes fitted to the towing vehicle
- A stabiliser fitted to the towbar

Answer

A stabiliser fitted to the towbar

It is highly recommended that you take a caravan manoeuvring course. The Camping and Caravanning Club provide a course for those wishing to tow trailers. They also publish literature and a really helpful video. For more information Tel: 01203 694995.

Question 14.12

Mark one answer

A trailer must stay securely hitched-up to the towing vehicle. What additional safety device can be fitted to the trailer braking system?

- Stabiliser
- Jockey wheel
- Corner steadies
- Breakaway cable

Answer

Breakaway cable

In the event of a tow bar failure the cable pulls on the caravan brakes, snaps and allows the car to run free of the stopped caravan.

Question 14.13

Mark one answer

If a trailer swerves or snakes when you are towing it you should

- ease off the accelerator and reduce your speed
- let go of the steering wheel and let it correct itself
- brake hard and hold the pedal down
- increase your speed as quickly as possible

Answer

ease off the accelerator and reduce your speed

Strong winds or buffeting from large vehicles might cause a trailer or caravan to snake or swerve. If this happens, ease off the accelerator. Don't

- brake harshly
- steer sharply
- increase speed.

Question 14.14

Mark one answer

Are passengers allowed to ride in a caravan that is being towed?

- Yes, if they are over fourteen
- No, not at any time
- Only if all the seats in the towing vehicle are full
- Only if a stabilizer is fitted

Answer

No, not at any time

Riding in a towed caravan is highly dangerous. The safety of the entire unit is dependent on the stability of the trailer. Moving passengers would render the caravan unstable and could cause loss of control.

Question 14.15

Mark one answer

You are towing a caravan along a motorway. The caravan begins to swerve from side to side. What should you do?

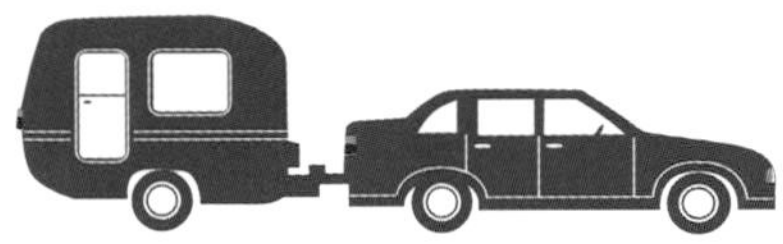

- Ease off the accelerator slowly
- Steer sharply from side to side
- Do an emergency stop
- Speed up very quickly

Answer

Ease off the accelerator slowly

Try not to brake or steer heavily, this will only make matters worse and you could lose control all together. Keep calm and regain control by easing off the accelerator.

Question 14.16

Mark one answer

If a trailer swerves or snakes when you are towing it you should

- ease off the throttle and reduce your speed
- let go of the handlebars and let it correct itself
- brake hard and hold the brake on
- increase your speed as quickly as possible

Answer

ease off the throttle and reduce your speed

Don't be tempted to use the steering to stop swerving or snaking. This won't help the situation. Ease off the throttle and reduce your speed.

Question 14.17

Mark one answer

How can you stop a caravan snaking from side to side?

- Turn the steering wheel slowly to each side
- Accelerate to increase your speed
- Stop as quickly as you can
- Slow down very gradually

Answer

- **Slow down very gradually**

Keep calm and don't brake harshly or you could lose control completely.

Question 14.18

Mark two answers

You are towing a small trailer on a busy three-lane motorway. All the lanes are open. You must

- not exceed 60 mph
- not overtake
- have a stabiliser fitted
- use only the left and centre lanes

Answers

- **not exceed 60 mph**
- **use only the left and centre lanes**

You should be aware of the speed limit for the vehicle that you're driving. Allow the faster-moving traffic to flow. Don't use the right-hand lane.

Question 14.19

Mark one answer

You have a sidecar fitted to your motorcycle. What effect will it have?

- Reduce stability
- Make steering lighter
- Increase stopping distance
- Increase fuel economy

Answer

- **Increase stopping distance**

If you want to fit a sidecar to your motorcycle

- make sure that your machine is suitable to cope with the extra load
- make sure that the sidecar is fixed correctly and properly aligned.

A sidecar will affect the handling of your machine. Give yourself time to adjust to the different characteristics.

Question 14.20

Mark two answers

When riding with a sidecar attached for the first time you should

- keep your speed down
- be able to stop more quickly
- accelerate quickly round bends
- approach corners more carefully

Answers

- **keep your speed down**
- **approach corners more carefully**

A motorcycle with a sidecar will feel very different to ride from a solo motorcycle. Until you get used to the outfit keep your speed down, especially when negotiating corners and bends.

Question 14.21

Mark one answer

A trailer on a motorcycle must be no wider than

- 1 metre (3 feet 3 inches)
- 1/2 metre (1 foot 8 inches)
- 1 1/2 metres (4 feet 11 inches)
- 2 metres (6 feet 6 inches)

Answer

- **1 metre (3 feet 3 inches)**

When you're towing a trailer you must remember that you may not be able to filter through traffic. Don't 'forget' that the trailer is there.

Question 14.22

Mark one answer

Before fitting a sidecar riders should

- have the wheels of their bike balanced
- have their bike's engine tuned
- pass the extended bike test
- check that their bike is suitable

Answer

- **check that their bike is suitable**

Make sure that the sidecar is fixed and is properly aligned. If your machine is registered on or after 1 August 1981 the sidecar must be fitted on the left side of the machine.

Question 14.23

Mark two answers

You want to tow a trailer behind your motorcycle. You should

- display a 'long vehicle' sign
- fit a larger battery
- have a full motorcycle licence
- ensure that your engine is more than 125 cc
- ensure that your machine has shaft drive

Answers

- **have a full motorcycle licence**
- **ensure that your engine is more than 125 cc**

When you tow a trailer

- your stopping distance may be increased
- any load on the trailer must be secure
- the trailer must be fitted to the machine correctly
- you must obey the speed limit restrictions that apply to all vehicles with trailers.

Question 14.24

Mark one answer

When may a learner motorcyclist carry a pillion passenger?

- If the passenger holds a full licence
- Not at any time
- If the rider is undergoing training
- If the passenger is over 21

Answer

- **Not at any time**

You are not allowed to carry a pillion passenger until you hold a full motorcycle licence.

This allows you to gain experience riding solo before carrying a passenger.

Question 14.25

Mark three answers

Which THREE must a learner motorcyclist under 21 NOT do?

- Ride a motorcycle with an engine capacity greater than 125 cc
- Pull a trailer
- Carry a pillion passenger
- Ride faster than 30 mph
- Use the right-hand lane on dual carriageways

Answers

- **Ride a motorcycle with an engine capacity greater than 125 cc**
- **Pull a trailer**
- **Carry a pillion passenger**

If you're a learner motorcyclist under 21 you must not ride a motorcycle on the road with an engine capacity over 125 cc.

Question 14.26

Mark one answer

Pillion passengers should

- have a provisional motorcycle licence
- be lighter than the rider
- always wear a helmet
- signal for the rider

Answer

- **always wear a helmet**

Pillion passengers must

- sit astride the machine facing forward on a proper passenger seat
- wear a safety helmet, which is correctly fastened.

Question 14.27

Mark one answer

Pillion passengers should

- give the rider directions
- lean with the rider when going round bends
- check the road behind for the rider
- give arm signals for the rider

Answer

- **lean with the rider when going round bends**

Pillion passengers should also keep both feet on the pillion footrests provided.

Question 14.28

Mark three answers

When carrying extra weight on a motorcycle, you may need to make adjustments to the

- headlight
- gears
- suspension
- tyres
- footrests

Answers

- **headlight**
- **suspension**
- **tyres**

Extra weight can affect a motorcycles feel and balance. To help, you can adjust the

- suspension
- tyre pressures.

You may find extra weight on the back affects the headlamp aim and this can be adjusted to compensate.

Question 14.29

Mark two answers

To carry a pillion passenger your bike should be fitted with

- rear footrests
- an engine of 250c c or over
- a top box
- a grab handle
- a proper passenger seat

Answers

- **rear footrests**
- **a proper passenger seat**

Pillion passengers should be instructed not to

- give hand signals
- lean away from the rider when cornering
- fidget or move around
- put their feet down to try and support the machine as you stop
- wear long, loose items that might get caught in the rear wheel or drive chain.

NI

Question 14.30

Mark one answer

To obtain the full category 'A' licence through the accelerated or direct access scheme, your motorcycle must be

- solo with maximum power 25 kw (33 bhp)
- solo with maximum power of 11 kw (14.6 bhp)
- fitted with a sidecar and have minimum power of 35 kw (46.6 bhp)
- solo with minimum power of 35 kw (46.6 bhp)

Answer

- **solo with minimum power of 35 kw (46.6 bhp)**

If you want to ride in countries that are members of the European Community you must have a valid driving licence. You will also want to find out what specific rules apply to any country you may be visiting concerning insurance, visas and other motoring regulations.

Question 14.31

Mark one answer

When you are going around a corner your pillion passenger should

- give arm signals for you
- check behind for other vehicles
- lean with you on bends
- lean to one side to see ahead

Answer

- **lean with you on bends**

A pillion passenger should not give signals or look round for you. They should lean with you when going around bends and corners so that you can maintain balance and stability.

Question 14.32

Mark one answer

Which of these may need to be adjusted when carrying a pillion passenger?

- Indicators
- Exhaust
- Fairing
- Headlight

Answer

- **Headlight**

Lights must be properly adjusted to prevent dazzling other road users. Extra attention needs to be paid to this if the vehicle is heavily loaded. This is important when carrying the extra weight of a pillion passenger which will mean that the machine will become lower at the back and cause the headlight to shine higher.

Question 14.33

Mark three answers

Your motorcycle is fitted with a top box. It is unwise to carry a heavy load in the top box because it may

- reduce stability
- improve stability
- make turning easier
- cause high-speed weave
- cause low-speed wobble
- increase fuel economy

Answers

- **reduce stability**
- **cause high-speed weave**
- **cause low speed wobble**

Because the weight is high up and over the rear wheel it can cause problems in maintaining control of the machine.

Question 14.34

Mark one answer

You are towing a trailer with your motorcycle. You should remember that your

- stopping distance may increase
- fuel consumption will improve
- tyre grip will increase
- stability will improve

Answer

- **stopping distance may increase**

When you tow a trailer remember that

- you must obey the speed limits
- your stopping distance will increase
- the trailer must be hitched correctly.

Above all, **don't forget it's there**.

Next steps

Passing your theory test means that you've taken the first step towards safe driving. However, it is only one stage in becoming a safe and competent driver. The knowledge you've acquired should be put into practice on the road.

DSA have produced a video that shows you

- how the practical test is conducted
- what happens at the test centre
- the standard manoeuvres
- some common errors
- how each fault is assessed at the time
- the myths of the Driving Test exploded.

Available from TSO by telephoning **0870 600 5522.**

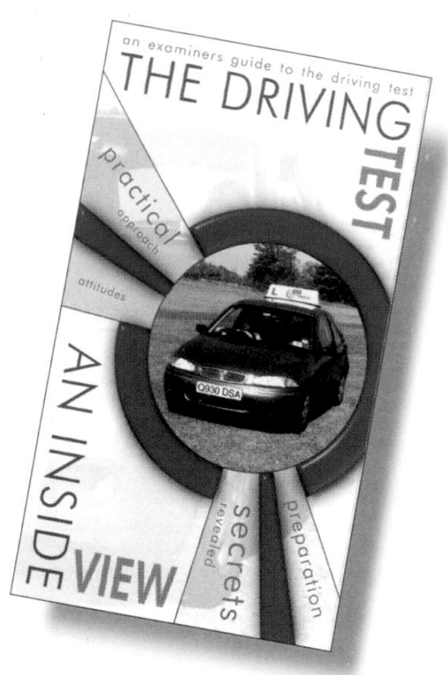

By passing a stringent two-part test, and continuing to apply the knowledge that you've gained on the way, you can make an important contribution to safety on our roads.

When you've passed your driving test you might like to have some additional training, and get a reduction in your insurance costs, by taking part in the 'Pass Plus' scheme. You should ask your driving instructor about it.

You'll never know all the answers. Throughout your driving career there will always be more to learn. Remember, any passengers you carry will be your responsibility. By being reliable, efficient and safe you'll be on your way to becoming a safe driver.

Service standards for theory test candidates

DSA and DVTA are committed to providing the following standards of service for test candidates.

1. Following routing by our call handling systems, ninety percent of telephone calls will be answered within twenty seconds.
2. Theory tests will be available during weekdays, evenings and on Saturdays. A test appointment should be available for 95% of test candidates within two weeks.
3. 99% of test notifications will be issued within five working days of receipt of a correctly completed application form and appropriate fee.
4. More time may be needed to make arrangements for candidates with special needs, but a test should be available for 95% of such candidates within four weeks.
5. 99.8% of all candidates should be able to obtain a test booking within two months of their preferred date at the centre of their choice.
6. A refund of test fees will be issued within three weeks of a valid claim with the supporting information.
7. No more than 0.5% of tests will be cancelled by contractors (acting on behalf of DSA and DVTA).
8. All letters, including complaints, will be answered within 15 working days.
9. 98% of all candidates should receive their test result within 30 minutes of completing their test.

Complaints guide for theory test candidates

DSA and DVTA aim to give their customers the best possible service. Please tell us

- when we've done well
- when you aren't satisfied.

Your comments can help us to improve the service we offer. If you have any questions about your theory test please contact DSA.

Tel: 0870 01 01 372

Fax: 0870 01 04 372.

Candidates with comments or queries about tests in Northern Ireland please contact DVTA.

Tel: 0845 6006700

Fax: 0870 01 04 372.

If you have any complaints about how your theory test was carried out, or any part of our customer service, please take up the matter with a member of staff if the circumstances allow. Alternatively you can write to the Customer Services Manager at the following address

Customer Services
Driving Theory Test
PO Box 148
Salford
M5 3SY

If you're dissatisfied with the reply you can write to the Managing Director at the same address.

If you're still not satisfied, you can take up your complaint with

The Chief Executive
Driving Standards Agency
56 Stanley House
Talbot Street
Nottingham NG1 5GU.

In Northern Ireland

The Chief Executive
Driver & Vehicle Testing Agency
Balmoral Road
Belfast BT12 6QL.

None of this removes your right to take your complaint to your Member of Parliament, who may decide to raise your case personally with the DSA or DVTA Chief Executive, the Minister or the Parliamentary Commissioner for Administration (the Ombudsman). Please refer to our leaflet 'If things go wrong.'

Compensation code for theory test candidates

DSA will normally refund the test fee, or give a free re-booking, in the following cases

- if we cancel your test
- if you cancel and give us at least three clear working days notice
- if you keep the test appointment but the test doesn't take place, or isn't finished, for a reason that isn't your fault.

We'll also repay you the expenses that you incurred on the day of the test because we cancelled your test at short notice. We'll consider reasonable claims for

- travelling to and from the test centre
- any pay or earnings you lost after tax (usually for half a day).

Please write to the address below and send a receipt showing travel costs and/or an employer's letter, which shows what earnings you lost.

DVTA has a different compensation code. If you think you're entitled to compensation write to

Customer Services
Driving Theory Test
PO Box 148
Salford
M5 3SY

This compensation code doesn't affect your existing legal rights.

Theory Test Centres in Great Britain and Northern Ireland

Scotland

Aberdeen
Ayr
Berwick-Upon-Tweed
Dumfries
Dundee
Dunfermline
Edinburgh
Elgin
Fort William
Gairloch
Galashiels
Glasgow NW
Glasgow Central
Greenock
Helmsdale
Huntly
Inverness
Isle of Arran
Isle of Barra
Isle of Benbecula
Isle of Islay, Bowmore
Isle of Mull, Salen
Isle of Tiree
Kirkwall
Kyle of Lochalsh
Lerwick
Motherwell
Oban
Pitlochry
Portree
Stirling
Stornoway
Stranraer
Tarbert, Argyllshire
Tongue
Ullapool
Wick

Northern

Barrow
Birkenhead
Blackpool
Bolton
Bradford
Carlisle
Chester
Doncaster
Durham
Grimsby
Harrogate
Huddersfield
Hull
Leeds
Liverpool
Manchester
Middlesbrough
Morpeth
Newcastle
Oldham
Preston
Runcorn
Salford
Scarborough
Scunthorpe
Sheffield
Southport
St Helens
Stockport
Sunderland
Wigan
Workington
York

Midlands & Eastern

Birmingham
Boston
Bury St Edmunds
Cambridge
Chesterfield
Coventry
Derby
Dudley
Grantham
Ipswich
Kings Lynn
Leicester
Lincoln
Lowestoft
Luton
Mansfield
Milton Keynes
Northampton
Norwich
Nottingham
Oxford
Peterborough
Reading
Redditch
Shrewsbury
Solihull
Stoke-on-Trent
Stratford Upon Avon
Sutton Coldfield
Wolverhampton
Worcester

Wales & Western

Aberystwyth
Bangor
Barnstaple
Basingstoke
Bath
Bournemouth
Bristol
Builth Wells
Cardiff
Cheltenham
Exeter
Fareham
Gloucester
Haverfordwest
Hereford
Isles of Scilly
Isle of Wight
Merthyr Tydfil
Newport
Penzance
Plymouth
Portsmouth
Rhyl
Swansea
Salisbury
Southampton
Swindon
Taunton
Torquay
Truro
Weymouth
Yeovil

London & South East

Aldershot
Basildon
Brighton
Canterbury
Chelmsford
Colchester
Crawley
Croydon
Eastbourne
Gillingham
Guildford
Harlow
Hastings
Ilford
Kingston
Palmers Green
Sidcup
Slough
Southend
Southwark
Staines
Stevenage
Uxbridge
Watford
Worthing

Northern Ireland

Ballymena
Belfast
Londonderry
Newry
Omagh
Portadown

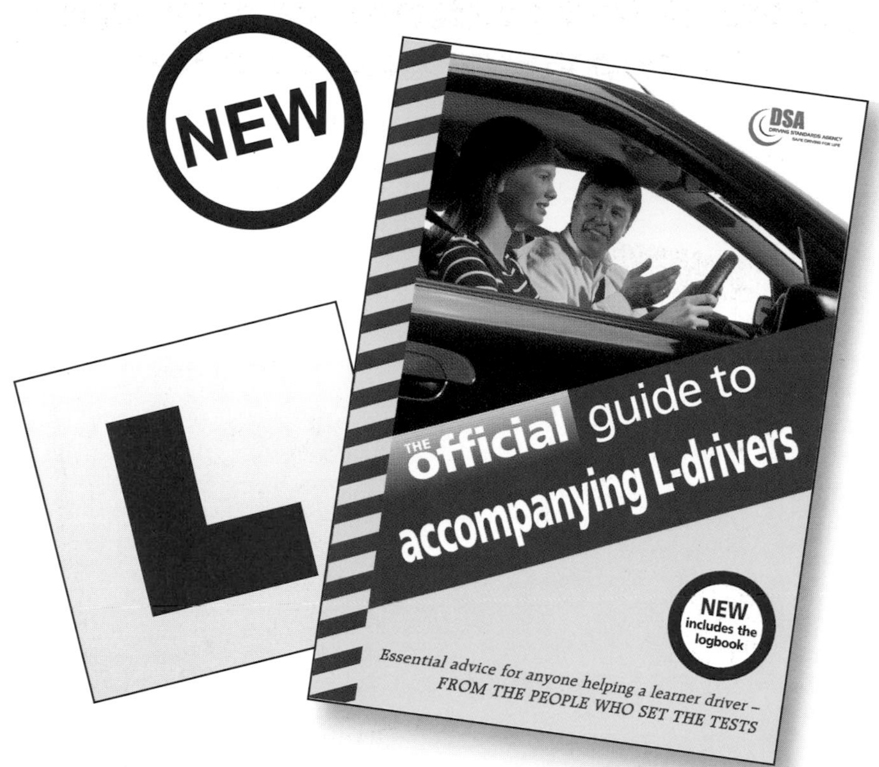

The Official Guide to Accompanying Learner Drivers

Understand what a learner driver needs to practice, and be aware of the potential hazards encountered in accompanying a learner driver. This new title ensures that the efforts of others complement the lessons given by their Approved Driving Instructor.

Essential guidance on

- ***What the law requires of the accompanying driver***
- ***Preparing your car for use by the learner***
- ***Planning your routes***
- ***Working in tandem with your learner's Approved Driving Instructor***
- ***Maintaining your learner's confidence***
- ***Dealing with potential hazards***
- ***Keeping your patience***

0 11 552178 X £7.49

The Official Driving Test

The practical driving test – fully illustrated and written in a clear and easy-to-understand style.

The full syllabus and tests, explained by the experts who set the standards. Help with your practical test and how to become a safer driver. What to do before the test, test requirements, skills, faults to avoid, plus CBT details for motorcyclists.

Fully updated with the officially recommended syllabus for learning to drive.

0 11 552190 9 £6.99

The Official Driving Manual

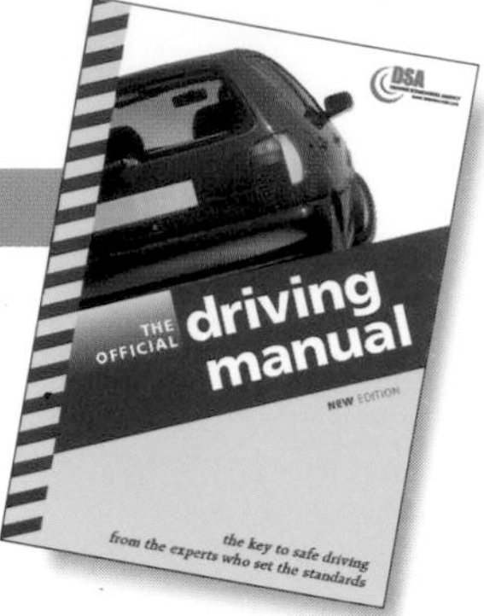

The essential reference manual for all motorists and instructors, from learners to advanced motorists - updated to include the very latest advice and legislation on good driving, covering subjects as diverse as defensive driving, bends and junctions, manoeuvring, towing and European driving, plus legal information.

0 11 552191 7 £12.99

The Official Compulsory Basic Training

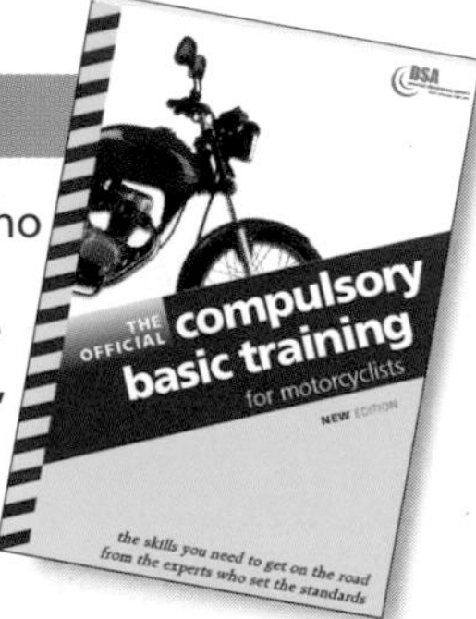

The skills you need to get you on the road, by the experts who set the standards. All the latest information for the first step for motorcycle learners: CBT is the course you must complete before riding on the road. Written and compiled by the DSA, this book explains each of the various elements of the training, plus helpful pre and post course information.

0 11 552192 5 £6.99

The Official Motorcycling Manual

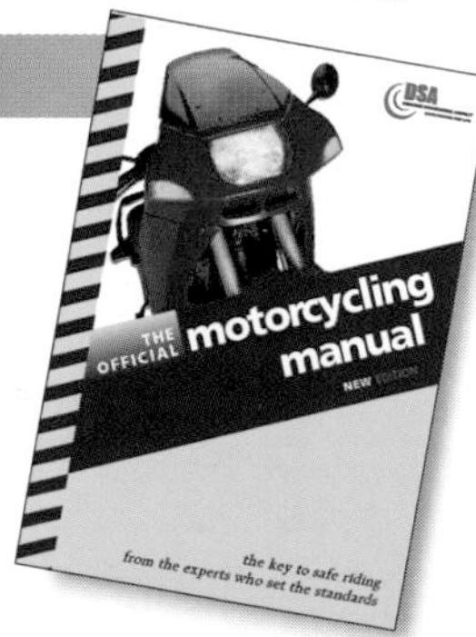

The authoritative guide to motorcycling, containing new graphics and photographs and updated to include the very latest information and advice. An essential reference book for motorcyclists who are keen to improve their machine handling and safety skills, including expert guidance on riding in traffic, defensive driving, in bad weather and at night.

0 11 552193 3 £9.99

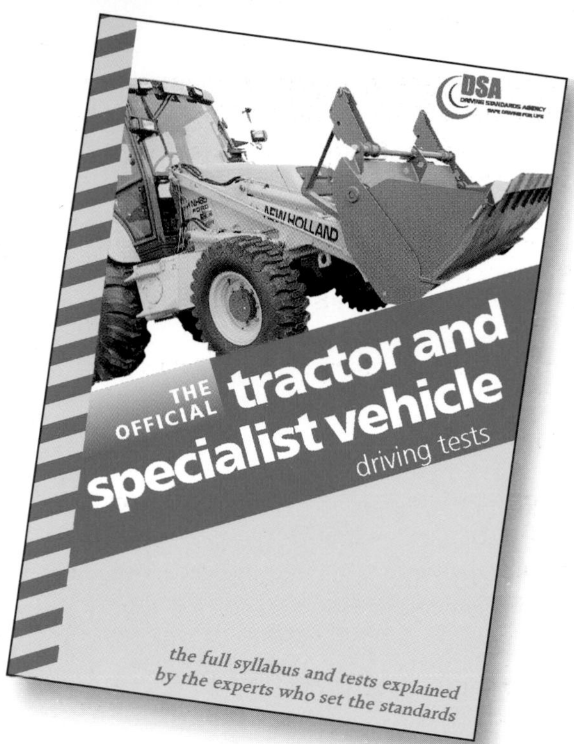

The Official Tractor and Specialist Vehicle Driving Tests

If you plan to drive a tractor or other specialist vehicle regularly - or even occasionally - as part of your job it is vital that you pass a specialist vehicle practical test to demonstrate your knowledge of basic road safety procedures. This new title explains the standards and principles that the examiner expects.

Unusual vehicles include

- ***agricultural tractors***
- ***bulldozers***
- ***road rollers***
- ***ride-on mowing machines***
- ***pedestrian controlled vehicles***
- ***track laying vehicles***
- ***three wheeled cars***
- ***motor tricycles/trikes.***

0 11 552170 4 £9.99

Printed in The United Kingdom for The Stationery Office TJ004076 04/01 C40 63789

Order Form

TSO publications are available from:

- **Mail Order:**
  The Stationery Office, PO Box 29, Norwich NR3 1GN
- **Tel:** **0870 600 5522** *quoting ref AJK/TT*
  Fax: **0870 600 5533**
  Online: **www.the-stationery-office.com**
- **The Stationery Office Bookshops**
  (See inside back cover for details)
- **Accredited Agents and all good booksellers**

Please send me the following publications:

Title	*ISBN*	*Price*	*Quantity*
The Highway Code	0 11 551977 7	£1.49	....
Know Your Traffic Signs	0 11 551612 3	£2.50	....
The Official Guide to Accompanying Learner Drivers	0 11 552178 X	£7.49	....
The Official Driving Test	0 11 552190 9	£6.99	....
The Official Driving Manual	0 11 552191 7	£12.99	....
The Official Compulsory Basic Training	0 11 552192 5	£6.99	....
The Official Motorcycling Manual	0 11 552193 3	£9.99	....
The Official Tractor & Specialist Vehicle Driving Tests	0 11 552170 4	£9.99	....
Handling charge per order:		£2.50	
	Total enclosed:	£................	

PLEASE COMPLETE IN BLOCK CAPITALS

Name ....

Address ....

....

.... Postcode .... AJK/TT

☐ I enclose a cheque for £.................. payable to: *'The Stationery Office'*

☐ Please charge to my account with The Stationery Office, No:

....

☐ Please debit my Mastercard/Visa/Amex/Diners/Connect Card Account No.

Signature... Expiry date ....

☐ Please send me information on TSO products. My email address is

....@...

Alternatively, contact us NOW to register at www.the-stationery-office.com

☐ Please tick this box if you do not wish to receive further information by conventional mail on products and services from The Stationery Office.

Prices are correct at time of going to press but may be subject to change without notice.
TSO account holders should note that credit card transactions will not be shown on their statements.
A full listing of terms and conditions of sale can be obtained on request from The Stationery Office PO Box 29, Norwich NR3 1GN.

The Stationery Office